ORCHESTRA... ...ES
COLLABORATIVE DESI...

Chris Risdon
Patrick Quattlebaum

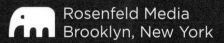

Rosenfeld Media
Brooklyn, New York

Orchestrating Experiences
Collaborative Design for Complexity
By Chris Risdon and Patrick Quattlebaum

Rosenfeld Media, LLC

540 President Street

Brooklyn, New York

11215 USA

On the Web: www.rosenfeldmedia.com

Please send errors to: rosenfeldmedia.com

Publisher: Louis Rosenfeld

Managing Editor: Marta Justak

Illustrator: Nick Madden

Interior Layout Tech: Danielle Foster

Cover and Interior Design: The Heads of State

Indexer: Marilyn Augst

Proofreader: Sue Boshers

ISBN: 1-933820-73-X

ISBN 13: 978-1-933820-73-6

LCCN: 2018930392

Printed and bound in the United States of America

CHRIS

*To my love Kathy and beautiful daughter Lucy
for being amazing, supportive, loving,
and making me a better person.*

PATRICK

*To my amazing partner in crime Katie
for her love, support, and patience.*

HOW TO USE THIS BOOK

Who Should Read This Book?

This book is written by designers, but it is for anyone who wants to make a greater impact in envisioning and making products and services in complex environments. Complex, in this case, refers to customer experiences with many moving parts—multiple channels, many touchpoints, and numerous contexts—and the departmentalized, fragmented organizations attempting to deliver them. Sound familiar? If so, you will likely identify with one of the following cohorts we had in mind when writing this book:

- **Practitioners of all stripes:** You define strategies for customer experiences, services, products, marketing, or technology. You design physical things, digital touchpoints, processes, communications, or systems. You deliver the objects, interfaces, platforms, or intangible interactions that enable value creation. Or you help manage all of these activities. In these pages, you'll find new approaches that expand your toolkit and facilitate others through a more collaborative design process.

- **Leaders and emerging leaders:** You work in cross-functional programs trying to create products and services that enable impactful experiences at scale. The common set of terms, models, and methods introduced here will increase your ability to help others engage in making the future together.

- **Executives:** You want differentiated, customer-centered experiences while defining focused strategies and leaner operations. The concepts we present will help you foster cross-functional collaboration, build customer empathy, and activate more effective customer journeys.

Regardless of your role, this book will equip you and your colleagues to design for better experiences, together. Bringing consistency and continuity to end-to-end experiences requires new concepts and methods. Creating broad empathy means helping your colleagues truly connect with your customers. Leaping from insights to vision to action necessitates increased facilitation and collaboration.

What's in This Book?

This book is organized into three parts, charting your course from embracing core concepts to orchestrating experiences.

Part I, "A Common Foundation," explores key concepts—channels, touchpoints, ecosystems, and journeys—related to understanding and improving the experience architecture of product and services. It argues for creating more consistency in how these terms are used in your organization and gives you tools to begin to do just that.

Part II, "Insights and Possibilities," outlines how to facilitate a cross-functional team through the process of better understanding customer needs and identifying opportunities for improving and reimagining end-to-end experiences.

Part III, "Vision and Action," explains how to generate ideas collaboratively and craft a vision that unites stakeholders and inspires action. It also shares techniques for carrying your intent into touchpoint design and moving your organization to orchestrate experiences more intentionally.

NOTE

Cross-functional collaboration is critical to improving or reimagining end-to-end experiences. For this reason, this book also contains several workshop examples designed to help engage the right people at the right time to envision orchestrated products and service experiences.

What Comes with This Book?

You'll find the book's companion website here (🐘rosenfeldmedia.com /books/orchestrating-experiences). The book's diagrams and other illustrations are available under a Creative Commons license (when possible) for you to download and include in your own presentations. You can find these on Flickr at www.flickr.com/photos/ rosenfeldmedia/sets/.

FREQUENTLY ASKED QUESTIONS

Do I have to do all these things in this book to orchestrate experiences successfully?

We cover many frameworks and tools, but you will likely gravitate to approaches that meet your unique needs. For example, you may find ecosystem mapping (Chapter 3) and storyboarding (Chapters 8 and 9) help you get the job done, while touchpoint inventories (Chapter 2) or improvisation (Chapter 8) don't resonate in your culture. The key: try out different approaches and build the toolkit that works for you.

Isn't this just a lot of deliverables?

No! Working collaboratively with your colleagues is *critical* to orchestrating experiences. It takes effort and skill. What you do make—such as experience maps (Chapter 5), experience principles (Chapter 6), and opportunity maps (Chapter 7)—should be approached as *tools* to build empathy, inspire ideas, create alignment, and take action towards the same outcomes.

You didn't mention [insert tool here]. Does that mean I shouldn't use it anymore?

We are constantly adding, dropping, and modifying design methods in our own toolkits. Those presented in this book have proven to be predictably effective when designing for complex ecosystems with cross-functional teams. In some cases, these approaches may displace other things in your toolkit. We think you will find, however, that most will complement other methods and tools that you commonly use. We also hope the book inspires you to find or invent additional approaches to orchestrate experiences better.

Does this take a lot of time?

More complex design problems in large organizations require more time as a rule. However, you will find that the approaches we cover can be leveraged when you need to run fast and lean. For example, you can use portions of the example workshops (Chapters 2, 3, 5, 6, 7, and 8) to design small working sessions. Or you could use the ideation techniques (Chapter 8) within a small team.

Isn't this service design? (Or isn't this just UX design or customer experience?)

Yes! And no! We've intentionally approached this book as a synthesis of best practices, regardless of tribal affiliation. The service design, user experience, customer experience, and other communities have contributed to the growth of the orchestration mindset. And you'll see us reference these practices and others (for example, see **Chapters 1, 2, 7, and 10**). At their heart, what they all have in common is human-centeredness. We will show you how to put it all together in action, regardless of whether you feel you're doing user experience design, service design, interaction design, or [insert discipline here].

CONTENTS

PART I: A COMMON FOUNDATION

CHAPTER 1

Understanding Channels   3

CHAPTER 2

Pinning Down Touchpoints   21

FOREWORD

Dear person who just bought this book,

I'm a little worried about you.

I'll say why, but I should first say that *this is a good book*. It is one of the few books about the place where the frontiers of design, management, and a systems view of innovation all come together.

You may already know that the world of design is embracing a systems and relationship view and that the same is true for management. These new practices involve orchestration—creative cooperation by people from across the old boundaries of roles, departments, and inside-or-out.

Let's look at some of the transformations described in these pages:

- From an us/them view of company and customer to an ecosystem view that tangles their world and ours

- From a focus on product to a focus on the way we participate in people's moments, days, weeks, and years

- From primacy of concepts to an emphasis on stories that matter to everyone who works to make them come true

- From specialized teams making specialized results to orchestrated teams who bring quality to each touch between people and organization

- From technical and usability metrics alone to including values and principles as new criteria for quality

In actual application, these are big changes for most organizations—not only because people resist the ideas, but also because shifting "the way we do things here" is uncomfortable. These approaches invite us into new ways to see roles, the definition of "good work," and what it means to be a thriving organization. And that is both exciting and scary.

Actually, that's why I'm worried about you.

I imagine that you are buying the book because you're excited by what it describes, and you aspire to implement these practices. But it will take time to see these ideas grow from the seeds in this book to exploratory sprouts and then to full flower in your organization. You'll need patience and persistence, and a habit of celebrating small steps. When persuasion doesn't work, you'll need other tools: story, vision, and invitations to the sandbox. And at the risk of being cliché, you'll need to find joy in the journey. This won't be easy.

So I ask myself, what could help? And here's my advice:

1. Find a collaborator or two. Don't try this alone.

2. Don't launch straight into one of the workshops. *Use Chapter 11.* Use it all year as the brief for applying the rest of the book. In our office, we often ask ourselves, "What conversation could we have in the next two weeks that would contribute to bringing our idea to life? Who needs to be involved, and do we need to make anything to support that conversation? Should it happen at a bar, in front of a working wall, or on a long walk together?"

These ideas can improve your ability to produce results that matter and last. But when you first pick up the book, there's no way to predict the particular way it will take root in your work. You have to live through the process of change to find out. That may take a bit of courage and persistence, but what does it serve you to play small?

And, of course, you're not alone. This book condenses the knowledge and experiences of a great number of people. With so many people setting out on this road, with a community of practice growing around these ideas, with so much enthusiastic exploration and imagination being captured in books like this, there is really no need for me to worry. I know you'll be fine.

Marc Rettig
Principal, Fit Associates
Faculty, SVA Design for Social Innovation

INTRODUCTION

We—Patrick and Chris—have known one another for several years now. We've worked at three organizations together—an agency, a consultancy, and a large financial services corporation. We've shared the stage at conferences and Adaptive Path events. We've co-taught thousands of people how to design for more human experiences.

Along the way, we've had a continuous dialogue about what challenges we've seen organizations facing and how they have approached solving them: for example, Design Thinking for unlocking innovation; Agile for speeding up product development; and Lean for creating operational efficiencies at scale. Each of these methodologies—some would say *religions*—has its strengths, but they all fail to address three critical challenges that organizations face today:

- How to evolve from shipping disconnected products and touch-points quickly to crafting end-to-end experiences that unfold gracefully over time and space

- How to break down operational silos and enable effective, efficient human-centered design collaboration

- How to bridge the gap between fuzzy-front-end strategy ("What should we do?") to nuts-and-bolts execution ("What we did")

This book takes aim at these challenges. Inspired and informed by our talented collaborators in service design and user experience, we will share language, concepts, and approaches that enable people across an organization to envision, plan, and design customer experiences together. We will help you guide others to understand the journeys of your customers and meet their needs better. We will expand your toolkit to generate better ideas and craft a compelling vision. Along the way, we hope to inspire you to become an orchestrator within your organization.

PATRICK **CHRIS**

PATRICK AND CHRIS

Because there are two of us, sometimes we have different viewpoints. Look for our specific sidebars with our pictures. In those sidebars, we will highlight important information, give case studies that we've worked on, or simply give our personal viewpoint about a topic.

We use the terms *orchestration, orchestrator,* and *orchestrating* throughout this book. In one sense, we are referring to approaches that help shift organizations from designing and delivering disparate parts to designing these parts to be aligned and in harmony with one another. This approach requires crafting channels and touchpoints intentionally as a system to support customers and their end-to-end experiences over time and in multiple contexts (see Chapters 1-4). In another sense, orchestrating means facilitating collaboration to achieve those outcomes. More and more, we are finding ourselves—product, design, IT, marketing, operations, and so on—in a room together attempting to solve increasingly complex problems. An orchestrator helps foster empathy, collaboration, creativity, and alignment, which result in better experiences and outcomes (Chapters 5–11).

Whichever meaning you pick for the word, let's face it: currently, orchestration runs counter to how most organizations operate. Although everyone has an agenda, we want to help you push your organization to be more thoughtful and collaborative in how it designs for experiences that result in real value. To support this objective, we have included workshop templates for facilitating the design process effectively. You can take these as is or adapt them to your unique needs.

We also provide examples of key outputs, both new and familiar—touchpoint inventories, ecosystem maps, experience maps, vision storyboards, and many more. Many of these artifacts are designed to be on walls—to be viewed by many, used as tools, and communicate lots of information. Our intent is not to load you up with more deliverables, but rather to give you tools that create impact.

While the latter portions of the book walk through approaches from research to prototyping, this is not a prescribed, rigid path. The methods we highlight are not required, nor are they the only ones to get the job done. Shipping products and delivering services is a continuum. Choose the methods that meet the needs of your team and organization. Play with your process. Invent your own tools.

As designers, we're wired to tackle ambiguous problems. We strive to give shape and form to products and services in an increasingly complex world. Whether you are a designer or not, there is an opportunity to be the glue that unites cross-functional teams around a shared vision and coordinated action upon a foundation of empathy. Organizations struggling to create better customer experiences need more than mapmakers. They need orchestrators. They require leaders armed with the right language, frameworks, and soft skills to *see* the forest and *make* the trees. We want this person to be you.

A Common Foundation

Organizations work constantly to engage customers in their products and services. Dispersed among multiple departments and people, these efforts result in many tangible and intangible things, each intended to create a positive customer interaction. Marketers produce commercials, banner ads, microsites, emails, and direct mail. Digital teams make mobile apps, websites, digital signage, and kiosks. Customer service people deploy online help guides, AI (artificial intelligence) chat bots, and IVR (interactive voice response) systems. Front-line employees assist customers in real time. Retail operations construct aisles, checkout counters, help desks, signage, and entranceways.

That's a lot of people, places, and things (and that's just scratching the surface).

Each discipline or function in an organization directly or indirectly impacts the customer experience. Distributing ownership and decision-making across these groups, however, comes with a challenge. How do different practitioners with different skills and philosophies own their piece of the puzzle while harmonizing with other customer interactions outside of their responsibility? And how does an organization build stronger relationships with customers more predictably, interaction by interaction?

To build strong internal partnerships and cross-functional collaboration, you must start to speak the same language and have common approaches for making sense of what all your disparate work produces. Four concepts are critical to getting on the same page: channel, touchpoint, ecosystem, and journey. For orchestrating experiences, it's critical to define these concepts consistently within a team, group, or an entire organization. They can serve as the connective tissue for creating more integrated, effective experiences across time and space. Let's start by looking at channels—the enablers of customer interactions.

Understanding Channels

The concept of channels pervades the modern business organization—for example, channel team, channel strategies, cross-channel, multichannel, omnichannel, channel preference, channel ownership, and on and on. Ideally, channels create connections to communicate and interact among people. However, they can also become silos that separate and create barriers between people, teams, and priorities.

From Theory to Reality

In the classic sense, a channel is a construct through which information is conveyed, similar to a waterway. Just as the Panama Canal delivers ships and cargo from one ocean to another, a communication channel connects the information sender with the information receiver.

In the world of designing services, *a channel is a medium of interaction with customers or users* (see Figure 1.1). Common channels include physical stores, call centers (phone), email, direct mail, web, and mobile (see Table 1.1). Behind these channels sit people, processes, and technologies. Channel owners count on these resources to reach their customers, deliver value, and differentiate them from their competition.

In addition, these channel owners are often evaluated and rewarded on the success of their individual channel metrics, which can be a detriment to connecting channels across an organization.

Social Media   Digital
Video   SMS   Native App
Print   Environment
Outdoor
Tablet   Mobile   Web   Software
Chatbot   Live Chat   Kiosk
Retail   Email   Native App   Mobile Web
Smart Phone   Call Center

FIGURE 1.1
Understanding and aligning with others on your channels is a foundational step toward orchestrating experiences.

TABLE 1.1 COMMON CHANNELS

Physical Store	Digital	Customer Service	Marketing
Signage	Web	Call Center	Broadcast
Kiosk	Mobile	IVR	Print
In-Store Screens	Mobile Web	Live Chat	Email
Environmental Displays	Native App	Chat Bots	Direct Mail
	Email		Digital Marketing
	Live Chat		Social Media
	SMS/Messaging		SMS/Messaging

Designing end-to-end experiences necessitates stepping into these channel-org dynamics. As an orchestrator, you need to understand how deeply engrained channel thinking (*vertical ownership*) can deter innovation and value creation. Your objective is to reframe channels as coordinated role players in the greater story of serving customers' journeys (*horizontal servitude*). The following four concepts will arm you to take on this challenge:

- Organizations are structured by channels.

- Channels don't exist in isolation.

- Channels are defined by interaction, information, and context.

- Channels should support the moment.

Structured by Channels

All companies start somewhere to market, deliver, and support their products and services to customers. For example, Lowe's Home Improvement started as a small storefront in a small town. Sears sold watches by mail order catalogs. UPS distributed paper forms filled out in triplicate to pick up, transfer, and deliver packages accurately. Netflix sent discs by mail. Amazon sold books on the web.

Over time, companies adapt and expand to engage with customers in new ways and new channels. Take Lowe's Home Improvement, a U.S. retailer, as an example. For decades, Lowe's primarily interacted with its customers through hundreds of retail stores and thousands of associates supported by television, radio, newspaper, outdoor and direct mail marketing, and advertising. In the 1990s, Lowe's (and its competitors) began moving into the digital realm both online and in the store. Now, two decades later, Lowe's has an expansive digital footprint including websites, apps, kiosks, associate tablets, and even a wayfinding robot (see Figure 1.2) that exists alongside the same channels that Lowe's has operated in from the first day it opened its doors. Lowe's answers customer questions through online chat, Twitter, in store aisles, and on the phone. It promotes sales on radio, via Google AdWords, in direct mail, and on physical and digital receipts. It teaches how to do home improvement projects in workshops, on YouTube, and in iPad magazines. That's a lot of channels.

FIGURE 1.2

LoweBot, developed by Lowe's Innovation Labs, opens a new channel to help customers find products in the store while also tracking and managing inventory.

Lowe's went online. Sears opened retail stores. UPS put digital tablets in its associates' hands and self-service websites in its customers' browsers. Netflix shifted to streaming. Amazon now sends their own delivery drivers (and drones!) to bring items to your door. Over time, organizations determine which channels to invest more or less in to meet their business objectives and connect with the evolving needs and behaviors of their target customers.

A good example of this evolutionary pattern can be seen in marketing. As the number of communication channels expanded in the last century, marketing groups (and their external agencies) formed teams to own newer channels, such as web, email, search engines, social media, and mobile. A typical marketing campaign, as a result, requires a lot of coordination. Multiple channel experts must align around a common strategy, the channel mix for tactics, and a plan on how to get all the right messages to all the right people at exactly the right time. Then they must coordinate with internal and external partners to define, design, and develop customer touchpoints for their channel.

That's a lot of people and a lot of coordination, and marketing is only one group among many looking to leverage the same channels to deliver value to customers.

NOTE WHAT'S A TOUCHPOINT?

That's a good question. Definitions—and whether it's spelled *touchpoint* or *touch point*!—differ as much as they align in disciplines from marketing to service design. For now, think of a touchpoint as what facilitates an interaction within or across channels between a person and a product or service. But, it's a little more complicated than that. Chapter 2, "Pinning Down Touchpoints," will delve into how to understand and codify your touchpoints.

These dynamics have only accelerated over the past 30 years as new digital channels—web, email, mobile, virtual reality, and so forth—have emerged as new ways to communicate, interact, and deliver products and services. The bright and shiny digital world often overshadows older media and channels. Yet, companies still invest in physical retail, direct mail, call centers, outdoor advertising, television, radio, and the like. (Just look at Amazon's 2017 acquisition of Whole Foods.) A greater focus on digital doesn't mean that the other channels go away—rather, it means that companies have more ground to cover than ever before.

Throughout this book, you will see the phrase "product and services" as a nod to the applicability of these approaches to multichannel, multitouchpoint systems. Services—such as traveling by air, staying at a hotel, or seeing your doctor— contain many products, and products—a digital camera or an automobile—can have many supporting services. Labels aside, if your offering operates in more than one channel with many touchpoints, you're in good hands.

Regardless of which channels it began operating in originally, a company's organizational chart often reflects this type of channel or business expansion (see Figure 1.3). With each emerging channel, companies typically follow a pattern of leaning on outside experts and then building those capabilities and skills internally as it becomes clear that they are core to the business' long-term success. New groups get built and slotted next to existing channel teams, each with its own strategies, visions, plans, and incentives for creating customer experiences. This redundancy leads to fragmented channel experiences, as well as more complexity in connecting touchpoints across functions and channels.

Channel proliferation (and its resulting effect on organizational structure) has made life complicated for even relatively small companies. How much should be invested in each channel? How can traditional channels be maintained while shifting into emerging

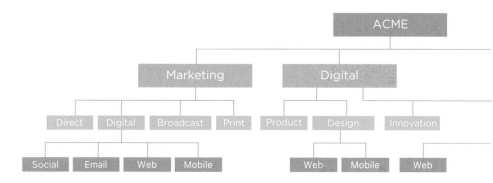

FIGURE 1.3

A representative organizational chart reflecting the separation of functions combined with channel proliferation.

channels? How do you manage all these channels? Who owns which channel and how do you get on their priority lists?

When taking this all into consideration, remember this one fact: customers don't really care about channels.

Channels Don't Exist in Isolation

What do customers care about? They want products and services that deliver for their explicit goals and implicit needs. Customers care about how organizations treat them, how their time is spent, and when and where they interact with products and services. In this landscape, channels are a means to an end.

Historically, organizations have viewed customer interactions and the channels that support those interactions—phone, store, and web—through a one-to-one lens. Each channel's team delivers solutions to support customer tasks with their channel. But this doesn't reflect the reality of how customers move across channels and connect with products and services.

People interact with many channels every day. They also switch among them—sometimes by choice, sometimes not. A commuter hears an advertisement on a podcast for ordering glasses online, checks out the website, and orders a sample kit, receives the kit a few days later, tries to chat online with customer service, and then finally calls a toll-free number to get her questions answered (see Figure 1.4). This type of scenario plays out millions of times every day with all sorts of products and services.

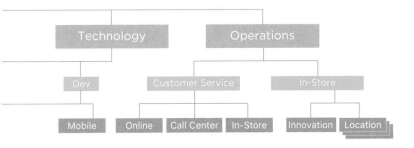

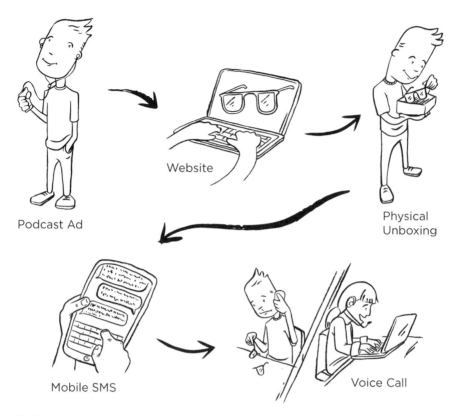

Podcast Ad

Website

Physical Unboxing

Mobile SMS

Voice Call

FIGURE 1.4
Companies organize by channel, but customers move across channels in predictable and unpredictable ways.

Yet, customers don't think about channels. They navigate the options available to them based on knowledge, preference, or context. Pathways can be designed to try to nudge customers to stay or move to a specific channel, but humans envision their own pathways where it is more attractive, useful, or expedient.

The general wisdom is that customers have these preferences, but organizations still spend a lot of time and energy to optimize channel investments and move customers to low-cost channels. Digital transformation efforts (common to most companies the last two decades) have moved jobs performed by employees to customers themselves (i.e., self-service).

Customers also do not care about what groups own the channels that support their experiences. An IKEA customer having an issue with the online store can easily walk into their local store to complain because, to the customer, it's *all IKEA*. The physical store team likely had little to no role in the online experience, yet consistency and continuity of experience is the customer's expectation.

Over the last 20 years, organizations have been told by analysts and consultants to strive to be omnichannel—available to customers in multiple, coordinated channels. Brand teams push to have a consistent look, voice, and tone in all their channels. Marketers attempt to create continuity in messaging while optimizing for high-impact channels. Technologists define architectures to share data and track customer actions across channels. As a result, much talk and effort goes into determining not only what channels to invest in, but also how to coordinate people, processes, and technologies to support and connect them.

This gets even more interesting when you look at the opportunities to mix and combine channels. A simple example is reflected in secure authentication experiences. In Figure 1.5, a user forgot her password to an online bank account. A typical pattern would be to ask her to

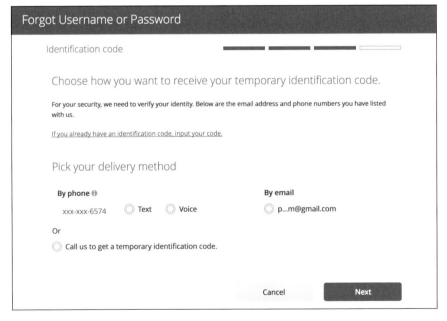

FIGURE 1.5
Most online banks offer customers the option to combine the web channel with text message, voice, email, or IVR to complete the password retrieval process.

fill in some information, such as the last four digits of a Social Security number and a bank account number. If she gets that right, then she is presented with the option to receive a passcode by email, text, voice, or (in unfortunate situations) by mail. This security requires the user to interact with two channels: web and text, web and email, mobile app and text, mobile app and email, or web and mail. The end-user here is trying to get one thing done—recover a password—but multiple channels are leveraged for security while offering the option of which channels to support user preferences.

As much as companies try to organize and optimize investments, people, and processes by channel, they don't exist in isolation. Customers maneuver among them, and smartly combining them can lead to innovation and delight. Yet, to be able to orchestrate experiences across channels, you must understand each channel's unique material.

Channels Reflect Interactions, Information, and Context

To design for good product and service experiences, you must know the capabilities and constraints of the different channels at your disposal. Designing a form delivered via a mobile channel is very different than designing one delivered in print. Creating advertisements for web, outdoor, and television requires different skills and expertise. This means that organizations need specialists for each form to be defined, designed, and executed. These specialists are typically organized by channel (i.e., digital) and then by a specialty in that channel (i.e., web, mobile, etc.). A hierarchical taxonomy of channels based on technology, however, gets muddy fast in the context of defining and executing end-to-end experiences.

As an exercise, list common channels in your business by media, and you will find overlap, redundancy, and conflict. Some of these channels are defined by their context of use (mobile), some by the means of interaction (tablet), others by their technological means of distribution (web), and still others by the content or information they distribute (social media).

A better approach is to define channels by three qualitative facets—interaction, information, and context.

- **Interaction:** What means does the customer use to interact with you? Examples include touch devices, mouse and keyboard, keypad, or voice (see Figure 1.6).

- **Information:** What is the nature of the content being provided to, or exchanged with, the customer? For example, social media.

- **Context:** What is the context—from environment to emotion—in which the interaction is happening. For example, physical stores.

CONSTRAINTS   OPPORTUNITIES

Small Screen   Portability

Awkward Input   Sensors

Distractions   Networked

FIGURE 1.6

The materiality of a channel creates opportunities and constraints.

A channel may be defined by one or more of these facets. Thinking explicitly about each channel through this lens ensures that you are not overlooking the unique material of a channel and how best to leverage it to support customer needs.

Channels Support the Moment

The concept of channels is just that—a concept. Channels help functions and support reaching a company's objectives—from marketing to operations to products.

This is where the challenge rears its ugly head again. Channel specialists, working in isolation, lack an overarching view of what customers will experience in other channels. They see their channel as the primary (if not only) point of customer interaction, not as one of many possible enablers for meeting customers' needs.

Put another way, defining channels as destinations obfuscates their supporting role of enabling and facilitating customer moments in different contexts. A customer shopping in a physical store while using her mobile phone to talk with her spouse and comparison price-check via an app does not represent three separate users in three different channels. She is a single person in a decision moment in which each channel can help or hinder her experience.

When a passenger books a ride with a ride-sharing service, she receives a confirmation message. This message can be delivered by text, push notification, within the application, or via a phone call from the driver. Each option, delivered via a channel, supports what really matters—the passenger knows the car is on its way (see Figure 1.7).

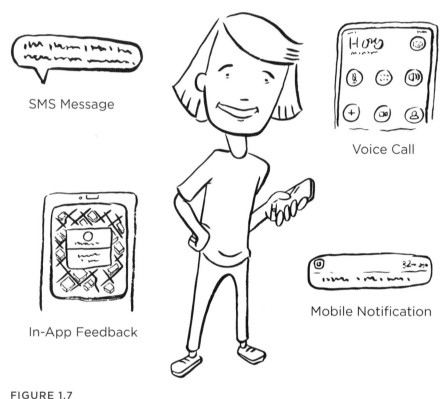

SMS Message

Voice Call

In-App Feedback

Mobile Notification

FIGURE 1.7
Multiple channels can deliver a confirmation message. Which channels are used by a customer depends upon their needs, context, and the capabilities of their mobile device.

Viewing channels as serving customer moments can empower you and your team to work backward from customer needs to which channel(s) will best facilitate meeting those needs. Instead of starting with one channel—digital—start with your customers' needs, context, and journey. What role could print, mobile, web, environment, voice, or people play to support those needs? Can you combine channels in interesting ways? Can you build bridges between channels that help customers move forward easily?

And, most importantly, how do these channels support great customer moments?

Changing the Channel-Centric Mindset

Evaluating your channels in this way creates the opportunity to rethink the relationship of the individual channels and how they may work together. You can readdress how they are defined or what each channel's role could be in a customer's end-to-end experience. At a minimum, you will shift your vantage point from channels as destinations to channels as moment enablers. This conceptual foundation is an important first step in changing the channel-centric mindset.

As discussed, this mindset creates barriers—both conceptual and organizational—that make defining and designing good end-to-end experiences difficult. Changing how your institution organizes people around channels and functions (rather than customers and journeys) is a long game. However, as shown in Figure 1.8, you can begin engaging your colleagues immediately by turning your world 90 degrees and looking at it from a customer's perspective.

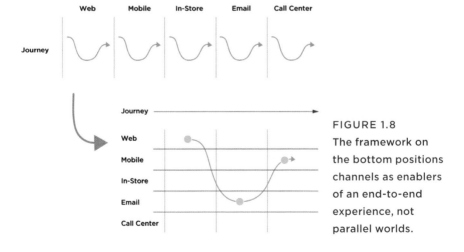

FIGURE 1.8

The framework on the bottom positions channels as enablers of an end-to-end experience, not parallel worlds.

Customers do not contain their actions to one single channel. Stating this to your colleagues will not set off fireworks, but showing it will flip on light bulbs. The next chapter will go into greater depth about how to use a simple framework—a touchpoint inventory—to inventory and visualize how customers interact with your product or service over time. To get ready to create your inventory, you will need to define your channels first.

Codify Your Channels

Your organization likely has some recognizable customer channels, such as websites, mobile apps, call centers, physical stores, and so on. A specific product or service may leverage all or only some of these channels. You also may have a greater or lesser presence in different channels. Here are some approaches to get you started. In general, remember to keep in mind the three facets discussed previously: interaction, information, and context.

1. **Start with the obvious.** What are the major channels you support or where you interact with customers? For example, a customer setting up, placing, picking up, and refilling prescriptions at a CVS Pharmacy at Target may interact with multiple channels owned by the two companies (see Table 1.2).

TABLE 1.2   COMPARISON OF CHANNELS

Target	CVS
Target.com: Pharmacy	CVS.com: Target
Store—Main Line	Pharmacy—Direct Line
Physical Environment (Parking, Signage, Displays, etc).	Physical Environment (Signage, Displays, etc).
	SMS/Messaging
Target Mobile App	CVS Mobile App
	Direct Mail
	Email

2. **Choose the right granularity.** As you identify channels, go beyond broad categories such as "web" or "print." A finer granularity will help you think more strategically about how to use specific channels and to identify where new channels are needed. If you have State Farm insurance, for example, the mobile channel has multiple native applications (see Figure 1.9). Differentiating each of these as separate channels helps clarify the current and future roles of each application in supporting different customer needs and contexts.

FIGURE 1.9

In larger, more fragmented product and service ecosystems, a more granular definition of your channels can help reframe what each subchannel really offers customers and how they relate to other subchannels.

3. **Be specific.** In some cases, you may be delivering different experiences based on the technological affordances of different devices. If your website has different features or touchpoints on larger screens than smaller screens that are assumed to be mobile, define those separately. For example, "Standard main website" and "Mobile main website." This will help you parse and reimagine how to design for varying intersections of technological affordances and customer context.

4. **Note who owns each channel.** As you take stock of relevant channels, you should note which groups and accountable executives own them. In some cases—as in the CVS pharmacy at Target example—you also want to determine what external vendors or partners make decisions related to specific channels. As later chapters will reveal, you will need to reach out and actively collaborate with these people in the future.

5. **Be ready to adapt.** You will probably discover new channels as you and your team go beyond the obvious. Over time, you will also see your channel mix change—either through your efforts or others. Just get a good foundation, start your digging, and adjust as needed.

Build the Orchestra

A helpful analogy for understanding and explaining to others this shift from channels as destinations to enablers of end-to-end experiences is an orchestra (unsurprising, given the title of this book).

What About Research?

Start exploring new frameworks by doing discovery alone or with colleagues. Doing so will help you get a feel for how to define your channels and identify the touchpoints within them.

However, this is merely a prelude to your first movement of work: engaging directly with the customers and other participants. Chapter 5, "Mapping Experiences," will cover the importance of performing qualitative research as a team to understand the needs of people and how they interact—or could interact better—with your organization.

In an orchestra, you have many instruments playing in concert with one another. The conductor determines (working from sheet music) which kinds of instruments will help bring the piece to life. What does each instrument need to play? When do they play solo? Where do they harmonize with other instruments?

Orchestrating experiences means approaching channels with this thoughtfulness and intent. Within each broad category—web, mobile, email, environments, call center, and so on—determine what channels exist. What is each channel's role? Where are your channels out of tune? Where are they creating dissonance? When you widen your lens beyond individual channels to customer moments enabled by channels, you will open new opportunities to orchestrate and reimagine the end-to-end experience.

We'll now move on to the notes your instruments play—touchpoints.

Coda

- A channel is a medium of interaction with customers or users.

- Channels are deceptively complex, as they enable how you interact with people, yet also create barriers within organizations to design across channels.

- Channels have three facets that define them: interaction, information, and context.

- To change the channel-centric mindset that dominates most organizations, start by defining your channels as enablers of moments, not isolated destinations.

- Approach your channels as a conductor would an orchestra. Choose, tune, and direct them with intent.

CHAPTER 2

Pinning Down Touchpoints

The term *touchpoint*, along with channel, has slowly made its way into the lexicon of organizations primarily via the marketing function. Marketing traditionally creates a demand for products and services through campaigns targeted at customer segments. Campaigns often include several tactics—from commercials, to direct mail, to banner ads, and so on—which, in concert, increase brand awareness and offerings. Each customer interaction with a marketing communication is called a *touch*; the communication itself is a *touchpoint*.

Marketing organizations have become increasingly scientific in the creation, deployment, and measurement of touchpoints. Approaches such as customer relationship management (CRM) have enabled marketers to define strategies for how often they touch customers through which channels and to what end. New tools now exist for customer experience managers to monitor and measure the performance of touchpoints. Thus, the term *touchpoint* has become more prevalent in branding and customer experience to quantify and delineate the different ways that customers interact with a brand.

Other disciplines—such as service design—also focus on defining and connecting touchpoints. Interactions such as the attention and detail of a restaurant staff, the way your ride service driver opens the door or drops you off at the airport, or the literal quality of the touch by a massage therapist create the service moments in real time. Many touchpoints are intangible; for example, conversations can leave a lasting impression but are not objects manufactured beforehand. Services also create tangible evidence to reinforce brand or invisible actions. For example, a hotel may put a card and mint on your pillow to bring focus to and amplify the service of a nicely made bed.

What's Service Design?

Service design is a human-centered design approach to defining a service's value proposition and designing interaction and operating models. This work results in more intentional and well-orchestrated service components (touchpoints, information, people, and so on) that deliver better outcomes for all service participants (customers, employees, and other stakeholders). Several methods and tools recommended in this book have their origins in the service design community or related disciplines.

The digitization of products and services (as well as growing interest in customer-centered approaches) has led to the language of marketing, customer experience, and service design mixing with digital and physical product design. The term *touchpoint* has become more prevalent, but also less precise. Much of this ambiguity exists because practitioners within various disciplines use the same terms with slightly (or dramatically) different meanings. When one of your colleagues says *touchpoint*, she may be referring to a digital product (e.g., mobile app), feature (password retrieval), channel (email), or even a role (call center agent).

Orchestrating experiences requires coordination across different disciplines. Touchpoints represent fundamental building blocks of support for customer journeys that cut across time, space, and channels. Therefore, a common definition and approach to touchpoints can lead to improved coordination and ultimately better customer experiences.

NOTE WHAT IS A CUSTOMER JOURNEY?

A journey is a conceptual framework used to understand and design for a customer's experience over time. Depending on the context, a journey can reveal what customers are doing, thinking, and feeling to achieve an explicit goal (owning a home) or implicit need (shelter) or interacting with a product or service (getting a home loan). These insights help identify opportunities for improving products and services or creating new value propositions and offerings. Chapters 4, "Orienting Around Journeys," and 5, "Mapping Experiences," cover these concepts in depth.

A Unifying Approach

Here's where things get tricky. To orchestrate experiences, you should think about touchpoints in two different but related ways.

First, customers encounter an organization, service, or product in a specific context. This encounter may be planned or unplanned; it may be designed or not designed. But they happen. You can observe the encounter, describe what is happening, and determine its effect. These encounters are touchpoints, and as branding folks will tell you, they will impact the customer's perception of a brand, product, or service positively or negatively.

Second, organizations can design proactively for specific customer moments. They can determine the value that they want to provide, choose channels to interact with customers, and use design craft to meet customer needs optimally. These series of choices result in a family of touchpoints that are produced in advance or cocreated with customers in the moment. For example, a greeter at a retailer's front entrance can be trained on how to greet customers while handing out a weekly specials coupon. The online store can welcome the customer with copy at the top and display the weekly specials below. The same touchpoint types—greeting customers and informing them about weekly specials—are delivered in different ways in different channels (see Figure 2.1).

FIGURE 2.1
Greeting customers and informing them of weekly specials are touchpoints that take on different forms when delivered via different channels.

Touchpoints represent an important architectural concept in experiences that can span channels, space, and time. An organization can *holistically* craft an interconnecting system with a better chance of consistently and predictably meeting customer needs in many contexts. This system should be adaptable and extensible as new channels and interaction types emerge over time.

Such a systematic approach to end-to-end experiences requires creating more consistency in how touchpoints are defined within an organization. In the previous example, your colleagues may ask: "Isn't the greeter a touchpoint?" or "Aren't the weekly specials on the website a feature?" Yes, in the language of the separate domains of store operations and product management, respectively. But to orchestrate experiences, these differences in language must be reconciled. To this end, touchpoints can be defined as having the following dimensions:

- Have a clear intent based on identified needs.
- Create customer moments individually or in combinations.
- Play varying but specific roles.
- Can be evaluated and measured for appropriateness and efficacy.[1]

What's Your Intent?

Touchpoints take different forms based on the channel, context, and interaction. An order status conversation with a call agent could be supported via phone, online chat, video, text message, or email. These touchpoints should share a common and clear intent behind their role in the end-to-end experience. They also should share a common set of principles that guide their definition, creation, and measurement. As Table 2.1 illustrates, product and service ecosystems typically have multiple channels—designed in silos—delivering similar touchpoints. Defining the underlying intent makes it possible to identify the same touchpoint types in different channels. This enables cross-functional teams to compare, connect, and increase the consistency of the superset of channel experiences.

TABLE 2.1   INTENT BY CHANNEL

Intent	Website	Mobile	Call Center	Store
Greeting customer	Welcome back copy	None	Enter phone number (IVR)	Conversation
Informing of specials	Special callout	Specials for you—push notification	Specials message during wait time	Coupon

---

1 This is mostly true. Indirect touchpoints—such as word of mouth—are important to consider and influence. They are the exception, however, not the rule.

INTENT VS. EXECUTION

Separating the *why and what* (intent) from the *how* (execution in different channels) is important. For example, in my work with libraries, I have seen lots of experimentation in programs and approaches to bring new value to the community. Libraries, however, must still stay true to a pillar of their traditional mission: helping the community find information and build knowledge. As Figure 2.2 shows, the touchpoint of asking a librarian brings this mission to life in multiple channels based on an evergreen intent.

FIGURE 2.2
The touchpoint of asking a librarian is available in many channels with the same intent.

Making the Moment

The intent behind any individual touchpoint should not be determined in isolation. A touchpoint's efficacy depends not only upon how it plays its unique role, but also how well the touchpoint connects with and conforms to the overarching experience. Because touchpoints can appear in different combinations in different contexts, it's helpful to view them as role players in the customer moments you hope to create.

Figure 2.3 illustrates this conceptual framework. As customers move from moment to moment in their product or service experiences, different touchpoints support their journey. A few of these touchpoints truly serve as features, helping to create signature customer moments. Some touchpoints support specific customer actions. Others may play a more ambient role, while still others are called upon to serve a subset of customers.

Experience over time

Moments

Touchpoints

FIGURE 2.3
Touchpoints appear in one or more customer moments, playing specific roles in each.

As an example, take the moment of checking in at the airport counter. Touchpoints in this customer moment include wayfinding signage, greeting and process conversations, mobile and print boarding passes, the baggage conveyor belt, and much more (see Figure 2.4). As illustrated here, touchpoints can be tangible (a sign)

FIGURE 2.4
Regardless of channels or who makes them, touchpoints should be orchestrated as one with the same underlying intent.

or intangible (a conversation). They can be analog (a conveyor belt) or digital (a mobile boarding pass). They can be manufactured beforehand (the check-in desk) or created in the moment (the length of the queue). Individually, each touchpoint plays its role; collectively, these touchpoints create the customer experience in the moment.

Different Moments, Different Roles

As you begin to rationalize the various definitions of touchpoints, it becomes easier to articulate the role and characteristics for each touchpoint. A few examples of touchpoint roles include *featured*, *bridge*, and *repair/recovery*.

- **Featured:** Not all aspects of a product or service uniquely deliver value to customers. Featured touchpoints play the role of helping create signature customer moments. Examples of featured touchpoints include USAA's first-to-market mobile checking deposit touchpoint, Zappos's easy returns, and Amazon Dash's physical reorder button (see Figure 2.5).

FIGURE 2.5
Amazon Dash is a signature shopping moment with a beautifully designed enabling touchpoint.

- **Bridge:** When you want to help a customer move from one moment to the next or one channel to the next bridge, touchpoints are important. Some bridge touchpoints serve as handoffs (Figure 2.6), such as when one customer service agent dials in a second agent and gracefully transitions the conversation. Other bridges require two or more coordinating touchpoints. For example, a PDF concert ticket attached to an email, the ticket printed from your printer (another touchpoint), the door person asking for and recognizing your ticket, and the scanning of your ticket's barcode are all touchpoints that bridge the moments from buying a ticket to seeing the show.

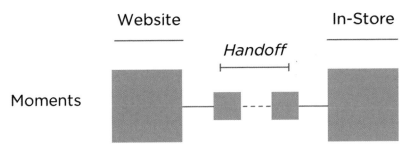

FIGURE 2.6
Bridge touchpoints (such as handoffs) often fall through the cracks as different teams focus solely on their own channel.

- **Repair/Recovery:** When customers fall off the happy path, repair and recovery touchpoints come to the rescue. If you can't recall your password, you interact with "Forgot your password?" touchpoints. Or if you receive damaged merchandise, a series of touchpoints aid you in getting a replacement via your channel of choice. Repair/recovery touchpoints often have sequential characteristics to them.

These are just three of the most common roles that touchpoints may play. You'll want to review your own moments and their respective touchpoints to determine what roles they play in your product or service experience. This becomes very helpful when you look at key moments through experience maps and service blueprints (see Chapters 5 and 9, "Crafting a Tangible Vision").

Making Sure That Touchpoints Do Their Job

When you approach touchpoints as a coordinated system of featured and supporting players on the stage of experience, you naturally segue to the thought: "Is everyone playing his or her part, and well?" From a measurement standpoint, some touchpoints—especially digital ones—can be tracked and reported on. Examples include the following: shopping cart abandonment rates, email offer click-throughs, usage rates for mobile versus paper boarding passes, and how many customers upgrade a service following a conversation with a call center agent.

Other touchpoints can be evaluated by asking customers questions in person or via surveys. Was the entertaining airline safety video not so entertaining? How satisfied were you with the call agent's problem resolution conversation? How would you rate your experience with our new packaging? This feedback can be used to improve specific touchpoints or flow among them.

As you will see in later chapters, great product and service experiences rely on orchestrating these good touchpoints well.

Two Helpful Frameworks

Touchpoints can be slippery. They take the form of the channels that deliver them, but work (or often don't work) in concert to help create a customer's experience. The same touchpoint—getting shipping status—can be offered simultaneously in different channels. Or a touchpoint can exist in only one channel. Understanding touchpoints, therefore, can require a couple of different (but helpful) frameworks:

- Touchpoints by moment
- Touchpoints by channel

Touchpoints by Moment

It's a given that touchpoints play an important role in creating customer moments. They facilitate interactions, deliver information, trigger emotions, and bridge one moment to the next. Figure 2.7 illustrates a simple but powerful framework for placing touchpoints in the context of the overarching customer journeys they support.

- **Journeys:** Customers experience product and services over time, often in the context of achieving an explicit goal or meeting an implicit need (see Chapter 4). A journey, in this context, is a conceptual frame to refer to the beginning, middle, and end of the customer's experience. Example journeys include going to the movies, saving for college, adopting a child, and a trip to the emergency room.

- **Stages:** A journey is not monolithic; it unfolds in a series of moments that tend to cluster around specific needs or goals. When mapping experiences, these clusters are known as *stages*. Stages are essentially chapters of the customer's journey, which use a level of granularity for creating strategies that the common customer needs. Table 2.2 provides a few examples of journeys and stages.

- **Moments:** Whether linear or nonlinear, moments occur throughout a journey as the customers make their way forward in time. Not all moments are created equal, and the most important ones are often referred to as *key moments* or *moments of truth*. Regardless, all moments matter.

- **Touchpoints:** Touchpoints enable interactions within and across moments. As we'll discuss in later chapters, defining a vision for each customer moment provides the right inputs for ensuring that each touchpoint plays its unique role while harmonizing with others.

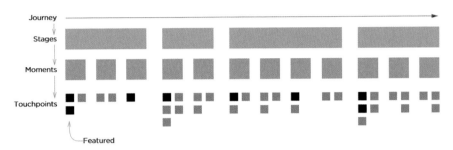

FIGURE 2.7

Touchpoints represent fundamental building blocks in the journeys of customers as they interact with a product or service in multiple channels over time.

TABLE 2.2 JOURNEY STAGES

Journey	Stages
Going to the movies	Exploring entertainment options, deciding what to see, going to the theater, buying a ticket, getting concessions, getting settled, watching the film, after the film
Buying a home	Searching for a home, getting prequalified, making an offer, applying for a loan, getting ready for closing, closing, moving, settling in
A trip to the emergency room	Experiencing a trauma, getting to the hospital, being admitted, waiting for care, getting care, recovering, paying medical bills

To put this framework to work, you will need to determine the journey and stages you want to dig into down to the touchpoint level. Chapters 4 and 5 will provide guidance as to how to make these decisions with the critical input of customer research. However, starting with an informed hypothesis can yield good results. See the tips on drafting your stages and channels in the next section.

Touchpoints by Channel

Channels enable touchpoints, so it is also helpful to make sense of which channels deliver which touchpoints. However, simply viewing your touchpoints by channel loses the context of how touchpoints align to the customer experience. As illustrated in Figure 2.8, a simple matrix with journey stages on the X-axis and channels in the Y-axis creates a structure that keeps customer context top of mind. This framework—called a *touchpoint inventory*[2] —also effectively provides an at-a-glance view of the density of touchpoints by channel and stage. The touchpoint inventory helps shed light on what touchpoints the organization has created and how they align—or fail to align—to the customer journey.

Online glasses purchase

		Explore	Try on	Select	Purchase	Wear	Extend
Channels of interaction	Web						
	Mobile						
	In-Store						
	Email						
	Call Center						
	At Home						
	Chat						
	Text						

Stages of journey

FIGURE 2.8

This simple framework organizes touchpoints by channel.

---

2 In some circles, this framework is called a *service blueprint*. In our usage, a service blueprint includes both customer touchpoints and operational elements to deliver an end-to-end experience across channels (see Chapters 3 , "Exploring Ecosystems," and 9).

As with any framework, you will need to customize your touchpoint for your organization. If you are creating your framework in advance or in the absence of a well-defined customer journey, you will need to create an educated hypothesis of your channels and stages. See Chapter 1, "Understanding Channels," for guidance on identifying your channels. As for your touchpoints, try one or more of the following:

- Bring together stakeholders that own various touchpoints in different channels. Collaborate with them to draft the journey stages that span all channels. (See the workshop agenda and approach following this chapter).

- Leverage any existing research you have on your customers, as well as the knowledge of your colleagues.

- Review business processes that customers must go through. Unfortunately, these processes may currently dictate where a stage begins or ends.

- Take your own journey. See how your experience breaks down into steps.

- Interview one to two customers to get a feel for their journey and its stages.

- Play with how many stages to divide the journey into. There is no magic number.

- Name your stages from the customer's perspective, not business or marketing language. Instead of "creating awareness" and "consideration," go with "researching and learning" and "exploring my options."

Identifying Your Touchpoints

After you select one (or both) of the above frameworks to try, it's time to get to work identifying all your touchpoints. This should occur in iterations. You can start by directly exploring each channel yourself. You can bring channel partners together to collaboratively build out a current-state touchpoint inventory (see the workshop example following this chapter). You will also discover more about your touchpoints (and even undiscovered touchpoints) when you conduct your customer research (see Chapter 5).

A QUICK-AND-DIRTY TOUCHPOINT INVENTORY

When Rail Europe wanted to better align its customer experience cohesively across channels, one of the starting points was identifying all the different touchpoints that existed where there was a specific need at a given time and place. We had everyone represented in the same room: marketing, digital, operations, call center, and more. Each stakeholder had a partial snapshot, but not a full view, one that reviewed interdependencies that they hadn't considered.

When we completed a draft of the touchpoint inventory shown in Figure 2.9, each stakeholder was surprised just how many moments there were and how each moment was an opportunity to deliver on the value proposition of the service. We knew what stages existed in the journey, but across the organization, we realized no one had an exhaustive picture of just where people were interacting with the brand. The touchpoint inventory wasn't a major endeavor, but it was an important one in getting everyone started with a clear picture of where the opportunity spaces were going to be as we later mapped out what people were experiencing on the rail travel journey.

Touchpoints by Channel for Travel Service

Stage	Research & Planning	Shopping	Booking	Pre-Travel (Documents)	Travel	Post-Travel
Website	Maps Test intineraries Timetables Destination Pages FAQ General product & site exploration	Schedule look-up Price look-up Multi-city look-up Pass comparison	Web booking funnel - Pass - Trips - Multiple Trips	Select document option (from available options) - station e-ticket - home print e-ticket - mail ticket	Contact page for email or phone	
Call Center	Order brochure Planning (Products) Schedules General questions	Site navigation help	Automated booking payment Cust. Rep booking Site navigation help	Call re: ticket options Request ticket mailed Resolve problems (info, payment, etc.)	Call with questions regarding tickets General calls re: schedules, strikes, documents	
Mobile	Trip ideas	Schedules	Mobile trip booking		Access itinerary Look up schedules Buy additional tickets	
Communication Channels (social media, email, chat)	Chat for web nav help	FB Comparator Email questions Chat for website nav help	Chat for booking support	Email confirmations Email for general help Hold ticket	Ask questions or resolve problems re: schedules and tickets	Complaints or compliments Survey
Customer Relations						Request for refund, escalation from call center.
Non-Brand Channels	Trip Advisor Travel blogs Social Media General Google searching	Airline comparison Kayak Direct rail sites	Expedia		Travel Blogs Direct rail sites Google searches	Trip Advisor Review sites Facebook

Non-linear, no time restrictions → Linear process ∿ Non-linear but time based

COURTESY OF ADAPTIVE PATH

FIGURE 2.9
Rail Europe touchpoint inventory.

Let's use our CVS Pharmacy at Target example again to look at how we might unpack a customer journey and its touchpoints by channel. This case study is interesting given the partnership between the companies (Target outsourced its pharmacy department to CVS following years of a well-regarded in-house approach).

To unpack each channel, you need to choose a method that works best for each channel's medium while also identifying the stage or stages that each touchpoint supports. We'll focus on identifying touchpoints for now. In the next section, we'll give you some guidance on how to catalog your touchpoints as you find them.

Target Website and CVS Website

Publically accessible websites and mobile applications are often the easiest channels to begin your discovery. You can simply click or tap your way through each screen and state, capturing your touchpoints along the way. Digital touchpoints are often, but not always, equivalent to product features, and can even be articulated as user stories common in an agile development environment.

For example, starting at Target.com, you quickly realize that you must navigate from the Target website to CVS.com (see Figure 2.10). You do so via a bridge touchpoint. (An improvement would be an additional wayfinding touchpoint that communicates that you are still "at Target," not a generic CVS.) Some of the CVS Pharmacy website touchpoints include: signing in, finding a pharmacy, transferring a prescription, printing prescriptions, and managing automatic prescriptions.

FIGURE 2.10

A bridge touchpoint ("go to CVS Pharmacy") connects the customer to a site that provides a full set of online services.

In addition to exploring these online channels organically, you may want to try flowing through them by simulating a common user scenario or task. For example, you could search on Google for "get a flu shot at Target" and see what touchpoints begin to appear in your path.

CVS Mobile App

Like many brands, Target has created mobile applications designed to support customers shopping the entire store or carrying out tasks specific to its different departments. For the pharmacy, you must download the CVS pharmacy app. To avoid any confusion, we call this channel "CVS mobile app" while also including "Target mobile app" to inventory the bridge touchpoint. (As with Target.com, the main Target mobile app just simply points you to CVS.)

It's easy to click through and see that many of the same touchpoints that are available on the website exist on mobile as well. As you click through, you will find that some touchpoints offer the same types of interactions as the website but others work differently based on the affordances of that channel. Refilling a prescription, for example, can be done by using your mobile's camera to take a picture of the label or by typing in the Rx number, similar to the website (see Figure 2.11).

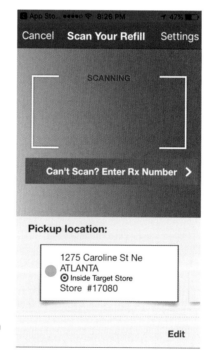

FIGURE 2.11

Refilling a prescription via mobile.

When doing your inventory, this is something specifically to look out for: How do touchpoints intended to meet the same customer need differ by channel? Doing so not only helps you understand if there are opportunities to meet needs in more channels, but also informs you of better ways to balance consistency and uniqueness across channels.

Physical Store

In a physical channel, such as a store, you can begin identifying your touchpoints as you did online by simply exploring. For Target, you can begin in the parking lot and find your way to the pharmacy. Is there signage or other wayfinding touchpoints to show you the way? Is there a store map? Are people there to assist? Are there pathways on the floor?

Observing customers and employees interact will also help you break down what exists in the space to support customer needs. Begin with building a list of the objects you see in the environment.[3] Within a few minutes of observing service in a CVS Pharmacy at Target, you can observe these touchpoints (and many more):

- Wayfinding signage

- A drop-off area

- A pickup area

- An order conversation

- A status conversation

- A bin with filled prescriptions organized by letter of last name

- Pill bottles with labels

- A digital signature component

- Rewards program marketing signage

---

3 There are many frameworks you can leverage to help you deconstruct the physical environment. For example, the widely used AEIOU method captures ethnographic observations in five categories: actions, environments, interactions, objects, and users.

INTRODUCING TOUCHPOINTS TO OTHERS

I often make identifying and cataloging touchpoints a group effort. For example, on a service experience strategy engagement with a public library system, I tasked key members of the library staff to catalogue the staff, touchpoints, activities, qualities, and types of customers at different branches. Each staff member was given a template to capture what he or she discovered through observation and experiencing of the libraries' services personally.

Distributing the inventory had several benefits. One was speed. We could pull together in a few days a great first pass. Just as important, the staff gained immediate experience in understanding what touchpoints were and which ones stood out in the current experience. By capturing them in a common template, my team was able to review and refine the inventory quickly. We then created a game (see Figure 2.12) in which participants determined which touchpoints to take into the future and what new touchpoints would be needed to serve customers better.

FIGURE 2.12
Playing with touchpoints and other elements that make up a current experience.

Phone—Voice

Many organizations provide voice channels supported by call centers or other means to sell, support, or deliver products and services. During your inventory, you likely will need to attack this and other communication channels from both the inside and outside to build a complete picture.

Let's start inside. Hopefully, you can get access to your call center or other locations in which people speak directly with customers. In this channel, your touchpoints will be conversations. For our CVS Pharmacy at Target example, the nature of a call might have been to place an order, update an address, or check status. It could have been all those things. Your objective is to identify what conversations exist to meet these different needs.

Conversations as Touchpoints

Many interactions between people and services occur through conversation. These conversations can be face-to-face, via the phone, or as an audio/video chat. It's helpful to approach these conversations as touchpoints, and even break them down into multiple touchpoints based on their intent and function.

For example, having your credit card stolen can be inconvenient and emotional. When calling your bank to report the theft, that conversation can be codified as a series of touchpoints:

- Understanding the issue

- Confirming your identity

- Capturing the details

- Explaining the process

- Confirming where to send the new card

- Offering further assistance

This level of granularity is helpful for rethinking the experience, as well as creating consistency and continuity across channels. The "confirming your identity" touchpoint could be moved to an interactive voice response (IVR) system preceding understanding the issue. "Confirming where to send the card" could also be delivered via email. The entire experience could be moved to a voice interface (e.g., Apple's Siri or Amazon's Alexa).

If your organization has one or more call centers, they are a gold mine for understanding the needs and language of customers. Call centers are also complex environments in which changing the customer's call experience requires equipping call center agents with the right concepts, tools, and training to deliver the intended experience. To understand the call center experience and the underlying processes, roles, tools, and policies, follow these procedures as much as possible:

- **Listen to calls.** Most call centers regularly record customer calls for compliance or quality assurance. Work with your call center team to identify calls related to the customer journeys or scenarios under investigation.

- **Analyze transcripts.** You can also read or search for key words in call transcripts.

- **Ask for a report.** Some call centers have sophisticated tools to analyze calls for key words and events. Try requesting a report (with audio clips) based on your needs.

- **Perform side-by-sides.** Call centers are typically set up for observers to plug in and listen to live calls. This is ideal for hearing the conversations and observing the environment and behavior of the agent.

- **Process documentation.** Process maps could clarify the flow of conversations and how processes trigger specific conversations. Be careful, however. Process maps often don't reflect what's happening on the calls.

- **One-on-one interviews.** Spend time interviewing agents to understand how they structure calls. You will need to keep these sessions to 30 minutes or less, as most call center managers are averse to taking their agents off calls for long periods of time.

- **Current-state service blueprinting.** This method is covered in Chapter 3, but consider doing service blueprinting sessions with agents to map how they work with tools and other employees to support customer conversations. Also, probe on what touchpoints the agents believe or know that customers interact with before and after their calls. For example, agents may have noticed that many customers call in after a digital touchpoint fails to meet their needs.

Other Channels

The methods we've outlined can also help you explore other channels. Target and CVS interact with customers via texts, push messages, physical mail, and email. In many cases, touchpoints are like voice communications—they may give status, prompt action, or connect to the next step. In other cases, they may contain unique touchpoints to that channel, such as a physical coupon.

Cataloging and Communicating Your Touchpoints

As you identify your touchpoints, you will need to document your findings. How detailed you get depends on the breadth and depth of your product or service, your goals, and the amount of effort you can (or should) commit to the inventory. You have lots of options, but your inventory should give people a complete picture of your touchpoints. Here are two approaches representing the two extremes on a spectrum from lean to finely detailed.

Keep It Lean

When you have little time, or just want to get a first iteration complete, your focus should be on nailing down the basics: stages, channels, and touchpoints. The Rail Europe example (see Figure 2.9) illustrates this level of detail. The stages should have clear labels in customer-centric language. It should reflect your primary channels, while less used channels can be summarized or combined. Touchpoints should then be organized at the intersection of stages and channels.

Figure 2.13 illustrates another approach on the leaner side of the spectrum. This inventory reflects a future-state vision of how to combine new and existing touchpoints into a better end-to-end experience. It includes specifications for each moment—required screens, content, and communications—to support the design process for different channels teams.

If you need to be even leaner and you have the wall space, build your inventory in sticky notes or take a picture of your workshop outputs and put up a large printout of it. Just make sure that your work stays visible to others so they can refer to it to inform strategy and design activities. Keep socializing the framework to unite others on its holistic view of where and when customers will interact with your product or service.

Hospitality Service Platform MVP *Touchpoint Inventory*

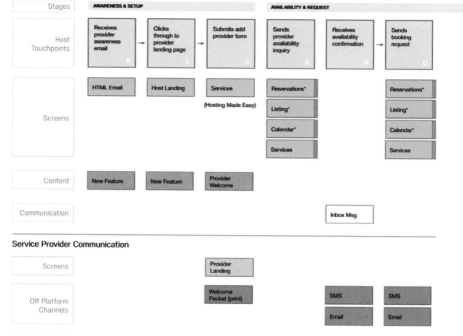

FIGURE 2.13

An example of a touchpoint inventory.

No Detail Left Behind

Beyond the basics, you can go much deeper into cataloging your touchpoints and describing their roles (and how well they play it) in the customer experience. This finely detailed approach is valuable in transformative work that involves reimagining customer journeys or creating sophisticated service experience architectures. While this takes time, the return on investment can be great in terms of better customer experiences and more easily managed operations.

A detailed inventory uses the same methods as outlined in this chapter, but with more information to collect and document. Like a content inventory, a spreadsheet tool provides the right functionality and flexibility to capture and analyze your work. You can then create different visual documentation with varying levels of information as needed. As Chapter 11, "Taking Up the Baton," advises, your

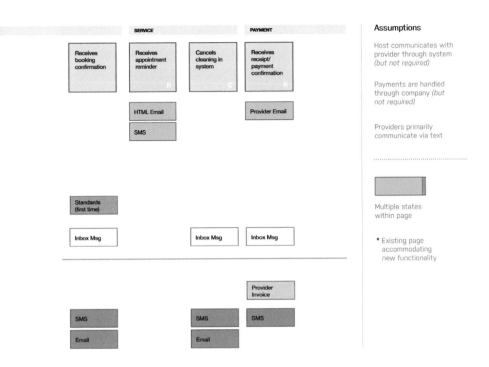

touchpoint inventory should be a living document for planning, creating, changing, and retiring touchpoints.

Below are common attributes helpful to capture and track your touchpoints throughout the design process.

- **Channel stage:** What stage(s) does the touchpoint support?

- **Moment:** What moment(s) does the touchpoint support?

- **Touchpoint name:** Make this clear and unique. If the touchpoint takes on different forms in different channels, keep the name consistent. For example, an Uber "ride confirmation" can be delivered via push notification or text message.

- **Needs:** What needs does the touchpoint meet? If none, do you need it?

- **Roles:** What roles—such as featured or repair/recovery—does the touchpoint play?

- **Connections:** If the touchpoint lives in a sequence or bridges to another touchpoint and channel, list those touchpoints here.

- **Quality:** Is the touchpoint good? Does it fail to adhere to basic heuristics or specific experience principles?

- **Measurement:** Do you have any performance metrics associated with the touchpoint?

- **Owner:** Who owns the touchpoint from the organization's viewpoint?

- **Status:** Is there a plan to change or replace the touchpoint in the future?

Nailing down all these details can be a collaborative effort by leveraging shared spreadsheets to have people contribute across the enterprise. Together, you can create a living document of the architecture that makes your customer experiences possible. This foundation will then pay off as you collectively research, imagine, and conceptualize the moments and touchpoints of the future.

Coda

- Touchpoints are critical architectural components of end-to-end experiences. Moment by moment, one or more touchpoints enables interactions between your customers and your product or service.

- While you can design and make them in advance, touchpoints come to life when a customer interacts with them in real time and in a specific context. Some touchpoints occur without any design intervention as customers make their own pathways through and around your organization.

- Create your touchpoints based on meeting specific customer needs and embodying one or more key characteristics. If there is no need or a clear purpose, why do you need it?

- You can use different methods—research, workshops, and discovery—to identify your touchpoints. A simple matrix showing which touchpoints exist at the intersection of journey stages and channels can have eye-opening impact on your colleagues.

- How much detail you capture as you identify touchpoints depends on your goals and time allocated. Start lean to change mindsets; go deep to fuel more advanced techniques in designing and managing your experiences.

This workshop is designed to engage your stakeholders in building your initial touchpoint inventory. If you have a draft already, you can easily adapt this workshop to fill in gaps and refine your understanding. The benefits of bringing collaborators together to build or refine a touchpoint inventory are many and include the following:

- **Jump-start your discovery:** Leveraging the knowledge of others, a first pass at the inventory can usually be completed in 2–4 hours, depending on the complexity of your product or service.

- **Teach new concepts:** Workshops are a great way to introduce new concepts (e.g., What is a touchpoint?) while focusing most of the time on creating a valuable framework.

- **Build relationships:** Scheduling the workshop will help you identify and build relationships with key people across functions and groups. It's also a great opportunity to test the waters on getting more time and partnerships to construct and then use the inventory.

Remember: This is just a start. You will uncover more about your touchpoints when you engage customers in your research (see Chapter 5.

Workshop Objectives

- Introduce key terms, including journeys, stages, channels, and touchpoints.

- Share the value of defining touchpoints consistently across functional areas.

- Build an initial list of existing customer touchpoints by channel and journey stage.

- Align on improving your inventory.

Example Pitch to Participants (and Their Managers)

How well you prepare and communicate will make or break the effectiveness of your session. Make sure that you have previously educated your collaborators and sold the value of your session. Here is a sample pitch that you can make your own:

Channel by channel, our work results in a multitude of customer touchpoints and interactions. But customers are not bound by channels. They move across them by choice or necessity, experience channels simultaneously, and see them as part of one whole—our company.

Here we will use a simple framework to inventory what our customers interact with in each channel. We'll examine the range of touchpoints we offer and how they relate to key stages of our customers' journeys. We'll share what we know is working or not working, and how we can work as a team to support our customers across channels and time.

Agenda

This workshop is designed to be completed in two to four hours, including a short break. Give yourself more time if you have a large group of participants (more than 20) or a larger number of channels and touchpoints. The times provided are based on a four-hour workshop.

TABLE 2.3 WORKSHOP AGENDA

Activity	Description	Duration
Introductions	Facilitate participants getting to know one another beyond just names and titles.	15 min
Review agenda and objectives	Share the activities for the day and what you want to accomplish by the end of the session.	10 min
Review key concepts	Share definitions and examples of journeys, stages, and touchpoints.	20 min
Agree to channels	List the major channels in which you operate for your selected journey.	30 min
Define journey stages	Use an existing stage or create a hypothesis for the stages of the customer journey.	40 min
Break	Recharge!	15 min
Fill in touchpoints	Work as a team to fill in your inventory.	20 min
Review and refine	Review and refine the inventory. Evaluate the performance of each touchpoint.	75 min
Reflect and determine next steps	Reflect upon the workshop process and outcomes. Determine the next steps.	15 min

Roles

- **Lead facilitator:** Workshop host and main facilitator for session activities

- **Co-facilitator(s):** Help(s) set up, break down, and assist in activities

- **Documentarian:** Takes photographs of the session to help nonparticipants understand the collaborative process

Participants

- Owners of specific channels or stages of the customer journey

- Subject matter experts who know the ins and outs of a channel or key customer processes

- Researchers (from design, marketing, and customer insights)

- Designers

- Product managers

Artifacts

- **Pictures or screenshots of touchpoints:** If you have done some previous discovery, bring screenshots of digital touchpoints and pictures of physical environments. These can help jump-start your inventory, as well as provide examples of touchpoints.

- **Example touchpoint inventory:** It's helpful for people to see an example of what they will be making together.

Materials

- Self-stick easel pad or butcher paper (to create a wall canvas)

- Painter's tape (for hanging butcher paper)

- Sharpies

- Sticky notes

- Red (sad) and green (happy) emotion stickers

- Camera

TOUCHPOINT INVENTORY: AN IMPORTANT FOUNDATION

A touchpoint inventory activity invariably helps people understand the potential transformation that orchestrating experiences can bring. For the first time, they can see what the entire organization has created to acquire and serve customers in one view. This tends to create a mix of emotions in workshop participants. Surprise. Confusion. Curiosity. Then the light bulbs go off and heads begin to nod. It never fails. And now the pump is primed to collaborate on further codifying and improving touchpoints as a system.

Preparing for the Workshop

As with any workshop, preparation includes identifying the right participants, clearly communicating intended outcomes, and getting your artifacts and materials ready in advance. Doing some light discovery to ensure that you hit the ground running in your session can pay dividends as well. Here are some tips:

- If you are new to your organization or client, do some digging to identify the right attendees. Channel and product owners should attend, but also invite people who make tangible touchpoints or interact with customers via intangible touchpoints (e.g., call center representatives).

- Track down any existing frameworks or models related to channel operations or customer journeys. This will help you understand the structures that currently govern participants' roles and work.

- Take some time to do your own exploration of your channels and touchpoints. This will give you better insight into whom to invite and how much time you will need to cover the breadth and depth of the customer experience. Take screenshots and take pictures of touchpoints.

Running the Workshop

To set up a workshop, use a few meters of butcher paper (or several sheets from a self-stick easel pad) to create a canvas on a wall. Build out your touchpoint inventory on this canvas, guiding participants through activities to define and fill in your framework (see Figure 2.14).

FIGURE 2.14
Scene from a touchpoint inventory workshop.

To begin, have people introduce themselves. Review your objectives and agenda, and then facilitate the group through the six activities:

1. Review key concepts.

2. Agree to channels.

3. Define journey stages.

4. Fill in touchpoints.

5. Review and refine.

6. Reflect and determine the next steps.

Review Key Concepts

Start with reviewing the definitions of channel, journey, journey stages, and touchpoints. Show examples from your products and services to make this tangible. Encourage people to embrace these definitions for the workshop, in order to ensure an effective session. There may be initial confusion (or even pushback) as you introduce concepts that challenge the status quo. In the end, you should find that most people will appreciate at least trying a new approach to document the ways your organization currently interacts with customers.

Agree to Channels

Take a first pass at your channels before the session and then validate and refine them with your participants. Go through each channel, one by one, and make sure that everyone understands the purpose of the channel at a high level. Each channel should be written on a sticky note and placed on your canvas as a row of your matrix.

Remember to push participants to break down overarching channels—such as "digital"—to more useful categories. For Amazon, a few useful channels for exploring entertainment journeys could be:

- Amazon.com
- Amazon app
- Echo and Alexa family
- Amazon Music app
- Amazon Kindle app
- Prime Video app

Define Journey Stages

If your organization has an existing journey model, place each stage on the canvas as a column of your matrix. Review each stage and make sure that everyone is in alignment before moving on to the next step. In the absence of a previously created journey model, you will need to build a quick hypothesis with your participants. Here is a quick way to do so:

- Give each participant a few sticky notes and a Sharpie.
- Ask everyone individually to capture what they think are the stages of the customer journey, writing one stage per sticky.
- Have participants present their stages one by one. As they do so, begin to cluster similar stages.

- Once everyone has presented, facilitate aligning around the names and sequence of your stages. Remember, there is no magic number, and your stages should be from the customer's perspective.

NOTE BE ITERATIVE

To create change, you must begin somewhere. This workshop essentially creates a hypothesis of your channels, stages, and touchpoints based on what the workshop participants know (or think they know). This starting point helps you introduce new concepts and get some traction in creating a shared understanding. You shouldn't create grand strategies and plans based on this initial hypothesis, however. More work—especially customer research (see Chapter 5)—and subsequent iterations will be needed to have a complete inventory.

Fill in Touchpoints

You can now begin populating your matrix. First, review the definition of a touchpoint again and ask for a few examples. Then instruct participants to write down individually, one per sticky note, as many existing touchpoints as possible and then place them on the canvas in the channel and stage in which they belong. For the best results, follow these simple guidelines:

- Timebox the activity at 15 to 20 minutes.

- Have people start with what they know. They may own a specific channel or stage of the customer journey. Encourage them to spend the most time on where they have the most knowledge.

- Some touchpoints may appear in more than one stage, so ask participants to add multiple sticky notes for those touchpoints.

- Group people together who have similar knowledge. By working together, they should be able to generate a good inventory while reducing duplicates or differences in language.

- Watch out for groups that get stuck on what to call things or what stages that touchpoints go in. Remind them this is a first pass and that you will refine everything in the next step.

Review and Refine

You will now have a wall covered in sticky notes and a room full of people surprised that there are so many. That's progress!

Next, facilitate a walkthrough of the matrix, going top to bottom, left to right. Your goal: review each touchpoint, combine duplicates, and fill in any gaps. Along the way, you will generate a valuable cross-functional conversation about why certain touchpoints exist, how they connect with others, and in general what is known about their performance. Take your time.

To get the most out of the discussion, we recommend the following:

- Get people to lean in. People should be actively putting up and moving sticky notes together.

- Assign some participants to document the walkthrough discussion. One person can write down new touchpoints; another can capture details of touchpoints (how they perform, if they are being replaced or improved, and so on).

- If you have time, give participants three green stickers and three red stickers. Ask them to put their stickers on touchpoints that are performing the best (green) and the worst (red). Facilitate a dialogue around how the organization defines and measures the success and failure of touchpoints.

> **NOTE** BUILDING BRIDGES, ONE STICKY NOTE
> AT A TIME
>
> The sharing of information and dialogue you facilitate in this workshop can generate more value than what ends up on the sticky notes. Bringing together colleagues from different functions with their varying perspectives to cocreate a tool happens too rarely in most organizations. When facilitated well, this workshop is enlightening and enjoyable. You will build a lot of goodwill and lay the foundation for other approaches outlined in this book. Make sure to take good pictures of the session so that you can share the process and results with others.

Reflect and Determine the Next Steps

Wrap up your session with a review of the workshop experience. What worked? What didn't?

Finally, discuss the next steps to improve your inventory. Engage stakeholders in doing some more discovery in their areas of ownership or expertise. Invite people to participate in field research to learn from customers about when, how, and why they interact (or don't interact) with your channels and touchpoints.

After the Workshop

Once the dust settles, you will need to assess the completeness of your inventory. You may need to circle back with some of the participants to make sure that you captured things accurately. Or, if you have not done primary discovery yet, you can take a deep dive into each channel and the journey as outlined earlier in the chapter. Remember, this is an iterative process. Keep filling in the blanks and continue to build consensus on a standard way to refer to your channels and touchpoints.

CHAPTER 3

Exploring
Ecosystems

All organizations sit within a complicated system of relationships of people, processes, technologies, regulations, and competitors. At every level, their employees make decisions to chart the best course through these ever-changing variables to support organizational objectives. Around each corner are risks and opportunities. Each choice affects the next; each action opens or closes new possibilities.

Customers, in turn, live within their own world—one in which *they* are the center, not your organization. Every day, between when they wake up and go to bed, customers navigate complex environments of people, places, and things (both seen and unseen) to meet their needs, chase their desires, and lead their lives. It's a giant sea of stuff, relationships, and possible futures.

These dynamics help shape each discrete interaction a person has with a product or service. These interactions, in turn, determine the health of the overall customer relationship. Therefore, understanding this greater context—the colliding worlds of an organization and its customers—comes with the territory of orchestrating experiences (see Figure 3.1).

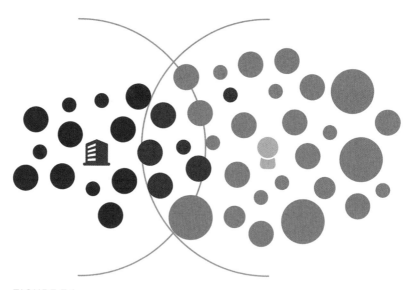

FIGURE 3.1
When they interact, an organization and its customers bring with them complex relationships, influencers, and objectives.

In this chapter, you will learn how to unpack an *experience ecosystem* to reveal relationships that influence customer needs, expectations, and behaviors today. These insights then can inform how you navigate and influence this ecosystem in the future. Before going too far, let's start with a refresher on the concept of ecosystems and its common application in business.

From Business to Experience Ecosystems

Your first exposure to the concept of an ecosystem was likely in grade school science. Perhaps it was explained as follows:

> *The sun shines on the river, causing water evaporation. Clouds form, and rain falls upon the land. Plants absorb the water and nutrients from the soil and then flower. Bees and birds travel from flower to flower, picking up and pollinating other parts of the land. The bees use the pollen to make honey. And so on, and so on.*

These simple stories helped us understand that ecosystems, while complex, are made up of many moving parts that can be identified and studied in relation to one another. Changing any of these individual relationships can have a profound effect on the rest of the ecosystem. Raise the temperature of the earth a bit, and you will lose the bees. With no bees, pollen isn't spread, and then you have a plant problem. These relationships, therefore, are critical to scientific observations and understanding of cause and effect within any given ecosystem.

Business Ecosystems

Over time, these concepts have influenced thinking in business strategy, innovation, and economic theory. In the early 1990s, James F. Moore published "Predators and Prey: A New Ecology of Competition," transforming companies' traditional views of competition. Moore argued that

> [A] company [should] be viewed not as a member of a single industry but as part of a business ecosystem *that crosses a variety of industries. In a business ecosystem, companies coevolve capabilities around a new innovation: they work cooperatively and competitively to support new products, satisfy customer needs, and eventually incorporate the next round of innovations.*[1]

---

1 J. F. Moore, "Predators and Prey: A New Ecology of Competition," *Harvard Business Review*, 71, no. 3 (1993): 75–86.

Moore saw business ecosystems as a changing set of relationships based on evolving factors, such as new technologies, regulations, environmental concerns, and other trends. To understand these changing dynamics, ecological frameworks would reveal which ecosystems to participate in, identify opportunities to provide new value to customers, and "[orchestrate] the contributions of a network of players."[2]

A good example of this in action is the frenemy relationship between Apple and Samsung. While these two giants compete vigorously in increasingly more product categories, Samsung is also a provider of components to Apple's computers, phones, and tablets. Similarly, Apple and Google partner and compete (and sue) in multiple ways.

Another example is the Amazon Marketplace (see Figure 3.2). While Amazon is viewed as a disruptive competitor in many retail segments, it actively recruits other retailers to sell directly on Amazon's platform. This enables Amazon to provide a greater selection of merchandise while keeping its customers in close orbit. This strategy also creates a greater return on investment on core capabilities, such

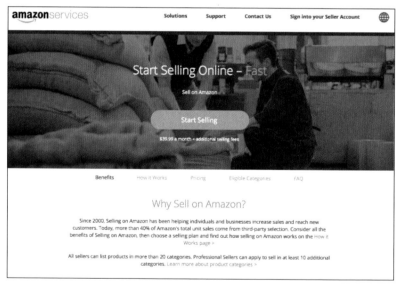

FIGURE 3.2

Amazon Marketplace is built upon the concept of keeping your friends close and your competitors even closer.

---

2 J. F. Moore, *The Death of Competition—Leadership and Strategy in the Age of Business Ecosystems* (New York: HarperCollins, 1996), 12.

as the technologies, partnerships, and processes behind transacting, shipping, and returning.

Experience Ecosystems

Your organization's business ecosystem should inform your work, but don't stop there. You can also codify the seen and unseen relationships that shape customer needs and behaviors. This vantage point—an experience ecosystem—places the customer at the center of the world to help make sense of their context. You then can see more clearly *if* and *how* you are a part of that world.

This simple reframing can help challenge inside-out thinking that tends to oversimplify the variables that determine customer needs and behaviors. This understanding can then inform the design of your system of channels and touchpoints from value propositions to discrete interactions. As illustrated in Figure 3.3, reminding stakeholders that their product or service is merely one part of the customer's life has rhetorical value on its own.

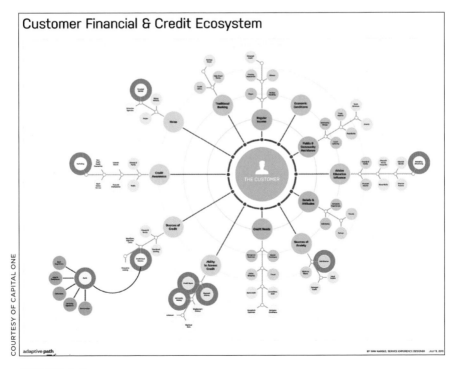

FIGURE 3.3
Placing a bank's products and operations in proper context.

An experience ecosystem complements other models, such as personas and customer journeys, which provide insights into your customers and their experiences. In fact, it's a best practice to gather qualitative and quantitative data to synthesize into multiple frameworks. The next section covers what entities and relationships you will need to identify in order to understand and document an experience ecosystem.

Unpacking an Experience Ecosystem

Unpacking an ecosystem is not unlike peeling an onion: there are many layers, and at some point in the process, you might start to cry. From our research, we have found varying approaches to breaking down the elements of an ecosystem. The same terms have different or overlapping meanings, depending on the methodology. Based on our experience, the following components can help produce good insights while keeping the focus on the customer:

- Actors
- Roles
- Artifacts
- Factors

- Places
- Interactions
- Relationships
- Boundaries

Actors

Ecosystem actors can come in different shapes and sizes. Most are simply people who participate (or could participate) in your product or service experience. Others are companies or institutions that compete, partner, regulate, or otherwise affect ecosystem dynamics. Overall, actors fall into one of four categories.[3]

- **Customers and external stakeholders:** It's common for organizations to focus myopically on customers (or users) of their products or services without considering the broader group of people who affect customer needs and behaviors. These people can be friends and family, professionals (such as realtors, financial advisors, or life coaches), or others directly or indirectly involved in the experience. Getting your arms around all of these external stakeholders is critical for understanding the human dimensions of an ecosystem.

---

3 Inspired in part by: J. F. Moore, *The Death of Competition—Leadership and Strategy in the Age of Business Ecosystems* (New York: HarperCollins, 1996), 63.

- **Internal stakeholders and agents:** Organizations are not people, but they are made of many people. Internal stakeholders include all of the different employees who play one or more roles in and gain value through the delivery of products and services. In a hospital, internal stakeholders might include doctors, nurses, technicians, administrators, marketers, and the board of trustees. Some of these actors interact with customers directly; others may be behind the scenes (see the section, "Current-State Service Blueprints"). Actors in this category may also be third parties, or *agents*, who act on behalf of your organization. For example, it is common in the cable industry for companies to contract third-party installers and technicians to deliver in-home service. Well-orchestrated experiences tightly integrate these agents to ensure consistency and efficiency.

- **Organizations and government:** Zooming out a bit, other organizations and institutions vie for your customers, influence product or service requirements, or provide capabilities for you to leverage. These actors include competitors, partners, suppliers, activist groups, government agencies, and other third parties. These relationships can be complex and constantly in flux.

- **Products and services:** It is useful to also think of individual products and services as unique actors in an ecosystem. For example, Apple may view Samsung as a competitor, but this level of granularity is not very useful if you are looking at the ecosystem around business communication and collaboration. Understanding these companies' phones, tablets, computers, and other products and services and their relation to the ecosystem provides greater insight.

Roles

It is sometimes helpful to distinguish actors from the roles that they play in an ecosystem. In a couple, one spouse may take on the role of handling paying the bills, while her partner handles the budget and investments. Different actors (a child, nurse, or hospice staff) may play the role of caretaker, each supporting an elderly patient in different ways. Roles (and how actors relate to them) give you a better handle on how other people provide value in an ecosystem. These insights can spark new ideas for supporting, replacing, or augmenting actors through new products, services, or artifacts.

Artifacts

The term *artifact* often trips people up, sometimes being confused with *customer touchpoints*. Broadly, artifacts are digital or analog things with varying dynamic or intelligent capabilities. Some of these may be product or service touchpoints; others may exist outside of your product or service, yet impact an actor's attitudes, expectations, and experiences. Within a healthcare ecosystem, artifacts could include cigarettes, warning labels on cigarette packages, a movie in which the hero constantly smokes, a lung cancer pamphlet, or a lung machine.

Typically, it's also useful to identify devices. Common devices include computers, laptops, mobile phones, tablets, smart watches, and so on.

Factors

Product and service ecosystems are also affected by various factors that trigger, constrain, or otherwise shape actor behaviors and relationships. Common categories of factors are regulations, technology trends, societal or cultural trends, and environmental changes. Some factors may be traceable back to certain actors, such as a government creating new regulations or laws (e.g., the Affordable Care Act being passed and implemented in the United States). Other factors can reflect macro trends in society. In our healthcare example, a small minority's concerns over the safety of vaccinations have influenced the behaviors of government, physicians, nurses, and other health officials. Studying current or emergent factors can provide great insight and fuel ideation on how to adapt a product or service in an ever-changing ecosystem.

Places

In many ecosystems, specific places play an important role in where, when, and how actors and artifacts interact. In San Francisco, the 1989 earthquake severely damaged a highway that ran along the bay (see Figure 3.4). Instead of rebuilding the structure, the city demolished the roadway, transforming a place dominated by shipping and cars to a place primed to support tourism, recreation, and local business development.

FIGURE 3.4
Same location, two very different places.

In product and service ecosystems, you want to identify the places that customers and other stakeholders live, work, and interact. For example, Richland Library in Columbia, SC, recognized that families from the suburbs congregated on weekends at festivals in the downtown area. To take advantage of this new place, the library staff developed a book trike to create a pop-up experience for festival goers with the goal of signing up new customers (see Figure 3.5).

FIGURE 3.5
Expanding the library ecosystem into the community.

SHOPPING THE ECOSYSTEM

The retail industry provides many great examples of exploring ways to extend services beyond going to a store, website, or mobile app. For example, HomePlus aspired to be the top grocer in South Korea, but its path to growth seemed to be restricted by competitor EMart's overwhelming dominance in store locations. So they asked the question: "How can we be number one, without opening any additional stores?"

HomePlus looked closely at the Korean culture and the larger ecosystem in which their stores lived. They discovered how unpleasant a single weekly visit to the supermarket could be in such a dense environment with hard-working, time-starved people. Convenience was going to trump price. In this research, they posed one hypothesis—instead of shoppers going to the store, could the store come to shoppers and blend into shopper's everyday lives?

In 2011, the retailer opened the world's first virtual supermarket at Seolleung Station, where shoppers could scan virtual store shelves where backlit display advertising would normally be. These shelves displayed some 500 items of food, toiletries, electronics, and more, for delivery within the same day. The results? An explosion in online membership and sales, making HomePlus South Korea's number one online supermarket and a close second offline. Many retailers around the world quickly adapted this innovation to their markets (see Figure 3.6).

FIGURE 3.6
Virtual shopping, such as this example from Well.ca, extends the retail ecosystem.

Interactions

Within any ecosystem, you will see patterns related to how different actors interact with other artifacts, places, and other actors. The nature, frequency, and importance of these interactions can reveal value exchanges that exist outside of your product or service. Understanding these patterns can inform new strategies, including partnerships, acquisitions, and competitive features and functionality.

A simple example of this is Pinterest and the home improvement ecosystem. Launched in 2010, Pinterest introduced a simple visual way to collect, organize, and share imagery found on the web. Many people quickly realized that Pinterest's functionality provided a convenient way to gain inspiration for home improvement projects, such as remodeling a kitchen. Instead of keeping a list of links, cutting photos from magazines, or printing web pages, home improvers could simply add items to Pinterest and get feedback from family members and friends.

These new behaviors and interactions came to the attention of home improvement retailers. Both The Home Depot and Lowe's Home Improvement actively offered online content, digital tools, in-store classes, and other services to interact with customers during the inspiration and planning stages of their projects. Pinterest represented a new actor in their ecosystem, and both companies eventually adapted to connect with the online service. For its part, Lowe's has benefited from hundreds of thousands of interactions between its site, Pinterest, and its customers (see Figure 3.7). These interactions enhance the customer experience and provide valuable insights into customer behavior related to project and product inspiration.[4]

---

4 Lowe's case study on Pinterest: **business.pinterest.com/en/success-stories/lowes**

FIGURE 3.7
The Lowe's Pinterest channel.

Relationships

To model an ecosystem, you must understand the relationships among its entities. Many types of relationships can exist in an experience ecosystem. Table 3.1 lists some common ones.

Relationships change over time. Mapping these relationships helps clarify not only what exists in an ecosystem, but also the dynamics within it. This can help you explore what might happen if you change or introduce something new into the ecosystem. Will there be a ripple effect? Will it be positive or negative?

Recall our example of the Korean grocer, HomePlus. There had not been a strong relationship between the mobile application and the environmental display advertising, but rethinking these two entities and creating a complementary relationship created a new opportunity.

TABLE 3.1 TYPES OF EXPERIENCE ECOSYSTEM RELATIONSHIPS

Competitive	Competitive relationships may seem obvious, but if you map your ecosystem well, you may find some unexpected indirect competitors. A streaming service may have other streaming services as a competitor, but going out to dinner and a movie competes for the same human needs of entertainment and escape.
Cooperative	Cooperative relationships can be easy to overlook. Examples include: merchants in a shopping district who want to build traffic to the district, and frenemy relationships, such as Apple and Microsoft.
Supportive	Supportive relationships can exist across channels, such as call centers, knowledge bases, and in-store support. A customer's family, friends, and other people can provide advice and counsel related to decisions big and small.
Transactional	Transactional relationships can exist in different forms. Simple transactions can be mediated or made possible by multiple third-parties. Services may depend upon subservices each bringing its own transactional relationship, such as getting financing and insurance when purchasing a car.
Regulatory	From healthcare to financial services, as well as new business models (such as car sharing), understanding regulatory relationships can impact the overall experience.
Complementary	Complementary relationships exist when different entities combine to create interactions, moments, and value. A smartphone maker depends upon the retailer selling and promoting its goods and review sites to help customers discover, purchase, and use their products.
Influencers	Customers come under the influence of other people, media, past experiences, and other entities as they attempt to get things done in their lives. Identifying and designing for these influencers can help ensure that a product or service is well-received and fits into the customer's greater context.
Emotional	People's experiences result in a set of emotional relationships with people, organizations, and even objects. Understanding the emotional connections people bring with them and create in their experiences provides valuable input interacting with them appropriately and effectively.

Boundaries

Exploring an ecosystem means also feeling your way through where it begins and ends. In the domain of healthcare, for example, customers must navigate a complex web of providers, policies, and regulations to receive care (see Figure 3.8). You could spend a lifetime understanding any one aspect of the ecosystem. You and your colleagues should discuss how wide and deep your ecosystem exploration will go. This should be an iterative process, as you gain more clarity on what insights provide the most value to the objectives of your project.

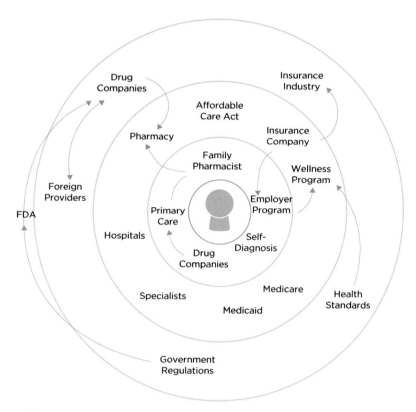

FIGURE 3.8

In complex ecosystems, draw explicit boundaries to guide your exploration.

Ecosystem Mapping Tips

Mapping an ecosystem takes time. The basic process includes identifying what makes up the ecosystem, identifying the relationships, and then modeling the data to communicate effectively to others. Typically, this will be an iterative process, as you analyze, synthesize, and visualize your model

As with touchpoint inventories, you can employ a collaborative workshop to jump-start the ecosystem mapping process. This approach also has the benefit of introducing the concept to colleagues and zooming out from simple product and service interactions to the greater ecosystem they live within. A collaborative workshop example—landscape alignment—is provided at the end of this chapter.

Uncovering the Components

Through interviews, observations, and other design methods, you can uncover different customers' ecosystems and then find the patterns across them. An effective approach—created by our former colleagues at Adaptive Path—involves facilitating customers through cocreating a model of their personal ecosystem.[5] Figure 3.9 shows this approach in action with a remote participant. Returning to our healthcare example, you could work with a patient to identify the people, conditions, resources, institutions, services, and other entities that impact their health and care. The resultant map combined with doing sessions with other patients provides rich data into patterns and relationships, as well as the common mental models.

Additional insights into an individual's ecosystem will also emerge via other qualitative research techniques. For example, doing one-on-one journey mapping with a customer. See Chapter 5, "Mapping Experiences," for more on this approach.

---

5 Tip of the hat to Maria Cordell and Ayla Newhouse for advancing this method at Adaptive Path.

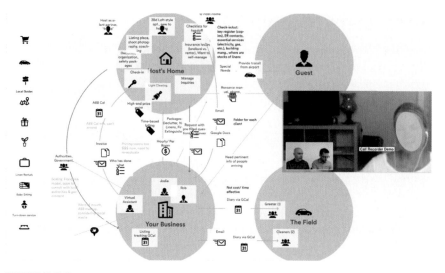

FIGURE 3.9
Remote ecosystem mapping session with a participant.

HYPOTHESIZING THE ECOSYSTEM

I'll often have project teams build initial hypotheses of both their business and customer ecosystems. This involves small teams using sticky notes to generate components for their ecosystem and then organizing the nodes into categories and relationships. By formally constructing a hypothesis of different customer ecosystems, stakeholders can identify assumptions and gaps in their knowledge of customers' context and relationships. This analysis then helps inform where to focus new primary research and begins the ideation process regarding what relationships may be ripe for improving or disrupting. The ecosystem models are then revisited after the research is finished.

Modeling an Ecosystem

Playing with different ways to model an ecosystem helps you identify and understand its dynamics. Finding patterns among the ecosystem components you have discovered creates an opportunity to collaborate with others. A good approach is to write individual components on sticky notes and then manipulate them iteratively, exploring affinities, relationships, and other dimensions (see

Figure 3.10). You should also sketch different modeling approaches. This will help you and your colleagues understand the ecosystem better, as well as how best to communicate it visually to others.

FIGURE 3.10
Collaboratively getting a sense of an ecosystem's complexity, relationships, and other dimensions.

Other things to keep in mind as you make sense of and model your ecosystem:

- **Putting the customer at the center.** As with any system or concept model, there are multiple ways you could represent an ecosystem. A common approach is to put the customer at the center of concentric circles. This type of model emphasizes varying degrees of direct and indirect influence of different entities on the customer. It also literally visualizes a customer-centered approach to look at the experience.

- **Playing with the center of gravity.** In addition to customer-centric ecosystems, it's a good exercise to model from different vantage points, or centers of gravity. For example, putting your organization in the middle, you can visualize the ecosystem in which your *business* lives. Imagine your business at the center of a universe surrounded by all the interconnected and interrelated parts that surround it and affect it. In this view, customers are one of many actors. This approach gives you a way of visualizing your organization's relationship with other organizations, customers, technological and societal trends, and so on (see Figure 3.11).

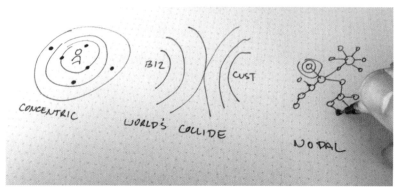

FIGURE 3.11
Exploring different vantage points.

- **Level of zoom.** Another variable you can play with is the level of zoom from which to view your ecosystem. This helps you explore the boundaries of the ecosystem, as well as what's useful to communicate and refer to in the design process.

  Whether you zoom in or out depends on the scope of what you're trying to tackle. You may just need to look at a certain area. Figure 3.12 illustrates this approach. This simple ecosystem map, zoomed in very tightly to the inside activities of a specific store-within-a-store, communicates key people, artifacts, and touchpoints—enough detail to get your bearings.

  Zooming out and looking at the wider landscape can also be helpful. Service systems are often inherently broad, particularly any that deal with regulations and have many interconnected parts, such as healthcare, financial services, hospitality. But even new technology disruptors may want to zoom out and take a broader view. Newer services like Lyft, Tesla, and Airbnb, must deal with regulations, leveraging existing entities in new ways, and accounting for completely new dependencies. Ultimately, the level of zoom is a judgment call based on your strategic focus.

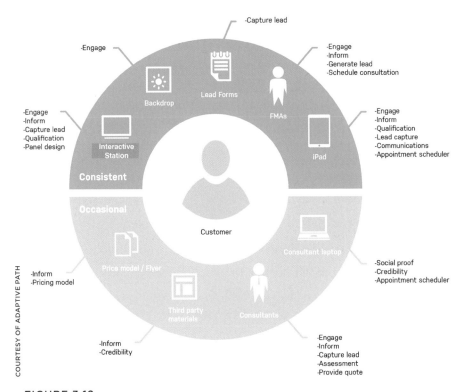

COURTESY OF ADAPTIVE PATH

FIGURE 3.12

A simple ecosystem map, zoomed in very tightly to the inside activities of a specific store-within-a-store.

Using an Ecosystem Map as a Tool

The activity of exploring an ecosystem can produce valuable insights to inform strategy and design decisions. This new knowledge may end up in other artifacts, such as personas and experience maps. You could stop there, but a well-designed ecosystem map can serve as a tool to support group collaboration when taking a fresh look at a problem space to spark ideas and take action.

In a workshop setting, you can play with ecosystem relationships. What if you removed something from the ecosystem? Added something? What would happen? You explore new ecosystem forces and their impact. What if the U.S. government went to a single payer healthcare system? What happens when self-driving cars are widely approved for use?

Forced provocation can be played as an idea generation game with your colleagues. Here's how to play:

- Using your ecosystem map, have each participant randomly pick two entities. For example, for a library and its community, you could choose books and grocery stores.

- Create a timebox to work within. Five minutes typically works well.

- Use the questions from earlier in this chapter to prompt ideas.

  - How *might* these entities be interconnected?

  - How *might* these entities interact?

  - How *might* these entities affect each other?

- Capture your ideas on sticky notes or sketch them. In the library example, these ideas could be: picking up or returning books at the grocery store, hosting book reading at the grocery store, or a curated service in which a cookbook and box of ingredients are delivered to patrons.

Another approach is called *forced provocation*. Forced provocation purposely combines two or more entities, perhaps seemingly unrelated, and explores their potential relationship to generate new ideas and strategies. The HomePlus example of combining display advertising and mobile to create a new shopping experience illustrates this approach in action. This technique can be used early in the design process or as an ideation exercise later when you know what opportunities exist to improve your service.

Other Sensemaking Approaches

Mapping ecosystems is one sensemaking approach to understanding the dynamics of complex environments or relationships and interactions among different actors. Three other models can also help you get your colleagues thinking bigger and broader: stakeholder maps, current-state service blueprints, and service origami. Each of these approaches is valuable on its own, but they are also good entry points into exploring and mapping the entities and relationships of a complex ecosystem.

Stakeholder Maps

Stakeholder maps focus on the actors in a product or service ecosystem. While more focused than full ecosystem maps, these models are useful for visualizing people and organizations that participate in value creation within a specific domain. Mapping stakeholders helps cross-functional teams keep people—rather than processes or technologies—top of mind when framing the product or service landscape.

Stakeholder maps are especially useful when initiating a project. When cocreated, they help facilitate a discussion around what you know about the actors (and the relationships among them) of your problem space (see Figure 3.13). This tangible approach makes it easier to discuss and determine trade-offs of how to engage various internal and external stakeholders.

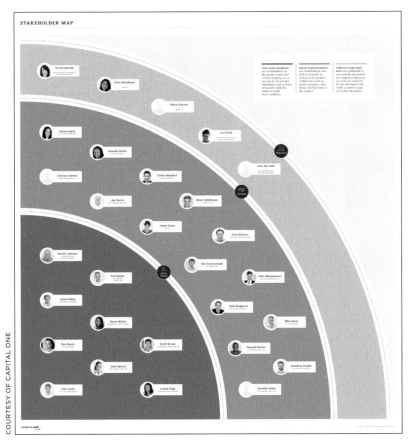

FIGURE 3.13

An internal stakeholder ecosystem.

Current-State Service Blueprints

Ecosystem maps can include an analysis of this inside world of the organization, but another method can often be of more use: the service blueprint. Approaches to service blueprinting vary, depending on your level of zoom (system or pathway). In this usage, a blueprint documents a key customer pathway, such as onboarding or resolving an issue, and shows how channels, touchpoints, people, processes, and technologies deliver that experience. Unlike a customer journey, it does not document (but is informed by) the greater context of the customer. The service blueprint framework brings together two worlds rarely seen together in operational documentation—the front stage of customer flow and interactions and the back stage of operational integration (see Figure 3.14). See Chapter 9, "Crafting a Tangible Vision," for more advanced approaches, including prototyping a operational approaches.

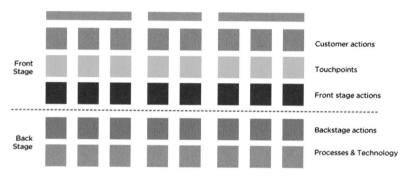

FIGURE 3.14
The basic service blueprint framework.

As a sensemaking method, you can use service blueprinting to deconstruct how your current product or service scenarios work. For example, imagine a retail client that wants to personalize a range of service journeys and make new connections in their ecosystem. To understand the current state, a cross-functional team could map the retailer's ecosystem, including its services, customers, employees, and so on. Then they might create a current-state blueprint of key customer pathways through that ecosystem. The ecosystem view would reveal the greater landscape of all the services that existed within, while the blueprint would show how different people, processes, and technologies played a role in specific service journeys.

Origami

A few years ago, Centre for Citizen Experience founder Jess McMullin popularized an effective experience modeling technique called *business origami*.[6] Originating in Hitachi's service design team, this technique employs three-dimensional artifacts (typically a tent-folded card) to model different components of product or service ecosystems. The original intent of the method was to be able to play quickly with different options for designing the connections and flow across channels and touchpoints.

Business origami is very game-like. Participants set up a board (the landscape) and place different actors upon it. As illustrated in Figure 3.15, places, interactions, and value exchanges among actors are then modeled. This technique, for example, could be used to create the proto-journeys described earlier in the chapter. In the context of service design, this method is called *service origami*.[7]

FIGURE 3.15
Teaching service origami.

---

6 Jess tells the story behind his approach to origami here: **www.citizenexperience .org/2010/04/30/business-origami**

7 Jamin Hegeman, Head of Design at Capital One Financial Services, coined this variation of the method.

ORIGAMI IN RESEARCH

While primarily used to explore future solutions, Chris and I have adapted it into a co-creation research method. For example, we used origami to better understand third parties within a service's growing ecosystem. We facilitated several groups of small business owners and their staff through modeling their service delivery. Being able to see the world of their service amazed our participants. We were then able to play with their ecosystem. We added, removed, or resituated actors and artifacts. We modeled new relationships and boundaries. As with many methods in this book, the technique made the current world more understandable and future possibilities more tangible.

Coda

- An ecosystem model provides insights into the entities and relationships within a specific context. It is the landscape upon which customer journeys play out.

- When applied to a business, product, or service, an ecosystem model focuses on competition, regulations, touchpoints, channels, customers, and other entities that relate to the creation of value.

- An experience ecosystem places focus on the world of customers—the people, places, and things that are relevant to meeting their needs.

- Combining these two views—business and customer—can reveal opportunities to create new products and services or adapt older ones.

- Through workshops, discovery, and research, you can piece together an ecosystem and then use that understanding to educate colleagues or use it as a tool to ideate.

Reframing your colleague's vantage point from vertical ownership to horizontal support is a foundational step in reimagining and orchestrating product and service experiences. Channel frameworks and touchpoint inventories can spark this shift, and an ecosystem view of your problem space can also aid you in this quest. To introduce the concept of ecosystems to your organization, the following workshop approach—landscape alignment—can get the ball rolling.

The key to this approach is taking the two vantage points covered in Chapter 3—business ecosystem and customer ecosystem—and mashing them together figuratively and visually. Through collaborative modeling, people will share their perspectives more easily. You will start to get more alignment on the landscape that your service and your customers inhabit. You can then collectively get to work.

Landscape alignment does not need to be a formal workshop. It's a good exercise for project teams, especially at the beginning of your initiative.

Workshop Objectives

- Introduce the concept of ecosystems and their value.

- Learn through collaboration how colleagues think about customers' context and its relation to your product, service, or organization.

- Share perspectives of what sits behind your product and service (operational entities) and forces (competitive, regulatory, and cultural) that can shape your decisions or the expectations/ behaviors of customers.

- Identify where you can start to understand your ecosystem better through research and discovery.

Example Pitch to Participants (and Their Managers)

While this workshop requires a small-time commitment, you need to set the table for its value and next steps. Here's an example for your invite:

In our collective goal of delivering great customer experiences, it's time to take a step back and take stock of the changing context of our customers and business. We'd like to invite you to a short workshop to share perspectives on the current relationships that shape our ecosystem and identify where we need to understand our solution landscape better.

In this workshop, we will use a simplified ecosystem framework to compare and connect the people, things, relationships, places, and other entities that shape our customers' behaviors and needs. We will also map the key roles, touchpoints, forces, partnerships, competitors, and other entities that create or impact our offerings. This will spark some enlightening and engaging conversations—and initiate the steps we can take together to make better connections with our customers and their context.

Agenda

This workshop is designed to be completed in 2 hours.

TABLE 3.2   WORKSHOP AGENDA

Activity	Description	Duration
Introductions	Facilitate participants getting to know one another beyond just names and titles.	10 min
Review agenda and objectives	Share the activities for the day and what you want to accomplish by the end of the session.	10 min
Review key concepts	Cover the basics of ecosystem entities and show examples.	20 min
Create maps	Organize into two cross-functional teams. Have one create a customer-centered map; the other will create an organization-centered map.	30 min
Share and analyze	Share out each map. Work together to identify relationships or opportunities across maps. Identify areas of investigation after the workshop.	40 min
Reflect and determine next steps	Reflect upon the workshop process and outcomes. Determine the next steps.	10 min

Roles

- **Lead facilitator:** Workshop host and main facilitator for session activities

- **Co-facilitator(s):** Help(s) set up, break down, and assist in activities

- **Documentarian:** Takes photographs of the session to help nonparticipants understand the collaborative process

Participants

- Product managers
- Marketing
- Business strategists
- Designers

- Researchers
- Business process engineers
- Customer support
- Technologists

Materials

- Self-stick easel pad or butcher paper (to create a wall canvas)
- Sharpies
- Sticky notes
- Camera

Preparing for the Workshop

This workshop requires little preparation. As with other workshops, reserve a space that supports hanging materials on walls or working while circling large tables. Avoid conference rooms designed for sitting and talking.

Before the session, set up your canvases (easel sticky pads or butcher paper) for two teams. If you have more than 14 people, you can divide into four teams.

Running the Workshop

Here is how to facilitate this activity. UberEats (a food delivery service prototyped by bootstrapping to Uber's existing service architecture and brand) is used as an example to help you visualize the activities.

Review Key Concepts

Following introductions and reviewing the agenda, spend 15–20 minutes educating participants on ecosystems and their entities. Chapter 3 gives you good definitions and examples to use in your presentation, but you should also include examples relevant to your organization. Also, create a simple handout with a list of the entities—actors, places, factors, and so on—for participants to reference during the exercise.

Create Individual Maps

Next, organize participants into two teams (see Figure 3.16).

- **Team 1:** Will create an ecosystem map with the customer in the center. This focus is on customers' context and relationships. Your organization, products, and services are a small subset of this ecosystem.

- **Team 2:** Will focus on the business ecosystem. Customer types are part of this landscape, but most entities are the channels, touchpoints, and people that deliver your product or service, and the competitors, partners, and forces that shape your strategies and tactics.

FIGURE 3.16

Two teams mapping the ecosystem from two vantage points—customer and business.

Once you are organized, give everyone a stack of sticky notes and a Sharpie pen. Set a timer for five minutes. Instruct each participant to brainstorm as many entities as possible for their ecosystem—customer or business. They should write down one entity per sticky. In the UberEats example, this could include the following for a customer ecosystem: Door Dash (a competitive service), friends/family, dining-out budgets, favorite dishes, and so on. For the business: the Uber app, drivers, restaurants, menus, locale regulations, neighborhoods, etc.

You should end up with two to three dozen sticky notes per person. Next, instruct each team to share their sticky notes and organize them into categories. Here are the steps:

1. Each person shares their sticky notes and places them on the canvas as they explain the nature of each entity. After the first share-out is completed, subsequent participants add new entities and note the ones that they also identified, which have been shared already.

2. After sharing, the participants should work together to organize their sticky notes into a model. As Figure 3.17 shows, a concentric circle approach works well for this activity, but you can experiment with other models. Be sure to show relationships among entities and their importance to the customer or business.

FIGURE 3.17
UberEats' ecosystem and the potential diner's ecosystem compared.

Share and Compare

Now it's time to share and compare. Have each team walk the other team through their map, highlighting entities and relationships that could have important strategy or design implications. Then facilitate a discussion about connections across the two views and what it could mean for your work. Example topics for UberEats might include the following:

- What is part of its service ecosystem and what are its boundaries? For Uber, the Eats service means extending into new relationships with restaurants, abiding by food safety regulations, and competing with the broader ecosystem of dining and food options.

- What do we know about our customers and what influences their choices around food and dining? The core Uber service's assumption on what riders need doesn't apply to what someone ordering and receiving food needs.

- Who are we competing with? What is their relationship to the customers we are targeting?

- What potential connections and relationships are ripe for innovation?

- What don't we need to worry about? What things seem to be in play but are outside of the boundaries useful to our service strategy and design?

- What do we need to learn more about? Do we need to conduct research?

- Do we have everyone involved in our effort who is required in order to improve the service?

- Where do we begin to make change?

During this discussion, you can combine elements of the maps to visualize connections you are seeing. You can also do a long workshop in which you use forced provocation to perform more structured ideation.

After the Workshop

In some cases, the conversation and next steps this workshop generates are enough. However, you may want to create a more polished map for distribution. See the tips and examples in Chapter 3 for inspiration on how to communicate your session's outputs to others.

CHAPTER 4

Orienting Around Journeys

U p to this point, we have unfolded a conceptual canvas of channels, touchpoints, people, places, things, and relationships upon which an infinite number of customer stories and interactions can play out. Now, let's explore one last framework integral to understanding experiences that occur over time and space—the customer journey.

With many proponents across customer experience, user experience, service design, marketing, and other tribes, the *customer journey* has become a ubiquitous term in academia and industry. The core concept is simple: a customer journey represents the current state of an end-to-end customer experience. Customer journeys, in general, help an organization better understand the pathways that customers follow when buying a product or using a service. As we will cover in more detail, customer journeys come in many shapes and sizes, from long and broad (e.g., buying a home) to short and compact (e.g., checking in for a flight).

Many methodologies exist for defining customer journeys and using journey frameworks to set strategy, inform design decisions, and measure the performance of touchpoints. The growing popularity of modeling customer journeys has also led to some backlash challenging whether they deliver upon their intended value. In many ways, customer journey maps have followed a similar pattern as personas: they are widely used but often misunderstood, created in silos without rigor, and shelved without being used properly in the design process.

Customer journeys can be an invaluable concept when framed appropriately and tied to a methodology that connects strategy to planning and execution. Later chapters will arm you with the mindset and methods to do just that. But first, what is a journey?

What Is a Journey?

In the context of orchestrating experiences, think of a journey as the conceptual trip a person embarks upon to achieve a goal or satisfy one or more needs. This may be a customer shopping for a product, a patient seeking treatment for an illness, an employee going through his first 90 days at work, or a citizen participating in an election. In all these cases, a person navigates the world around them, interacting with various people, places, and things across time and space. These journeys likely have highs and lows, differ from what was expected, and lead to other journeys, planned or unplanned. This book focuses on the journeys of customers, but the concepts and approaches outlined are applicable to other types of people and contexts.

JOURNEYS ARE CONSTRUCTS

Journeys are constructs, not mental models. I once had a client who was concerned about calling a specific experience a *journey* because a marketing research team had shown in their findings that customers did not "think of their experience as a journey." It's important to remember that journeys are a construct to aid in the design of better experiences, not a customer mental model. A customer may not think of their experience as beginning before or ending after a major interaction with your product or service (that's a finding!), but a journey framework can help put that key moment in a more useful context.

Journeys Are Made of Moments

A journey unfolds one moment at a time. These moments occur in many contexts and with different intensities of emotion. Booking a ticket online. Checking in at the airport. Having lunch in the premium lounge. Boarding the plane. Using the entertainment system. Collecting bags. Checking loyalty points. And on and on.

Each moment constitutes an opportunity for an organization to clarify its relevance and provide value through information and interactions. Information can be communicated in different ways— via a person, a recorded message, in print, static text on-screen, in video. Interactions can be simple or complex, one-sided or responsive, and with people or things. The basic equation, however, is simple: interactions with a product or service invoke both emotions and thoughts. These can be positive, negative, mixed, or neutral. These interactions can create a lasting memory or disappear into the ether.

An interaction does not happen in isolation. One moment can impact the next moment and others that follow. An eye-catching ad may inspire someone to try a new service. However, if signing up for the service is overly complicated or calling customer service creates more confusion than clarity, the value promised in the advertisement becomes a broken promise.

New experiences can color our memories of previous interactions with a company and its offerings. A handwritten apology for poor service can lessen the intensity of one's recollection of the events that generated the apology. An automated "how was our service" call that wakes you up in the early morning can obfuscate positive memories of your service experience.[1]

In the end, the accumulation of these moments, the value they deliver, and the memories they create constitute a customer's journey.

There Are Many Types of Journeys

Customer journeys come in many shapes and sizes. Journeys that teams have mapped and designed for include the following:

- Taking a day trip to a museum
- Obtaining and using a customer loyalty card
- Applying for a credit card
- Shopping for insurance
- Becoming a first-time investor
- Traveling by train in Europe
- Taking on a large home improvement project
- Buying a home
- Hiring and firing in the employee lifecycle
- Discovering and dealing with mental illness
- Surviving cancer

As you can see from this sample, a customer journey is a flexible concept. A journey can frame a relatively short and simple experience (e.g., a day at the museum), a long and complex one (e.g., buying a home), or the entire arch of a relationship over potentially many years (e.g., the employee lifecycle). You can use a journey model to define the pathways you want to create for customers, such as onboarding, switching services, or canceling a service. Or you can study relevant customer journeys to your service. For example, mapping the journeys of parenthood to identify unmet needs and pain points.

---

1 See the work of Daniel Kahneman, specifically, the peak-end rule.

Figure 4.1 illustrates one example. Imagine that you were hired to recommend opportunities for providing more value in the customer experience for a major airline. Where does the journey begin? Where does it end? Is it even one journey? It depends on what you want to explore. Consider the following information:

- The travel experience: how does air travel fit within the overall journey of taking a trip?

- The overall airline service: from the trigger when the customer begins shopping for air travel through receiving a loyalty miles credit two days after returning home.

- The core air travel experience: from arriving at the airport through leaving the airport at your destination.

- A smaller service journey: getting a refund for a cancelled flight, using your loyalty miles to book a trip, or what happens when your bag goes missing.

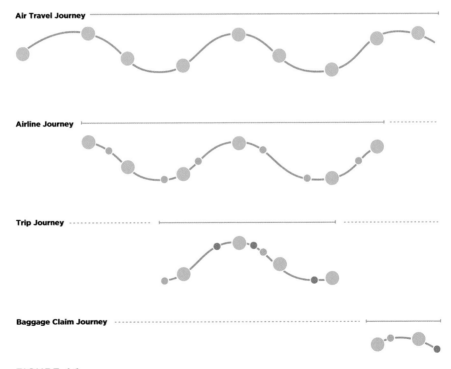

FIGURE 4.1
Journeys within journeys.

Each of these journeys involves an experience that unfolds over time and across multiple touchpoints and channels. The broadest journey (e.g., the travel experience) approaches air travel as one service with a larger experience; the journey of using loyalty miles to book a trip is a service within the overarching service an airline provides. Conceptually, each of these levels provides insight into different (but likely related) customer needs and pain points, experiential context, and service opportunities. Where you focus is a strategic decision based on what you need to learn and what journeys you can directly impact.

Journeys Are Valuable to Everyone

Many disciplines have gravitated toward the concept of customer journeys to define strategies, design for experience over time, and modernize operations. Why? A convergence of several new best practices is underway, including:

- Staging experiences, not selling products and services
- Using data to build and manage customer relationships
- Measuring each touch
- Adapting to the mobile customer
- Meeting expectations for experience continuity
- Embracing emotions

Staging Experiences, Not Selling Products and Services

While many organizations preach "putting customers first," the C-suite has dramatically increased its focus and investments in moving employees from thinking inside-out to outside-in. This evolution has been largely driven by consultancies of all stripes—management consulting, service design, marketing, and even technology—influencing their executive customers to shift their mindset from feature-laden products and services to creating differentiating experiences. Whether it's the Voice of the Customer (VoC), design thinking, user experience, or customer-centric marketing, organizations are swimming in competing philosophies and frameworks for attracting and retaining customers over time. Against this backdrop, customer journeys have emerged as a valuable framework to understand how to stage experiences better.

Using Data to Build and Manage Customer Relationships

Marketing, once viewed with advertising as an art form of persuasion, has increasingly embraced more sophisticated data and modeling approaches to underpin where, how, when, and why a brand interacts with current and prospective customers. Conceptually, relationship management depends upon understanding who the customer is, measuring the quantity and quality of interactions with that customer, and determining what the next offer or interaction should be. Most medium-to-large organizations employ a customer relationship management (CRM) platform to manage customer models and track interactions with customers in every channel. Journey frameworks fit nicely with the intent of relationship management: it's not about one touch—rather, it's about how many touches build a relationship with a customer over time.

Measuring Each Touch

As interactions with products and services become increasingly digitized, organizations have greater insight into how each touchpoint impacts the customer experience. Did the customer open the marketing email? Did she read the product description? Was the product abandoned in her shopping cart? What search term did she use to find a better product? The collection and analysis of this data help reveal the pathways that customers take, stay with, and abandon. Journey models are useful for analyzing these pathways and identifying patterns to meet customer needs at and across touchpoints more predictably.

Adapting to the Mobile Customer

More widespread mobile computing has challenged organizations to rethink how they interact with digital customers. Overly simplified customer pathways, such as starting online and then coming into a store, neither reflect the fluidity of customer actions nor the reality of digital and physical channels merging in real time. Customer journeys capture the range of customer actions and help organizations identify where to optimize paths and design for channel pairing, not conflict.

Meeting Expectations for Experience Continuity

In a world of digital data and tracking, customers expect organizations to provide more continuity across channels and touchpoints. Have a problem with the flight you booked online? You expect the call center agent to have that information at his fingertips. Searched for a vinyl record on a mobile app? You want to pick up your search on your laptop. Framing customer experiences as journeys can help identify how customers move or want to move across and within channels, as well as where inconsistencies in utility, interactions, or language lead to confusion or frustration.

Embracing Emotions

The growing science around how emotions impact decision-making and brand perception have found their way to organizational leaders through books such as *How We Decide*, *Nudge*, and *The Art of Choosing*. The popularity of these concepts has aided marketers, designers, and others to lean confidently into new techniques for better understanding of customer emotions. Customer journey mapping meets this need, helping researchers identify and report upon the variety and intensity of customer emotions in product and service experiences.

Journey: The Hub of Empathy and Understanding

Hopefully, you see the value that customer journeys can bring to organizations grappling with the complexity of orchestrating experiences across many touchpoints and channels. Before we go further, we do want to be explicit: articulating your customers' experiences as journeys does not replace other research approaches and models. It's not always appropriate to gear your research toward understanding an end-to-end journey. You still need other frameworks and models, such as personas, to communicate critical insights into the needs, behaviors, and goals of customers. As with all concepts, customer journeys have their place; like all tools, experience mapping should not become the proverbial hammer searching for a nail.

To orchestrate experiences, however, a customer journey model effectively provides insights and context to stakeholders responsible for a range of decisions related to the strategy, design, and implementation of products and services. Other traditional user experience tools for connecting different parts of the experience, such as concept models, lack the elements of time and context. Scenarios communicate experiences over time, but their strength lies in individual customer stories, not a view of the broader range of actions, emotions, and needs among many customers. User stories tactically break down touchpoints into functionality, but they focus on minute tasks, not larger outcomes.

A customer journey provides insights into customer needs while also clarifying how different touchpoints and channels work or don't work well as a system. For this reason, we call the customer journey the *hub of empathy and understanding*. Why a hub? As illustrated in Figure 4.2, the customer journey sits at the center of a continuum from the smallest customer interactions to the most critical organizational strategies and frameworks. Let's explore the model in both directions.

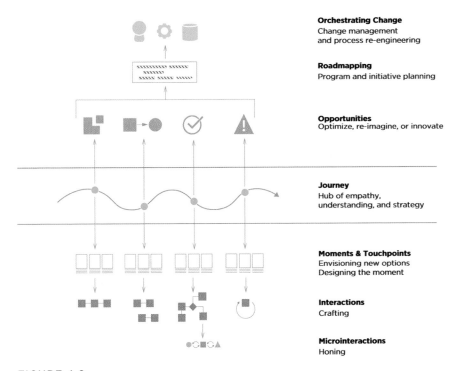

FIGURE 4.2

The customer journey provides a hub of empathy, connecting the needs of customers from microinteractions to organizational strategy.

From Journey to Microinteraction

Any meaningful moment a customer has with a product or service exists within a greater context. The customer journey is a bird's-eye view of the moments that matter and how they relate to existing or missing touchpoints. Customer journeys are invaluable for understanding where specific product or service touchpoints can better meet a need in the moment while bridging one moment to the next.

For example, most airlines include the ability for travelers to obtain a digital boarding pass. This pass is needed to check luggage, go through security, and eventually to board the plane. The question for airlines to answer in their end-to-end experience is: How do touchpoints that support "getting a boarding pass" bridge the traveler to the later moments in which "showing the boarding pass" is required? Your check-in experience can be smooth and delightful, but if the traveler struggles to produce their boarding pass later in the journey, the "getting a boarding pass" moment likely has room for improvement.

If you are responsible for experience strategy, viewing the experience as a journey can help identify the greater flow that a product or service should create. As a hub, the customer journey informs the design of each touchpoint to shine in concert with other touchpoints to make great moments. This also provides scaffolding—what we call the *DNA of the journey*—to guide more detailed interaction and microinteraction design decisions that are critical to create continuity and consistency across the end-to-end experience.

From Journey to Enterprise Strategy

In addition to guiding more detailed design and implementation decisions, a customer journey should be used as a strategic tool to inform strategic planning. As a hub, the customer journey can help a product or service team do the following:

- **Identify pain points and opportunities.** By providing an appropriate customer-centered context, opportunities for improving or creating touchpoints become clearer. These insights help drive what to do next and how to prioritize what will align business and customer value across the end-to-end experience.

- **Make a plan.** Customer journeys provide a good framework for roadmaps or evolution maps to communicate and organize efforts over time. These plans can clarify how typically disparate projects connect and result in an improved end-to-end customer experience.

- **Organize across silos.** The customer journey also clarifies what touchpoints are critical to the end-to-end experience and, as a result, what parts of the organization should be collaborating more closely. When a customer journey is embraced as the hub, aligning people and making trade-offs across silos become easier.

Moving further up in strategic importance, a customer journey is typically one of many your organization must create or support to reach its strategic objectives. Smart organizations holistically codify existing and emerging journeys that matter to their customers and business. They look across these journeys to identify patterns of needs to drive enterprise strategy for evolving their offers. They streamline and organize operational capabilities to support the prioritized journeys and moments.

Unpacking End-to-End Experiences

Understanding the end-to-end experiences of multiple customers with often dozens of touchpoints over time may seem like a fool's errand. Fortunately, you can gain valuable insights into the customer journey by focusing on manageable sets of what we call *building blocks* of end-to-end experiences. As Figure 4.3 illustrates, these building blocks fall into four distinct categories: the journey, the customer, the ecosystem, and the context.

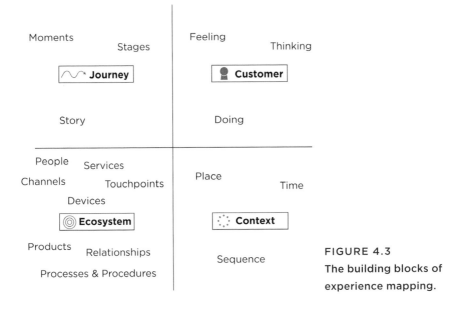

FIGURE 4.3
The building blocks of experience mapping.

The Journey

An experience map synthesizes the experiences of multiple customers. Approach each customer's individual journey as a story with the following elements:

- **The overarching story:** What is the journey's raison d'être? Why do customers embark upon the journey, what value is created, and what are their lasting impressions at the end?

- **Moments:** What events take place in the journey? Which moments do your products and services produce or play a role in? Which moments are more important to your customer? Or to your product or service?

- **Stages:** Do these moments occur in clusters that reveal a useful narrative structure? For example, the stages of an airline journey might be researching options, booking a flight, making other preparations, checking in, and so on.

When researching people's end-to-end experiences, you need to stay open to letting the answers to these questions emerge from your data. What you find may differ from your organization's current frameworks (e.g., conversion funnels or business-centric journeys) or your hypothesis greatly.

The Customer

Since customers are the protagonists of their own journeys, a key objective is to nail down how their behaviors, perceptions, and emotions change moment by moment and interaction by interaction over time. You also want to identify other underlying factors of their journey. The following three customer building blocks are important to understand: feeling (emotions), thinking (perceptions), and doing (behaviors).

Feeling (Emotions)

To design better products and services, you need to get closer to the messiness of customers' lives and the feelings they bring to their interactions across your entire product or service (see Figure 4.4).

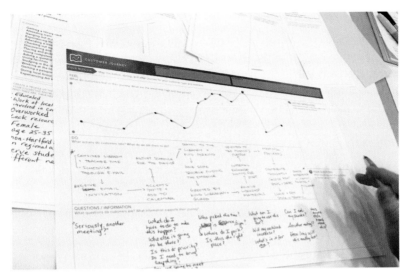

FIGURE 4.4
Emotions in specific moments should be placed within the context of the entire emotional journey.

You may be told that you have these insights already thanks to Voice of the Customer reports and Net Promoter Score (NPS) surveys.[2] These qualitative approaches are not designed to understand the context and nuances of interaction. Therefore, you must conduct qualitative research that answer questions such as:

- What emotions do customers experience throughout the journey?

- What moments or interactions dramatically impact how customers feel?

- How do emotions affect decision-making?

- To what extent do emotions reveal deeper motivations behind people's actions?

- How well does the product or service identify, accept, and adapt to a customer's emotional state?

---

2 Net Promoter Score (NPS), developed by Fred Reichheld, Bain & Company, and Satmetrix, is a widely used methodology intended to measure customer loyalty. Grappling with NPS and its fans in marketing comes with the territory when orchestrating experiences. For a thoughtful critical analysis, see "Net Promoter Score Considered Harmful (and What UX Professionals Can Do About It)" by Jared Spool, **https://blog.usejournal.com/net-promoter-score-considered-harmful-and-what-ux-professionals-can-do-about-it-fe7a132f4430**

Thinking (Perceptions)

Thinking concerns a customer's mental model and how it is met or challenged and changes over time. For example, if you have purchased a home in the past, you have specific assumptions, expectations, and preferences that you take to your next home-buying journey. Each interaction with a product or service intended to help you find, finance, and move into your new home either matches or differs from that previous mental model.

The questions related to thinking that you need to answer include the following:

- What do different customers expect will happen at each key moment of their journey?

- When a part of the experience fails to meet the customer's expectations, how does this impact their actions, emotions, and needs?

- What other products, people, or information help shape a customer's mental model?

- How well does the product or service experience anticipate, address, or acknowledge existing mental models?

Doing (Behaviors)

Doing is about actions and behaviors. Some of these actions involve interactions with your product or service touchpoints; others reveal the broader ecosystem of people, things, and places (see Chapter 3, "Exploring Ecosystems"). Learning what customers actually *do* is typically an eye-opening moment for stakeholders who are used to looking at a limited set of data related to customer interactions.

Valuable insights related to behaviors include the following:

- What range of customer behaviors exists in the end-to-end experience?

- What do customers do to address specific needs during their journeys?

- How do customers' actions deviate from their preferred or your organization's desired behaviors?

- How do touchpoints, people, or places impact customers' behavior?

The Ecosystem

A customer's personal ecosystem greatly shapes their experience when intersecting with an organization's product or service ecosystem (see Chapter 3). Think of a customer's end-to-end experience as a distinct pathway through these colliding ecosystems (see Figure 4.5).

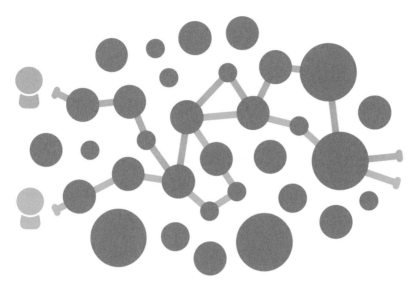

FIGURE 4.5
Different customers, different pathways.

Ecosystem entities that often appear in customers' journeys include:

- **Channels:** What channels do your customers gravitate toward in certain moments or to meet specific needs? How well can they switch channels?

- **Touchpoints:** Which touchpoints do customers interact with and to what degree? What is the quality of those interactions? What touchpoints are missing from specific channels or missing completely?

- **People:** What role do agents of the product or service play in the customer journey? Are there other people—friends, family, and so on—who impact experiences, decisions, and behaviors?

- **Other products and services:** What other products and services make up the customer journey? Where do people turn to for information? What competitors are being considered, chosen, or rejected?

- **Devices:** What types of devices—laptops, kiosks, mobile phones, and so on—do people interact with and why?

- **Relationships:** How do different parts of the ecosystem relate to one another? Can you identify cause-and-effect relationships below surface behaviors and emotions?

- **Processes and procedures:** How do regulations, processes, and procedures dictate pathways, behaviors, and barriers for customers, as well as the employees who serve them?

The Context

Experiences do not happen in a vacuum. Experience mapping involves understanding and embracing how context impacts behavior, emotions, and mental models. When you are attempting to understand and codify context, consider elements such as:

- **Place:** Where are customers during their journeys? How do geographic locations impact their experiences?

- **Time:** What is the range of durations for different customers' journeys? How long do they spend in each stage or moment? How do your customers think and feel about how they spend their time?

- **Sequence:** What patterns exist in customer behaviors from one moment to the next across the journey? How does one moment impact the next or future moments later in the journey?

Getting Started with Journeys

A journey paradigm can create strategic clarity, improved cross-functional collaboration, and more successful products or services. When journey frameworks are embraced to drive strategy, transformational change can result in new customer value propositions and the reorganization of people and processes to better support the end-to-end experiences of customers.

Big organizational changes start with small efforts that demonstrate better ways of learning, making decisions, and having an impact together. To gain support for making customers and their journeys the centerpiece of your product or service strategy, start with *one journey.* Step away from intent statements, product backlogs, sprints, and NPS scorecards. Step into the lives and stories of your customers to understand their experiences.

Coda

- Journeys—in the form of maps, models, and frameworks— are becoming commonplace in organizations. But the concept doesn't always translate to impact.

- The journey concept is powerful, but you have to tie the model proactively to how experiences are defined, designed, and executed in matrixed organizations.

- There are many types of journeys, not just the pathways you create for customers. Understanding the different journeys that customers undertake can unlock different types of insights.

- Journeys should function as a hub of empathy for an organization, grounding product and service decisions in the real experiences of customers.

- Journeys provide the right context and inputs to create inspiration for new products and services, as well as crafting the microinteractions between you and your customer.

- Experiences are complex, but you can identify common building blocks to deconstruct what customers do, think, and feel in context and their interactions with your product or service.

PART II

Insights and Possibilities

In Part I, "A Common Foundation," we introduced concepts and frameworks helpful for shifting organizational perspectives from dividing and conquering to uniting and orchestrating. The recommended methods aid codifying your channels, touchpoints, ecosystems, and journeys as elements of a greater system. This sets the table for collaboration and change. But you can't stop there.

As you move forward, it is critical to test your own hypotheses and challenge internal thinking of what customers need. You must get out of your work environment and take a deep dive into what people do, think, and feel in their journeys. You must uncover the barriers they face, the nuances of their context, and, ultimately, the value they seek. Your objective: *build* empathy and *identify* true opportunities to create positive change for your customers and organization.

Collaboration is also critical as you learn, reframe, and prepare for action. The next three chapters will prepare you to guide others through a three-step process. First, you will conduct *generative research* to better understand your customers' end-to-end experiences. Next, you will synthesize what you learn into an *experience map* and *experience principles*. With these new insights, you can then identify and prioritize *opportunities*.

As you will see, this process is not a solo endeavor in which you report back what you have learned. It's a facilitated group effort to build empathy and create alignment for address-ing the needs of customers and your organization holistically. While this level of collaboration may seem radical, the trust it engenders in your colleagues is a key building block in creating better orchestrated experiences.

Let's start with how to facilitate mapping experiences.

> "There's gold in them thar hills."
>
> —Mark Twain

CHAPTER 5

Mapping Experiences

It's become a standard practice in most organizations to make artifacts that model customer journeys. Approaches to creating and using visual models of customer journeys vary widely, as do their names. In this book, they are referred to as *experience maps*.

If journeys serve as the hub of empathy for an organization, you must do more than make a map. *You need to use the activity of mapping to catalyze change.* Your goal should be to create a human-centered mindset and shared ownership of customer experiences in as many of your colleagues as possible.

This chapter will help you facilitate others through an experience mapping process based on the principles of collaboration, codesign, storytelling, and the power of visualization. Let's look at the experience map artifact and the insights it should communicate.

What's an Experience Map?

Based on qualitative and quantitative data, an experience map visually articulates the range of behaviors, emotions, mental models, and needs of customers within a conceptual journey framework (such as home buying or travelling). An experience map illuminates customer interactions with your product or service via touchpoints and channels across time and space. A good experience map also reveals the salient elements of the wider ecosystem—other products, services, people, and places—that customers experience as they attempt to meet their explicit goals and implicit drivers. Figure 5.1 shows a basic example of looking beyond touchpoints to the greater landscape as a journey unfolds.

There are meaningful insights across your organization buried in research reports and the tacit knowledge of colleagues. An experience map surfaces and synthesizes this information. For the first time, stakeholders across an organization can see their channel or touchpoints in a broader context. This shared understanding and empathy serve as a foundation for forming and executing upon a singular vision of the customer experience.

Yet, an experience map represents more than a synthesis of insights. Early in the strategy and design process, an experience map identifies new opportunities, generates ideas and concepts, and clarifies the gap between the current state and a desired future state. As Figure 5.2 illustrates, it doesn't have to be a polished deliverable to provide this value. To get this value, however, you must approach the design of your experience map as a *tool*, not a *deliverable*.

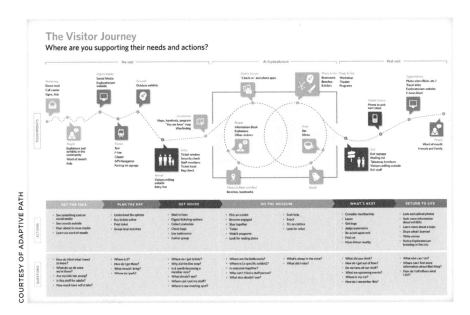

FIGURE 5.1

An experience map showing opportunities to meet visitor needs both inside and outside a museum.

FIGURE 5.2

In this example, a workshop team has used a rough journey map (the sticky notes) to generate ideas (the white pieces of paper on top).

Mapping with Confidence

Experiences have many moving parts to identify and understand. While it takes time and effort to create an experience map, you can proceed with confidence following a few straightforward rules:

- Map with intent.
- Choose your level of zoom.
- Don't go solo.
- Do your homework.
- Be iterative.
- Build into your process.

Map with Intent

As with any design method, you should employ experience mapping for the right reasons, at the right time, and with the right level of time investment and organizational support. Regardless of the complexities of your organization and the journeys you support, experience mapping makes sense to use in the following circumstances:

- You don't have a clear understanding of your customer experience across channels and touchpoints and don't know which customer pain points or opportunities might add value to your organization.

- Different functions—marketing, product, customer insights, operations, and so on—are working in silos, each coming up with its own vision for the customer's experience. When placed into market, the resulting end-to-end experience is fragmented and inconsistent.

- Business leadership has made the shift to customer journeys, but business strategy approaches are not balanced with an understanding of customer needs and translating those insights into effective designs.

- Strategic initiatives—defining new products and services—lack insight into unmet customer needs in common cultural journeys, such as home ownership, healthcare, parenting, and travel.

- Process design drives the definition and sequencing of customers' pathways. This process work—such as lean process design and value stream mapping—is divorced from other efforts related to customer experience.

- Your organization needs to evolve from Voice of the Customer to embracing the full complexity of customers' lives and the stories that play out (for good and bad) every day.

One or more of these factors may apply in your case. Just be clear to yourself and others why it's the right time to get a shared perspective on your customers' end-to-end experiences. You will also need to communicate what you will do with the insights and opportunities that the experience mapping process generates. This will prepare you for the inevitable *why* questions you will get, and tee you up to ask for the time and involvement of others.

Choose Your Level of Zoom

You can apply a journey construct across a spectrum of macro and micro customer narratives. However, different levels of zoom (or conceptual laddering) can provide different insights, so you must choose the level of granularity that you want to learn about and model (see Figure 5.3).

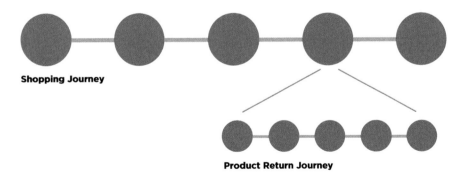

FIGURE 5.3
Choose your level of zoom carefully to support your strategic aims.

Choosing your journey depends on the strategic question(s) you want to answer. For example, a customer experience team for a big-box retailer could look at many different journeys:

- **30,000 feet:** You want to expand and diversify your product and service offerings. What types of experiences are your target customers having that could reveal where you are only a small part of their journey?

- **10,000 feet:** You want to find better ways to create a seamless experience across channels. How do your customers shop across physical stores, web, mobile, and call centers?

- **5,000 feet:** You want to look for innovative ways to connect with millennials. What unmet needs do millennials have when they shop with you?

- **2,500 feet:** You want to turn more casual shoppers into loyal customers. Where are the opportunities to build stronger relationships before, during, and after a transaction online or in store?

- **1,000 feet:** You get many complaints about your return experience. How do you improve how customers buy online and then return the merchandise in the store?

As you conduct your research, you may find that you need to zoom out more to understand a broader journey. Or you may determine that a greater context (e.g., shopping across channels) is valuable, but your map needs to zoom in on a subset of customers (such as millennials) to provide input into a specific initiative. You should enter the experience mapping process with a strong hypothesis of the journey you want to investigate, while setting expectations that new data may lead you to a more valuable level of zoom.

Don't Go Solo

Most organizations operate on an internal service model in which departmental specialties—such as customer insights, design, and business analysis—provide capabilities for the business to use, or not use, to further its aims. In some cases, the job of researching and modeling customer journeys is owned by one group or outsourced to third parties. Assigning experience mapping to a select team of people, however, sacrifices long-term impact to short-term efficiencies.

When you involve more of your organization in experience mapping, it has these benefits:

- **Builds customer empathy:** A customer-centered mindset does not happen through a cursory reading of Voice of the Customer reports or observing focus groups. Experience mapping, as with other human-centered research approaches, creates the opportunity for stakeholders to meet face-to-face with the customers they serve.

- **Establishes cross-functional rapport:** When bringing together people from different functions, you quickly learn that many of them do not even know one another, or they work together infrequently. Establishing these new relationships bears fruit later in the design process.

- **Shifts from vertical to horizontal:** Most organizations operate on distributed, vertical ownership. Getting your colleagues out of the weeds to explore the big picture together chips away at these dynamics. Through building customer empathy and coworker rapport, your colleagues will become more open to working across functions toward an end-to-end experience. This buy-in is critical for ensuring that your insights turn into action.

- **Creates efficiency:** The more collaborative and inclusive you are in your process, the more time you will spend mapping and using your map instead of talking about what you have done and will do.

- **Speeds adoption:** All of the above will help lead you to where you were headed all along—adoption of your experience map as a tool to work collaboratively toward new solutions.

Getting these benefits depends not just on bringing more people into the process, but rather on selecting the *right* people. You want to get colleagues who will commit to participating in the full process, as well as people who will benefit from using the map as a tool. Questions that can help guide your decision include:

- Who is responsible for key channels and touchpoints of your product or service ecosystem?

- Which groups would benefit from having a better understanding of the customer journey?

- Which functions might already have information or data so that you don't have to reinvent the wheel?

- Who will be responsible for making decisions and acting on using the experience map?

As a best practice, here are typical organizational roles you should consider including:

- **Executives:** Leaders who set strategic objectives, fund product or services, and hold the budget for activities, such as experience mapping, that they expect to bring value to the organization

- **Owners:** Product managers (or owners) or key business partners responsible for making important or final decisions related to product strategy

- **Strategists:** People responsible for setting business strategy related to products and services

- **Researchers:** Specialists responsible for designing or conducting research studies for marketing, products, or other functions

- **Data or business analysts:** Specialists in gathering and analyzing quantitative data related to product or service touchpoints

- **Marketers:** Roles responsible for creating awareness and consideration of a product or service

- **Process engineers or process designers:** Specialists responsible for identifying requirements and designing business processes

- **Technologists:** Roles related to the architecture, design, and implementation of digital solutions

- **Channel owners or practitioners:** People responsible for or knowledgeable of various customer channels, including stores, call centers, mobile, and so on

- **Front-line staff:** Employees or other agents—such as call center staff and service personnel—who interact directly with customers

- **Legal:** Specialists responsible for ensuring that company activities are lawful and interests are protected

As you spread your net to engage a broader range of stakeholders, you need to clearly define and communicate what level of involvement you are asking from each person. How central a specific stakeholder is to the mapping process depends on his or her level in the organization, their dedication to your mapping initiative, the knowledge they have, or their ability to help you navigate your organization's processes and procedures.

The various roles include:

- **Facilitators:** People like you! They know how to design an experience mapping initiative and guide others through it. They get their hands dirty in doing discovery, defining research plans, conducting research, generating insights, and making artifacts.

- **Experience Mappers:** Stakeholders ready to roll up their sleeves and go out into the field or participate in analyzing and synthesizing the data into maps. In later stages, they also help make the leap from insights to action (see later chapters).

- **Subject Matter Experts (SMEs):** People who have or can point you to existing wisdom in the organization regarding who your customers are and their current experiences.

- **Enablers:** Managers, legal, participant recruiters, executive assistants, and others who can help you get the right people together, go into the field, and clear other unforeseen obstacles.

- **Influencers:** Other like-minded employees of all levels who can support or benefit from your work. These could be teams who have successfully adopted experience mapping or others rooting for you to get a green light to do something similar in their neck of the woods.

- **Executive Leadership:** High-level executives whom you need to keep abreast of the work and get buy-in for not only conducting the research but also using the map as a strategic tool.

Do Your Homework

In addition to conducting new research, you should be layering in existing insights and data. This discovery will be invaluable for two reasons. First, you always have limited time to conduct primary research. Learning what your organization already knows will help you make proper trade-offs of time and energy. Second, requests for new research typically attract questions of "Don't we already know this?" like honey attracts flies. Being buttoned up on the knowledge gaps you need to fill will protect you when you are challenged.

As part of your discovery at the beginning of an initiative, consider hosting an experience mapping hypothesis workshop. In this type of session, a group of stakeholders works together to create one or more maps representing what they *believe* is the end-to-end customer experience. Figure 5.4 shows the output of this approach. The hypothesis is built upon the information collected from discovery or from the existing knowledge provided by subject matter experts.

Common discovery activities that can help you get a sense of what you know and don't know include the following:

- **Existing qualitative research:** Review relevant research from marketing and design, including studies that resulted in useful models, such as personas or decision frameworks.

- **Existing quantitative research:** Analyze studies related to customer preferences, channel or touchpoint feedback, Voice of the Customer, or other marketing or design studies.

- **Touchpoint inventory:** See Chapter 2, "Pinning Down Touchpoints," for how to identify and document your channels and touchpoints.

- **Ecosystem mapping:** See Chapter 3. "Exploring Ecosystems," for how to begin mapping your product or service ecosystem. (You may also choose to research and map your ecosystem in your primary research.)

- **Channel scorecards:** Review metrics related to customer volume, interactions, and satisfaction in different channels.

- **Call center data:** Look at reports regarding common customer needs, complaints, and issue resolutions.

- **Web analytics:** Analyze data that shows the volume by touchpoint, movement between touchpoints and channels, where customers enter and exit experiences, and so on.

- **Competitive research:** Research studies that contain information on competitor touchpoints and channels.

FIGURE 5.4
Multiple hypotheses of what customers' experiences are in their
end-to-end journeys. This exercise helps build the case for primary
research and what questions are most critical to answer.

The value of this approach is three-fold. First, a workshop is an efficient way to go through tons of existing information and make sense
of what it is telling the team. This helps to inform the research plan
with regard to the most critical knowledge gaps. Second, it's an opportunity to teach the basic concepts of experience mapping. This helps
stakeholders buy in to the approach and collaborate more effectively
in later activities. Finally, as humans, we can all suffer from confirmation bias—the tendency to map new information to existing mental
models or theories. A hypothesis workshop surfaces the biases among
the group for everyone to be aware of as new insights come to light.

Iterate

Your discovery efforts will likely begin before you go into the field. In general, strive to work iteratively as you move through various sensemaking activities. An experience map reflects the collection of many disparate pieces of information and ongoing analysis, synthesis, storytelling, visualization, and using your map. Set expectations with your colleagues so that you will continue to refine your understanding and how to communicate that knowledge throughout the mapping process.

Build into Your Process

Selling this collaborative approach to other people depends greatly on their understanding of how it helps to define or design better end-to-end product and service experiences. Make sure that you communicate that what you learn will inform downstream activities, such as opportunity identification, ideation, concept development, vision creation, and roadmap planning. Later chapters will set you up for success in getting the most out of your mapping investment.

Learning Your Customers' Stories

Mapping your customers' experiences requires a certain level of research expertise. Since this is not a research book, you may need to turn to other resources that cover the specifics of designing a research plan and protocol, recruiting participants, and how to perform qualitative and quantitative research methods.[1] Experience mapping does seek to gain specific insights and has best practices in methods and analysis. To that end, the rest of this section will cover the answers to the following questions:

- What participants should you recruit?
- What are you trying to learn?
- What methods get the best results?
- What about quantitative research?
- How do you involve different stakeholders successfully?

---

1 Please see Steve Portigal's book, *Interviewing Users* (New York: Rosenfeld Media, 2013), for great advice on how to get the most out of your research conversations with people.

What Participants Should You Recruit?

As with any research study, an overarching strategic intent should inform the types of customers that you recruit. Using the retail example from earlier in the chapter, Table 5.1 illustrates different participant approaches based on common mapping objectives.

TABLE 5.1   DETERMINING YOUR PARTICIPANTS

Objective	Participant Approach
We want to expand and diversify our product and service offerings. What types of experiences are our target customers having that can reveal where we are only a small part of their journey?	Recruit a good representation across your existing product or service customer segmentation, with current and prospective customers both represented.
We want to find better ways to create a seamless experience across channels. How do customers shop across physical stores, web, mobile, and call centers?	Identify customers who have shopped in multiple channels during the last six months. Participants should reflect the range of demographics, psychographics, geography, loyalty, and other dimensions believed to impact behaviors and needs. Recruit some frequent customers to participate in longitudinal research, such as a diary study.
We want to look for innovative ways to connect with millennials. What unmet needs do millennials have when they shop with us?	Recruit current and prospective customers born between 1982 and 2004. Participants should reflect the range of demographics, psychographics, geography, loyalty, and other dimensions known to impact behaviors and needs.
We want to turn more casual shoppers into loyal, frequent customers. Where are the opportunities to build stronger relationships before, during, and after a transaction online or in store?	Identify customers who have purchased 1–2 times in the past 12 months either online, in store, or both.
We get many complaints about our return experience. How do we improve how customers buy online and return in store?	Recruit customers who have made a purchase online and returned in store in the past 3–6 months. Stores should represent locations with few complaints and many complaints. Product returns should represent different product categories. If you can, observe customers going through the return experience in store and intercept them afterward to probe on their high and low points.

Your recruiting screener in each case will require different combinations of customer attributes to cover your bases.[2] As with any qualitative research study, you won't need a large sample size to get good results. Three to five participants per segment should get you good insights before diminishing returns kick in.[3]

WHAT DO YOU MEAN WHEN YOU CAN'T TALK TO CUSTOMERS?

Many organizations make it difficult for their employees to speak directly to their customers (or even forbid it). Instead, research is outsourced, conducted only by a research or insights department, or simply not funded. These practices run counter to making an organization more customer-centric. This book recommends approaches that challenge this business as usual. If your organization does not support this new paradigm, try the following:

- Do some secondary research. There are a growing number of case studies from the design thinking, service design, innovation, and other communities on building empathy directly with customers.

- Meet informally with the gatekeepers of customer research. Share key examples of how design research is critical to organizational success.

- Hold lunch-and-learns to educate peers and create more demand for new research approaches.

- Pitch an experiment. See if you can get partnership on a small study to try out a new way of working.

- Bring in outside experts to support your case. Look for someone who is not only an expert in experience mapping and research, but who is also committed to helping you and your organization build new capabilities (i.e., not outsourcing experience mapping).

---

2 A recruiting screener outlines the criteria for what types of people you want to participate in your study. It typically includes demographic, attitudinal and behavioral requirements, and the type of customer relationship with your product or service.

3 This rule of thumb is based on both experience and best practices in qualitative research within the design community. See Sarah Elsie Baker and Rosalind Edwards' excellent paper on this topic: blog.soton.ac.uk/dissertation/files/2013/09/how_many_interviews.pdf

What Are You Trying to Learn?

With your strategic intent in mind, experience mapping involves understanding how different customers take different paths in different contexts in relation to your problem space. This entails answering the following questions (which map back to the building blocks outlined earlier):

- What **triggered** the customer's journey?
- What were her **expectations**?
- What **actions** did she take?
- What did she **feel** at different points in time?
- What was she **thinking** at specific moments?
- Which **touchpoints** did she interact with?
- What **people** were involved?
- What **technologies** (screens, devices, etc.) were involved?
- What was the **sequence** of events?
- What were the **key moments**?
- What **places** did actions take place in?
- How much **time** elapsed within and across the journey?
- What was her **lasting impression**?

You won't ask these directly. The answers will emerge simply by customers telling their stories or observing their experiences directly. In addition to understanding each journey taken, you will also learn about each customer's unique needs, goals, motivations, and context. You will generate insights into specific pain points and opportunities and find inspiration for what solutions may meet their needs better.

Which Methods Get the Best Results?

The research methods you select or create to uncover your customers' stories in depth depend greatly upon your context. As with other research studies, the breadth and depth of your customer segments and the type of access you have can push you toward certain approaches. Research protocols for a large, global customer base versus a less diverse, local group of customers will look quite different. And, of course, the constraints of time and money also will play a big role in your options.

Regardless, you should combine multiple methods—both qualitative and quantitative—to support your team learning about your customers' ecosystems and journeys from different angles. Here is an overview of three common approaches and several methods that can help you get the job done well. Quantitative methods will follow later in the chapter.

Face-to-face Customer Sessions

Sitting down face-to-face (either in person or over video) with your customers is a go-to approach when conducting experience mapping and for good reason. Talking directly with customers has the advantages of building direct empathy, requiring relatively less logistical wrangling, and affording maximum flexibility in the methods you employ during the session. Another plus is that you can create roles for less experienced researchers to add value and participate in the sessions. While not perfect—people's memories may reflect some past actions, thoughts, and feelings inaccurately—you will still get good results and plenty of bang for your research buck.

How you structure your face-to-face sessions depends partly upon how physically close you can get to your customers and their world. When possible, get as close as you can! Going out into the field to hold in-context sessions is preferable. Lab environments, especially those located at your organization's building or campus, create barriers for client comfort as well as bias. For this reason, you may also consider using neutral third spaces, such as a coffee shop.

In some cases, remote sessions will be necessary to reach customers when you cannot go to them. Video sessions—using video conference tools, FaceTime, Google hangouts, or similar services—can mitigate not being in the same space. While not ideal, you can use screen sharing to support interactive methods. Table 5.2 provides additional pros and cons related to different research environments.

During face-to-face sessions, the methods you employ should support uncovering the key building block categories: the customer, the journey, the ecosystem, and the context. You also want to make the session enjoyable for your participants so that they feel their time was well spent and you receive open and honest information. Table 5.3 illustrates what a 90-minute session might look like.

TABLE 5.2   RESEARCH ENVIRONMENTS PROS AND CONS

Approach	Pros	Cons
Video	Low cost Access to wide geography Easy for other stakeholders to observe or participate in sessions	Requires specific tool and being tech savvy More difficult to build rapport More difficult to use co-creation methods
In-Person—Lab	Relatively low cost Easy for other stakeholders to observe or participate in sessions Effective use of co-creation methods	Limited geographies covered (based on where labs are) Most inconvenient for customer Lab setting creates barriers to creating optimum comfort and rapport
In-Person—Neutral	Ability to choose environments that are comfortable and reduce bias Effective use of co-creation methods Can hit a broad geography	Limitations to stakeholders' observation and participation Travel costs related to number of locations Can be inconvenient for customer Extra effort related to finding appropriate neutral locations
In-Person—in Context	Most convenient for customer Effective use of co-creation methods Ability to observe and more fully understand context Can hit a broad geography	Travel costs related to number of locations Limitations to stakeholders' observation and participation More logistically challenging (but worth it!)

TABLE 5.3 A FACE-TO-FACE SESSION AGENDA

Time	Objective	Method
10 min	Build rapport	Get-to-know-you conversation, focusing on who they are as a person, what makes them tick, and their relationship to your product or service (if any)
25 min	Understand context	Personal ecosystem mapping (see Chapter 3)
30 min	Understand journey	Experience mapping using directed storytelling and visual mapping
20 min	Further understand needs and solutions	Cocreate solutions to pain points and opportunities uncovered in previous methods
5 min	Close session	Conversation

In this example, the session has been designed to create a comfortable, safe, and interactive discussion regarding the participant's experiences and how those fit into the greater context of who they are and their personal context. Specific methods used include:

- **Get-to-know-you conversation:** A brief discussion to build rapport with the participant and lay the ground rules for the session. Treat this as you would a conversation with a stranger at a cocktail party. What do they do for a living? Do they have a family? What are their interests? Then segue into topics related to the domain you want to discuss in the session. This could be your product or service (e.g., getting a mortgage), or the greater context in which they exist (e.g., finding and buying a home).

- **Personal ecosystem mapping:** As discussed in Chapter 3, you can cocreate the participant's personal ecosystem to dig into important people, places, things, and relationships. This approach helps you understand context and gives you a preview of what may be mentioned when you map their end-to-end journey.

- **Experience mapping:** This approach leverages two methods: directed storytelling and visual mapping. Directed storytelling is an interview technique in which a participant recalls an experience (in this case, a recent journey). As the participant recalls his story, you or another facilitator can visually map the journey as it is revealed. This helps you make sure that you have captured the actions, emotions, thoughts, and moment accurately.

- **Cocreate solutions:** Before closing the session, take some time to consider the future with the customer. Use the unmet needs, pain points, and opportunities you have uncovered to explore new solutions.

COCREATING THE JOURNEY VISUALIZATION

During research sessions, I strive to get a participant leaning in and cocreating artifacts with me. This gets the participant more engaged and leads to deeper insights. For example, after visualizing the customer's journey, you can place a translucent sheet of vellum over your diagram (see Figure 5.5). You and the participant can then discuss and sketch improvements.

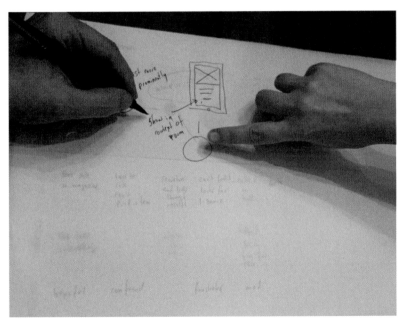

FIGURE 5.5
Visualizing the journey, now and in the future.

In the Moment and in Context

In addition to talking with customers about past experiences, observing customer journeys as they happen can yield incredibly valuable insights. The type of methods you employ will depend upon the nature of your product or service. Regardless, your goal is to reduce the time between when a journey moment occurs and your understanding and interpretation of it.

In industries where physical channels play a critical role—such as retail, healthcare, banking, and travel—there is a high return-on-investment for getting directly into the environments in which key moments occur. Specific approaches include:

- **Observation:** Watching customers interact with different people and things in the environment (see Figure 5.6).

- **Intercepts:** Following and observing customers; brief interviews with them to dig deeper into what you saw and the moments that occurred outside of direct observation.

- **Ride-a-longs:** Using contextual inquiry to follow the journey of your customer while asking questions and validating your observation.

- **Apprenticing:** Training as a service provider and interacting directly with customers to understand needs, touchpoints, and interactions more deeply.

FIGURE 5.6
Observing customer interactions directly requires interpretation.

For more digital products and services, similar techniques can be leveraged. Intercepts, for example, may involve soliciting participants while interacting with a website to discuss their experience, previous moments, and what they may do next. A ride-a-long in this context involves recruiting participants pre-journey and observing as they interact with digital channels in context.

More observational techniques require some interpretation for nailing down building blocks such as thinking and feeling. Pairing them with intercepts and other methods can help balance seeing what happened with understanding why and what it means.

First-Person Documentation

A third research category involves equipping your customers to capture their own journeys as they unfold. Multiple common self-reporting methods work well for experience mapping, including:

- **Textual:** Analog or digital journals in which the customer records their journey moments

- **Photographic:** Annotated photographs of key journey moments

- **Video:** Real-time or post-moment capturing of the journey

- **Snippets:** Micro reflections as moments occur sent via text or mobile app

First-person studies require careful design and lots of scaffolding for participants to be successful. However, the richness of data collected in situ and in follow-up interviews can be well worth it.

> **NOTE** SYNTHESIZING QUALITATIVE DATA
>
> As with quantitative data and statistical analysis, it takes great skill to unpack qualitative research and find patterns within it. It also takes time, typically in the magnitude of weeks, not days, for medium to large research studies. You will need one or more experienced people who can guide the larger group through making sense of what you learned.[4]

---

4 A great resource on research synthesis is John Kolko's *Exposing the Magic of Design: A Practitioner's Guide to the Methods and Theory of Synthesis* (Oxford: Oxford University Press, 2011).

What About Quantitative Research?

Quantitative and qualitative research should go hand-in-hand. You may have a number of sources for quantitative research: analytics, Net Promoter Score (NPS), and Voice of the Customer, just to name a few. This is incredibly valuable data to ensure that you understand the range of behaviors and interactions customers have with your product or service during their journeys. In general, three types of quantitative data can add value to your experience mapping effort:

- **Pre-existing marketing data:** Most marketing organizations invest in regularly surveying customers. Look for studies that touch upon moments of your customer journey to see if any valuable insights lurk within them. For example, a previous survey may have asked customers which channels they prefer or moments in which they were most or least satisfied.

- **Business metrics:** Businesses ask their functional departments to measure their performance and report back trends to inform strategy. Within common reports such as NPS, channel performance, conversion funnels, and many others, you can get a feel for trends in performance that can be mapped back to what you learned in qualitative research.

- **Channel data:** Each channel has best practices for measuring interactions with customers. Web and mobile analytics can reveal usage rates, user flows, entrance and exit points, and more granular conversion data. Call center reports include call volumes, types of assistance requested, and resolution paths. Dig into this data to piece together which pathways customers take more often and what happens when they do. Then use your qualitative research to understand why.

- **Journey-based survey data:** In addition to pre-existing data, you should consider conducting your own survey to see how your qualitative insights play out at scale. You may have individual data about the usage of any given channel, but doing journey-based surveys helps you look at the channels utilized across an individual's experience and how they perceived their touchpoint interactions and the overall experience. Figure 5.7 shows this approach when visualized in map form.

Quantitative data, of course, does not provide the *why* behind behaviors, the thoughts and emotions that customers experience, or the different contexts in which interactions take place. When asked, tell your colleagues that quantitative research is valuable, but not adequate on its own. However, when you interview a handful of people but can bolster your findings with data representing a great sample size, then you can have more confidence that you have painted a full picture of the range of experiences your customers are having.

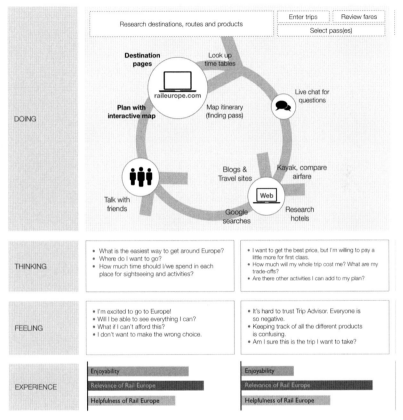

FIGURE 5.7
In this Rail Europe experience map, survey results were mapped by journey stage.

How Do You Involve Different Stakeholders Successfully?

As you go through your iterative discovery and research process, it's important to keep your colleagues engaged and active along the way. Here are a few techniques to involve different stakeholders from experience mappers to influencers:

- **Build a question map.** Before you design your protocol, hold a session with a broad range of stakeholders. Run an exercise to gather questions that each stakeholder would like to know about the end-to-end experiences of customers. Analyze everyone's input as a group to identify key topics to incorporate into your protocol.

- **Rotate experience mappers.** Most of your colleagues will not have the skill to facilitate research sessions, nor the time to participate in all of them. It's important, however, to bring several stakeholders into the field to understand the viability of your approaches and build direct empathy with customers. A good approach is to rotate these colleagues in the role of note-taker. To ensure that you get good notes, make sure that you train everyone who will go into the field and design a note-taking template with instructions to provide sufficient scaffolding for their role.

- **Do a gallery tour.** Often, too much time goes by between gathering insights and sharing them. A powerful technique that builds team rapport and customer-centered culture is to hold a post-research gallery tour. At the conclusion of field research, gather everyone who participated in the field and build out a room displaying raw information from your sessions. Items could include a picture of each participant, the journey and ecosystem maps you created with them, and sticky notes with key insights from each session. Then, do an open house for other stakeholders to tour your research gallery (see Figure 5.8). Have each experience mapper tell stories from the field, referencing the materials.

FIGURE 5.8
A gallery tour presenting field research to the greater organization.

Making Sense of What You Learned

The collaborative research approach does not end once you complete your sessions. Bring your cross-functional team together to dig in and find the larger story within your data.

To get to that story, you and others will need to find the patterns within your discovery and research outputs. This will take time and get a little messy. Approaches common to research—unpacking your data, finding patterns through affinity mappings, and then laddering up to generate insights—apply to experience mapping. In addition to those fundamentals, these steps should be followed to go from raw stories to insights:

1. **Go deep into each customer's story.** Go through each session's outputs at a high-level, sharing with one another the stories you heard. Start building a list of findings, story by story.

2. **Group cohorts and break down their journeys.** Begin looking for patterns across your different customer findings. Group together similar customers. Then go through your research notes and artifacts for each group to understand each journey and how they compare with others in their cohort.

3. **Compare cohorts.** Look for patterns across cohorts. Regroup customers as you find deeper patterns.

4. **Nail down your structure and key themes.** Using the building blocks and frameworks recommended in Chapter 4, "Orienting Around Journeys," define a structure for your experience map. Take a first pass at the themes that it should communicate.

5. **Correlate with other models and data.** Take the structure from your mapping activities and merge it into what you have learned through touchpoints, inventories, quantitative data, and any observational research.

6. **Keep refining.** Getting your structure right and choosing what details to include will take several iterations. Keep at it.

These activities can take place in a multiday workshop or across several working sessions. See the "Experience Mapping" workshop following this chapter for how to tackle the steps outlined previously.

Communicating What Matters

A good experience map should serve as a catalyst for action. For it to do so, you have to translate your findings into a compelling artifact. You should design your experience map (or maps) to support your next steps, whether that is strategic planning, idea generation, or tactical execution. Approach your experience map as a tool to be used, not a research deliverable to be consumed.

There is no experience map template; however, best practices have emerged in recent years. Here are some tips to guide your design decisions.

- **Design for your context.** You have a lot of options in designing your map. Craft your artifact to the needs of its users and ensure that it fits the greater system of tools that support your strategy and execution.

- **Create a clear structure.** The stages and moments that emerged during your analysis serve as an important structural frame for your map. As with chapters and sections in a book, these elements should help users navigate the story you want to tell. Both stage and moment labels should reflect the language of your customers in order to reinforce their experiences. Avoid business jargon such as awareness, consideration, conversion, or loyalty. Go for labels that summarize the overarching customer actions or needs from their perspective, such as "exploring my options," "getting to the hotel," or as in Figure 5.9, "I think I need help." Often, you will find inspiration in the conversations that you had with customers to phrase your stages and moments authentically.

- **Show relationships among the customer building blocks and touchpoints.** Make sure that your customer and their interactions with your organization take center stage. Moment by moment, highlight the nature and quality of your customer touchpoints and the range of what customers do, think, and feel.

  As you explore options for communicating the relationships, look at options for using one of the customer building blocks to drive your story. Is it about the customer's emotional journey (see Figure 5.10)? Is it about what they are doing? Thinking? Depending on the themes or insights you want to communicate, one of these should stand out as central to how you visualize the journey.

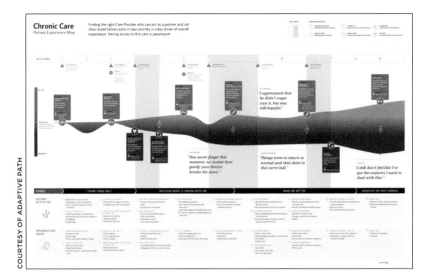

FIGURE 5.9

"I think I need help"—as opposed to "awareness"—communicates the customers' actual experience clearly.

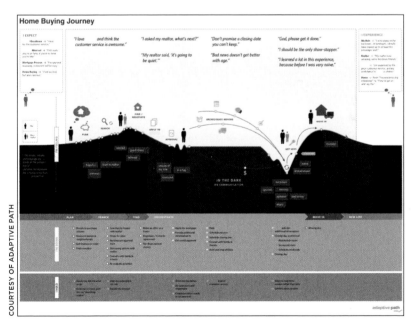

FIGURE 5.10

In this example for home buying, the feeling building block takes center stage with other building blocks mapped against it.

- **Emphasize that not all customers are the same.** You will have found a range of needs and experiences within your customer base, perhaps leading to creating profiles of archetypes. How you indicate this in your artifact depends on the story you want to tell. You can represent this diversity by calling out the breadth of experiences, comparing the emotional journeys of different customer types (see Figure 5.11), or designing separate maps for different customer profiles. Your map doesn't have to carry the entire load of your customer insights, but make sure that you critique your map to ensure that it doesn't overgeneralize your *customers* as *the customer.*

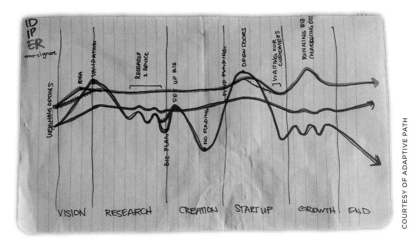

FIGURE 5.11
Comparing emotional journeys of different customer types.

- **Share the big picture.** While highlighting touchpoints is job one, make sure that you include insights into moments or needs outside of those with your product or service. How much you include will depend on the level of zoom you choose—shopping and buying for a home vs. applying for a mortgage—and how critical the insights are to your understanding of your customers' stories.

- **Give prominence to what matters most.** Everything you choose to include in your map should be important, but you should have a strategy for what should stand out the most and what can serve as secondary or supporting information. Figure 5.12 shows a good approach of including a clear overarching story with salient highlights, while providing detail to "drill down" for more information. Follow solid information design principles—such as hierarchy, contrast, scale, and color theory—to make the most effective map that you can.[5]

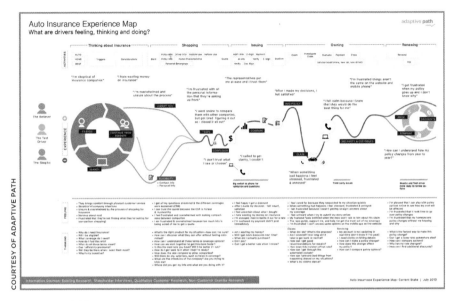

FIGURE 5.12
There's lots of good information to drill down on, but the salient highlights are immediately clear.

- **Bring in the customer's voice.** Using verbatim quotes from your customers adds richness and authenticity to your map. Use quotes sparingly to double-down on key insights and further synthesize data presented throughout your map. Less is more.

- **Highlight some, but not all, quantitative data.** As noted earlier, bringing quantitative data that provides more insights into customers' experiences or the role of touchpoints and channels adds some weight to your map. As with customer quotes, don't go overboard in putting numbers and graphs in your map. High-light insightful data and let other supporting documentation get deeper into the numbers if you have them.

---

5 A tip of the hat to all the talented visual and communication designers we have worked with who could write a whole book themselves on best practices in designing experience maps. They get a big "thank you!" in the acknowledgments.

- **Play with form to create tools.** Later chapters will detail how experience maps can be used as tools in the design process. Again, you want to avoid your map being just a pretty deliverable filed away never to be seen again. This goes back to designing for your context. Figure 5.13 illustrates different ways to present your map for use in socialization, downstream design activities, and ongoing updating and maintenance.

FIGURE 5.13
Get creative with the forms your map can take to be useful and effective in your culture.

- **Tell a story.** Finally, and most importantly, work backward from the story you want to tell. Before you start exploring ways to visualize your map, write down the key points it should communicate and what you want people to take away. Just as you can deconstruct an experience into building blocks, you can design for what you want users of your map to think and feel as they experience the artifact. Try to craft a story and a tool for what you hope they will do with their insights. Then use your key points and takeaways to critique how you visualize the map and refine it accordingly.

TELL A COMPELLING STORY

When done correctly, a map tells a story with depth and richness around the human experience. I love telling stories with visuals and models because it is easier and faster for people to comprehend than a few paragraphs of words. A good model of the journey tells a story through the layering of qualitative and quantitative information. With the element of time, this visual model is the quickest and most effective way to tell a story.

Coda

- An experience map is a visual articulation of research insights related to the end-to-end customer experience. It illuminates how customers interact with your product or service as well as the greater ecosystem around them.

- Experience mapping is a team activity that should begin with a clear intent and include iterative discovery and primary research to uncover the stories of your customers.

- You have many options in how you structure your qualitative research. Be sure to mix methods and leverage quantitative data along the way.

- Moving from raw data to a synthesized understanding of the end-to-end experiences of customers takes time. Keep engaging your cross-functional team to ensure that you continue to build rapport and buy-in into the value of mapping.

- Design your map for your context. Have a clear structure and work backward from the story you want to tell. Through thoughtful editing and visualizations, you can create an effective tool to inform and spark strategic and tactical action.

A n experience-mapping workshop uses a co-creation approach to build an initial experience map with the colleagues that joined you in field research. This workshop assumes that you followed many of the approaches outlined in Chapter 5, "Mapping Experiences." You should have several people— experience mappers—who spent time directly with customers and know their stories. Facilitating this workshop involves guiding participants through a series of activities to understand each customer's experience in detail and synthesize those findings into key insights. Depending on the scope of your focus, this workshop may happen in a couple working sessions, or it may take several days and sessions. This is structured research synthesis, but the hard work results in an experience map that you can stand behind.

Workshop Objectives

- Get all participants up-to-speed on the key findings from each customer session.

- Perform a detailed analysis of each customer's journey.

- Find patterns across customers to generate key insights.

- Synthesize the individual journeys in an initial experience map.

Agenda

This workshop typically takes two to three days, depending on how many interviews and observations you performed with customers. The times below provide timing for each key step across a two-day workshop. This agenda also includes structured breaks and meals, but you can build breaks in more organically.

TABLE 5.4 DAY 1 WORKSHOP AGENDA

Activity	Description	Duration
Review agenda and objectives	Share the activities for the day and what you want to accomplish by the end of the session.	30 min
Go deep into each customer's story (Part I)	Go through each session's outputs at a high-level, sharing with one another the stories you heard. Start building a list of findings, story by story.	90 min
Break	Recharge!	15 min
Go deep into each customer's story (Part II)	Continue to go through the stories.	120 min
Lunch	Eat!	60 min
Go deep into each customer's story (Part III)	Finish going through the stories.	90 min
Break	Give people a rest while you set up for the next activity.	15 min
Group cohorts and break down journeys (Part I)	Look for patterns across your different customer findings. Group similar customers. Then deconstruct each journey into its building blocks.	120 min

TABLE 5.5 DAY 2 WORKSHOP AGENDA

Activity	Description	Duration
Group cohorts and break down journeys (Part II)	Continue breaking down the journeys.	120 min
Break	Give people a rest while you set up for the next activity.	15 min
Compare cohorts	Look for patterns across cohorts. Regroup customers as you find deeper patterns. Mine your data to pressure-test your sensemaking.	90 min
Lunch	Eat!	60 min
Nail down structure and key themes (Part I)	Using the building blocks and frameworks recommended earlier in this chapter, define a structure for your experience map.	120 min
Break	Recharge!	15 min
Nail down structure and key themes (Part II)	Complete your structure and document key themes.	90 min
Review and reflect	Review the workshop process and outcomes. Determine the next steps.	15 min

Roles

- **Lead facilitator:** Workshop host and main facilitator for session activities

- **Co-facilitator(s):** Help(s) set up, break down, and assist in activities

- **Documentarian:** Takes photographs of the session to help nonparticipants understand the collaborative process

Participants

- Facilitators from field research
- Experience mappers from field research

Artifacts

- **Research documentation:** Written notes, photographs, and video from your sessions.

- **Co-creation artifacts:** Journey visualizations or other artifacts created with customers in your sessions.

Materials

- Self-stick easel pad or butcher paper (to create a wall canvas)

- Tape or drafting dots to place artifacts and documentation on walls

- Sharpies

- Sticky notes

- Camera

Preparing for the Workshop

As with the other workshops recommended in this book, how well you prepare and communicate will make or break the effectiveness of your session. Make sure that you have previously educated your collaborators and sold the value of experience principles. (See the handy list earlier in the chapter.) You want your workshop to be laser focused on getting feedback on your principles, not the process. You do not want the session to go off track explaining in detail what experience principles are or defending their usefulness. People should be excited to collaborate on shaping a tool together, not being introduced to the concept for the first time.

Running the Workshop

This workshop can be challenging to facilitate. You will have lots of data to comb through in your notes, transcripts, and session artifacts (e.g., journey maps made with customers). Your participants will have varying expertise in unpacking research effectively and efficiently. The days will be long, and participants will run into conflicts related to their "day jobs."

Trust us, it's worth the hassle. This type of detailed work builds empathy for customers and partnerships within your organization. Be patient, but firm, as you guide the group through these steps:

- Go deep into each customer's story.

- Group cohorts and break down their journeys.

- Compare cohorts.

- Nail down your structure and key themes.

Go Deep into Each Customer's Story

Your colleagues will have experienced one or more research sessions directly. Very few (if any) of your team, however, will have spent time with every customer. Therefore, your first objective is to get your team familiar with each customer and their unique story. You can do so by kicking your analysis off with introducing one another to what you learned in each session. Here is one approach:

- Assign each research participant to a colleague who participated in the corresponding session.

- Ask each person to go through the session's outputs (typically: notes, co-creation worksheets, transcripts, photography, and debrief sheets) and pull out the key findings. They can write each finding on a sticky note. Instruct people to be thorough. This will take some time. *Note: The same approach can work for self-reported journeys generated using diary methods.*

- After everyone has analyzed their session outputs, take turns introducing each customer. If you have visual artifacts from your session, they should be used to help make the insights more tangible. Focus on the key categories of building blocks at a high level:

  - Who is the customer?

  - What did you learn about her ecosystem and context?

  - What sparked her journey?

  - What were the major moments?

  - What were her motivations, key needs, and emotional high and low points?

  - What's the moral of her story?

- As people present, have other colleagues capture notes (one per sticky) of things that stand out to them. This will help speed up the synthesis of key themes later in the process (see Figure 5.14).

FIGURE 5.14
Finding patterns in the personal ecosystems of customers.

Group Cohorts and Break Down Their Journeys

Once you have unpacked each session and created a high-level understanding of each customer, you need to take an initial pass at how your customer falls into cohorts. What defines a cohort in your research depends on the variables that you believe most affect customer behaviors, emotions, and needs. This may or may not map to the segmentation that you used to recruit or codify pre-existing customer models, such as personas. Here are a few examples:

- Investing: Customers on a mission vs. customers in exploration mode

- Travel: First-time fliers vs. seasoned fliers

- Home loans: New mortgage vs. refinancing

- Healthcare: Going to the emergency room vs. going to primary care

- Shopping: Casual vs. loyal customers

At this stage, don't get too hung up on how you organize your customers. Your goal is to identify customers to compare as you break down their journeys into more detail. Often, your first segmentation won't be where you end up. Don't get stuck. Make an informed call and get to mapping.

After you have your cohorts, organize your colleagues into small teams. Your next objective is to take the journey of each customer and break it down into its constituent building blocks. Here are some tips to manage the process:

- Set up a large canvas for each team to work and give them sticky notes in five to six different colors. This canvas can be on the wall or a long table.

- Each team should start with one customer. Recap again the customer's background and ecosystem.

- Then—leveraging notes, transcripts, visual journeys, and other assets—begin breaking down the customer's journey moment-by-moment, step-by-step. Focus first on what the customer did, thought, and felt, as well as what she interacted with from one end of her experience to the other. Fill in other details—people, places, and so on—as you go along.

- It's best to define clear lanes for each building block. As illustrated in Figure 5.15, different color sticky notes can be used to differentiate building blocks, or you can pick a different color for each customer.

- As the journey takes shape, look for natural breaking points in the journey. These chapters of the customers' stories will help you determine your journey stages.

- Identify and add quotes from customers that illustrate key findings.

- Do the same process for all customers in each cohort, mapping them to the same canvas. This will take some maneuvering of sticky notes, but this approach helps you compare the experiences of different customers more easily.

FIGURE 5.15
Breaking down a journey into its building blocks.

SKETCHING AND CLUSTERING MOMENTS

If you did visual mapping of each participant's journey in your sessions, you can use another approach to jump-start the mapping process. Take one of your illustrated journeys and identify the key moments. For example, when ordering from Warby Parker, your package of samples arrives at your home. You then try them on, choose which one you want, and pack up the samples to return (among other moments). Then, as illustrated in Figure 5.16, take a quarter sheet (A6) of paper and capture the following for each moment:

- The name of the moment
- A sketch representing that moment
- Details on the actions, thoughts, feelings, and ecosystem entities

Doing this for each journey produces dozens of moment cards that you can compare, contrast, and organize to identify patterns. You can then go deeper into your notes and transcripts to flesh out the details by using the sticky note approach outlined previously.

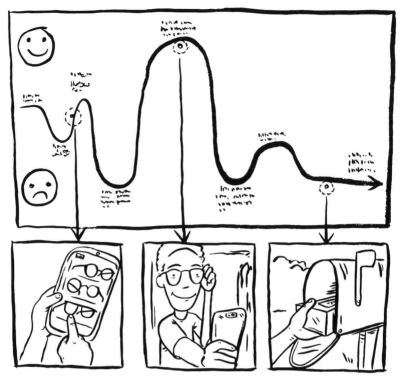

FIGURE 5.16
Pulling moments out of an individual journey.

Compare Cohorts

When the dust settles from your detailed mapping, take a step back. Work as a team to identify the patterns within and across cohorts. Look to answer these questions:

- Did your segmentation hold up? What would be a better way to group your customers? Do you need to group them at all?

- What needs emerged? Which ones were common? Extreme?

- Did customers go through similar moments? How did those moments cluster into stages?

- Were there common high and low points? Did you find lots of divergent experiences?

- What expectation gaps, pain points, and opportunities did you discover?

- What time did customers spend in different stages or moments?

- What breakdowns did customers experience in changing channels?

- What did you learn about the quality of your product or service touchpoints? Did any new touchpoints emerge?

- What did you learn about the experiences outside of your control? What other products, services, people, and things impact customer behaviors, emotions, thoughts, and needs?

Nail Down the Structure and Take-Aways

The results of this discussion (which you should diligently capture) will lead you to nailing down a draft of some important structural elements and the key take-aways from your research. Here is a checklist of what you and your colleagues need to align around:

- An approach to grouping customers based on their needs and experiences

- The stages and moments of the end-to-end journey

- The range of actions, thoughts, and feelings by stage and moment

- Ecosystem elements (touchpoints, other products and services, people, etc.) that play a role in or impact the customer experience and that customer's greater context

- The channels in which interactions take place

- Key customer needs by stage and moment

- Time durations and places within the journey

- Customer quotes that reflect key insights

- Pain points and opportunities

- What it all means: what your experience mapping tells you about the qualitative experiences for customers and what it means for them and your organization

HOLD A GALLERY TOUR

Previously, we mentioned doing a gallery tour to engage stakeholders, and immediately after this workshop is a perfect time for one. You and your colleagues play the role of docents, guiding visitors through your work and telling stories and anecdotes from the field. I typically do this as an open house for 1–2 hours, and often show video clips as well. These sessions help build empathy, show the rigor behind the work, and expose high-level executives to the collaboration happening across their teams. It's always a big hit and creates buzz (and often demand) for these types of approaches.

After the Workshop

This workshop jump-starts your journey mapping, but you will still have a good bit of work to do. As noted earlier in Chapter 5, you will continue to iterate on your experience map and the story it needs to tell. This includes correlating with other data and research, sketching approaches to visualize your map, and using a draft of your map in opportunity and ideation workshops to identify additional improvements you can make. (See the workshops after Chapters 7, "Identifying Opportunities," and 8, "Generating and Evaluating Ideas.")

CHAPTER 6

Defining Experience Principles

If you embrace the recommended collaborative approaches in your sensemaking activities, you and your colleagues should build good momentum toward creating better and valuable end-to-end experiences. In fact, the urge to jump into solution mode will be tempting. Take a deep breath: you have a little more work to do. To ensure that your new insights translate into the right actions, you must collectively define what is *good* and hold one another accountable for aligning with it.

Good, in this context, means the ideas and solutions that you commit to reflect your customers' needs and context while achieving organizational objectives. It also means that each touchpoint harmonizes with others as part of an orchestrated system. Defining *good*, in this way, provides common constraints to reduce arbitrary decisions and nudge everyone in the same direction.

How do you align an organization to work collectively toward the same *good*? Start with some common guidelines called *experience principles.*

A Common DNA

Experience principles are a set of guidelines that an organization commits to and follows from strategy through delivery to produce mutually beneficial and differentiated customer experiences. Experience principles represent the alignment of brand aspirations and customer needs, and they are derived from understanding your customers. In action, they help teams own their part (e.g., a product, touchpoint, or channel) while supporting consistency and continuity in the end-to-end experience. Figure 6.1 presents an example of a set of experience principles.

Experience principles are not detailed standards that everyone must obey to the letter. Standards tend to produce a rigid system, which curbs innovation and creativity. In contrast, experience principles inform the many decisions required to define what experiences your product or service should create and how to design for individual, yet connected, moments. They communicate in a few memorable phrases the organizational wisdom for how to meet customers' needs consistently and effectively. For example, look at the following:

- Paint me a picture.
- Have my back.
- Set my expectations.
- Be one step ahead of me.
- Respect my time.

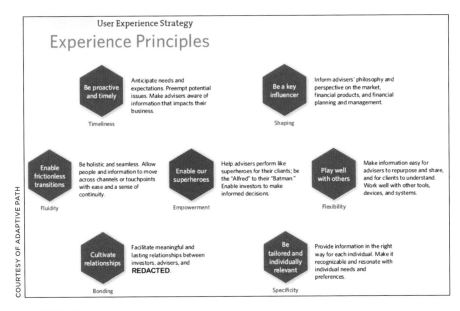

FIGURE 6.1
Example set of experience principles.

EXPERIENCE PRINCIPLES VS DESIGN PRINCIPLES

Orchestrating experiences is a team sport. Many roles contribute to defining, designing, and delivering products and services that result in customer experiences. For this reason, the label *experience* best reflects their value beyond designers and the design process. *Experience principles* are outcome oriented; *design principles* are process oriented. Everyone should follow and buy into them, not just designers.

Experience principles are grounded in customer needs, and they keep collaborators focused on the why, what, and how of engaging people through products and services. They keep critical insights and intentions top of mind, such as the following:

- **Mental Models:** How part of an experience can help people have a better understanding, or how it should conform to their mental model.

- **Emotions:** How part of an experience should support the customer emotionally, or directly address their motivations.

- **Behaviors:** How part of an experience should enable someone to do something they set out to do better.

- **Target:** The characteristics to which an experience should adhere.

- **Impact:** The outcomes and qualities an experience should engender in the user or customer.

FOCUSING ON NEEDS TO DIFFERENTIATE

Many universal or heuristic principles exist to guide design work. There are visual design principles, interaction design principles, user experience principles, and any number of domain principles that can help define the best practices you apply in your design process. These are lessons learned over time that have a broader application and can be relied on consistently to inform your work across even disparate projects.

It's important to reinforce that experience principles specific to your customers' needs provide contextual guidelines for strategy and design decisions. They help everyone focus on what's appropriate to specific customers with a unique set of needs, and your product or service can differentiate itself by staying true to these principles. Experience principles shouldn't compete with best practices or universal principles, but they should be honored as critical inputs for ensuring that your organization's specific value propositions are met.

Playing Together

Earlier, we compared channels and touchpoints to an orchestra, but experience principles are more like jazz. While each member of a jazz ensemble is given plenty of room to improvise, all players understand the common context in which they are performing and listen and respond to one another (Figure 6.2). They know the standards of the genre, which allows them to be creative individually while collectively playing the same tune.

Experience principles provide structure and guidelines that connect collaborators while giving them room to be innovative. As with a time signature, they ensure alignment. Similar to a melody, they encourage supportive harmony. Like musical style, they provide boundaries for what fits and what doesn't.

FIGURE 6.2

Jazz ensembles depend upon a common foundation to inspire improvisation while working together to form a holistic work of art.

Experience principles challenge a common issue in organizations: isolated soloists playing their own tune to the detriment of the whole ensemble. While still leaving plenty of room for individual improvisation, they ask a bunch of solo acts to be part of the band. This structure provides a foundation for continuity in the resulting customer journey, but doesn't overengineer consistency and predictability, which might prevent delight and differentiation. Stressing this balance of designing the whole while distributing effort and ownership is a critical stance to take to engender cross-functional buy-in.

To get broad acceptance of your experience principles, you must help your colleagues and your leadership see their value. This typically requires crafting specific value propositions and education materials for different stakeholders to gain broad support and adoption. Piloting your experience principles on a project can also help others understand their tactical use. When approaching each stakeholder, consider these common values:

- **Defining good:** While different channels and media have their specific best practices, experience principles provide a common set of criteria that can be applied across an entire end-to-end experience.

- **Decision-making filter:** Throughout the process of determining what to do strategically and how to do it tactically, experience principles ensure that customers' needs and desires are represented in the decision-making process.

- **Boundary constraints:** Because these constraints represent the alignment of brand aspiration and customer desire, experience principles can filter out ideas or solutions that don't reinforce this alignment.

- **Efficiency:** Used consistently, experience principles reduce ambiguity and the resultant churn when determining what concepts should move forward and how to design them well.

- **Creativity inspiration:** Experience principles are very effective in sparking new ideas with greater confidence that will map back to customer needs. (See Chapter 8, "Generating and Evaluating Ideas.")

- **Quality control:** Through the execution lifecycle, experience principles can be used to critique touchpoint designs (i.e., the parts) to ensure that they align to the greater experience (i.e., the whole).

Pitching and educating aside, your best bet for creating good experience principles that get adopted is to avoid creating them in a black box. You don't want to spring your experience principles on your colleagues as if they were commandments from above to follow blindly. Instead, work together to craft a set of principles that everyone can follow energetically.

Identifying Draft Principles

Your research into the lives and journeys of customers will produce a large number of insights. These insights are *reflective*. They capture people's current experiences—such as their met and unmet needs, how they frame the world, and their desired outcomes. To craft useful and appropriate experience principles, you must turn these insights inside out to *project* what future experiences should be.

WHEN YOU CAN'T DO RESEARCH (YET)

If you lack strong customer insights (and the support or time to gather them), it's still valuable to craft experience principles with your colleagues. The process of creating them provides insight into the various criteria that people are using to make decisions. It also sheds light on what your collaborators believe are the most important customer needs to meet. While not as sound as research-driven principles, your team can align around a set of guidelines to inform and critique your collective work—and then build the case for gathering insights for creating better experience principles.

From the Bottom Up

The leap from insights to experience principles will take several iterations. While you may be able to rattle off a few candidates based on your research, it's well worth the time to follow a more rigorous approach in which you work from the bottom (individual insights) to the top (a handful of well-crafted principles). Here's how to get started:

- Reassemble your facilitators and experience mappers, as they are closest to what you learned in your research.

- Go back to the key insights that emerged from your discovery and research. These likely have been packaged in maps, models, research reports, or other artifacts. You can also go back to your raw data if needed.

- Write each key insight on a sticky note. These will be used to spark a first pass at potential principles.

- For each insight, have everyone take a pass individually at articulating a principle derived from that insight. You can use sticky notes again or a quarter sheet of 8.5" x 11" (A6) template to give people a little more structure (see Figure 6.3).

- At this stage, you should coach participants to avoid finding the perfect words or a pithy way to communicate a potential principle. Instead, focus on getting the core lesson learned from the insight and what advice you would give others to guide product or service decisions in the future. Table 6.1 shows a couple of examples of what a good first pass looks like.

- At this stage, don't be a wordsmith. Work quickly to reframe your insights from something you know ("Most people don't want to . . . ") to what should be done to stay true to this insight ("Make it easy for people . . . ").

- Work your way through all the insights until everyone has a principle for each one.

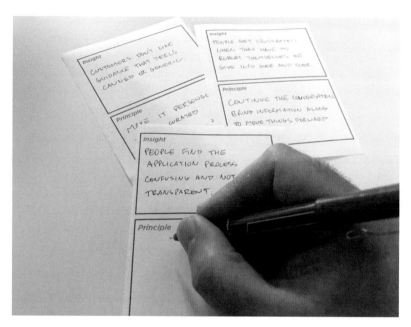

FIGURE 6.3
A simple template to generate insight-level principles quickly.

TABLE 6.1   FROM INSIGHTS TO DRAFT PRINCIPLES

Insight	Principle
Most people don't want to do their homework first. They want to get started and learn what they need to know when they need to know it.	Make it easy for people to dive in and collect knowledge when it's most relevant.
Everyone believes their situation (financial, home, health) is unique and reflects their specific circumstances, even if it's not true.	Approach people as they see themselves: unique people in unique situations.

Finding Patterns

You now have a superset of individual principles from which a handful of experience principles will emerge. Your next step is to find the patterns within them. You can use affinity mapping to identify principles that speak to a similar theme or intent. As with any clustering activity, this may take a few iterations until you feel that you have mutually exclusive categories. You can do this in just a few steps:

- Select a workshop participant to present the principles one by one, explaining the intent behind each one.

- Cycle through the rest of the group, combining like principles and noting where principles conflict with one another. As you cluster, the dialogue the group has is as important as where the principles end up.

- Once things settle down, you and your colleagues can take a first pass at articulating a principle for each cluster. A simple half sheet (8.5" x 5.5" or A5) template can give some structure to this step. Again, don't get too precious with every word yet. Get the essence down so that you and others can understand and further refine it with the other principles.

- You should end up with several mutually exclusive categories with a draft principle for each.

Designing Principles as a System

No experience principle is an island. Each should be understandable and useful on its own, but together your principles should form a system. Your principles should be complementary and reinforcing. They should be able to be applied across channels and throughout your product or service development process. See the following "Experience Principles Refinement" workshop for tips on how to critique your principles to ensure that they work together as a complete whole.

Crafting for Adoption and Impact

Defining a set of principles collaboratively with other people creates alignment, but crafting the language and presentation of your experience principles will fall on fewer shoulders. This detailed work is critical to ensure a broader understanding and adoption in your organization. Therefore, it's important to spend the time and have the right skills handy to write and communicate your intent effectively.

Here are a few rules of thumb that we follow and recommend. However, it's important to remember that every context is different. Use these as inspiration, not as hard standards.

Use a Consistent, Two-Tiered Structure

Experience principles need to be easy to recall and to use. As a system, it's appropriate that all your experience principles share the same schema. We recommend a two-tiered structure consisting of a clear, memorable headline and supportive content to ensure that the intent is understood. In use, the headline is your short-hand principle, while the additional details put flesh on the bones. Figure 6.4 is an example of this approach.

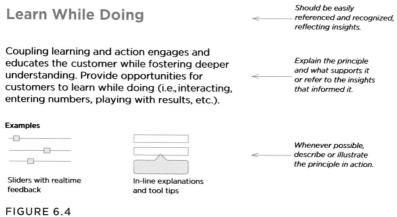

Learn While Doing

Should be easily referenced and recognized, reflecting insights.

Coupling learning and action engages and educates the customer while fostering deeper understanding. Provide opportunities for customers to learn while doing (i.e., interacting, entering numbers, playing with results, etc.).

Explain the principle and what supports it or refer to the insights that informed it.

Examples

Sliders with realtime feedback

In-line explanations and tool tips

Whenever possible, describe or illustrate the principle in action.

FIGURE 6.4

Schema of an experience principle.

Make Your Headline Brief but Memorable

An experience principle should strike a good balance between brevity and clarity. One word, such as "guide," doesn't fully communicate a thought or inspire action. Too many words—such as, "provide me with the knowledge, tools, guidance, and people to help me succeed"—would be difficult to recall and is too specific to spark new ideas effectively. Strive for something relatively short but clear.

Good principles also have effective creative writing without crossing into cuteness or unintended ambiguity. "Be the Robin to my Batman," may seem memorable, but its cultural specificity fails in terms of universal accessibility. On the other end of the spectrum, "support me" is too broad and less inspirational. "Always have my back," however, clearly and memorably communicates important customer needs and emotions.

FIRST PERSON OR THIRD PERSON?

You may have noticed that some of our examples are in the Voice of the Customer (e.g., "Have my back"), while others are in third person (e.g., "learn while doing"). We have found both approaches to be effective and impactful. Experiment to determine what works best for your collaborators and culture. Whichever way you go, just be consistent—make them all first- or third-person, not a mixture of both.

Provide Supportive Details but Don't Go Overboard

In addition to a brief, memorable phrase, supportive details help people understand the intent of an experience principle better. We recommend keeping this to one to three sentences. These should flesh out relative information regarding customer needs, emotions, mental models, behaviors, or the target experience. Follow the same rules as for your headline: your details should be clear, unambiguous, and easy to apply. For example:

> *Always have my back*
>
> *I get uneasy if I think my best interests are not being protected. Clearly communicate that you respect my needs and incorporate that understanding into our interactions.*

Avoid writing many paragraphs that explain the principle in detail. Too much detail risks crossing the line into being too prescriptive of a singular solution or specific product, service, or feature ideas. Flesh out your principle enough to make it easy to understand and useful, but don't be overly prescriptive.

Design for Adoption

In addition to being well-written language, you will need to design multiple communication vehicles to ensure that your experience principles are integrated into your process and culture. Every organization is different, but the following tactics should give you some traction.

- **Give examples of good and bad outcomes.** Once crafted, your experience principles can be used immediately to critique current experiences or in-progress work. Hold some brown bags or more formal sessions to illuminate good and poor examples.

- **Integrate into other deliverables.** Experience principles should start to make their way into other artifacts, such as experience maps, opportunity maps, experience storyboards, and concept presentations (see Figure 6.5).

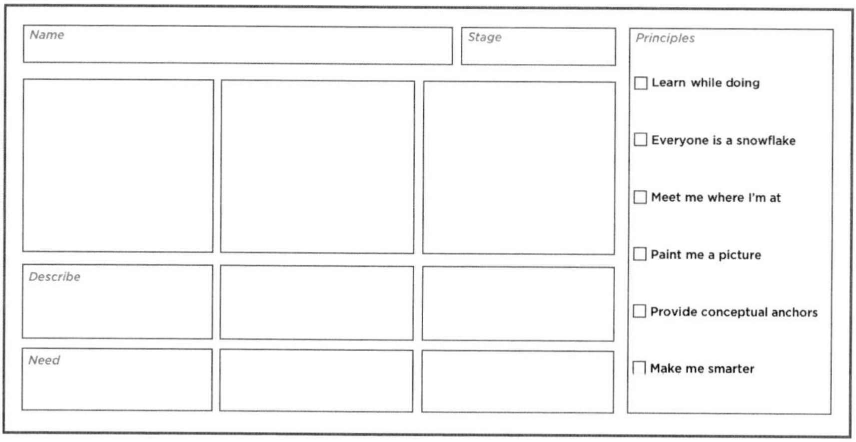

Name		Stage	Principles

Describe

Need

☐ Learn while doing

☐ Everyone is a snowflake

☐ Meet me where I'm at

☐ Paint me a picture

☐ Provide conceptual anchors

☐ Make me smarter

FIGURE 6.5

Experience principles are incorporated into a storyboard tool.

- **Make contextual decision-making tools.** It's important that your principles are easy to use by different roles. Take the time to design tools for use during ideation workshops, in agile pods, design critiques, and other contexts. For example, you can produce experience principle scorecards for sprint demonstrations and retrospectives. Or you can build them into ideation kits for workshops or individual brainstorming (see Chapters 8, "Generating and Valuing Ideas," and 11, "Taking Up the Baton").

- **Pilot with some teams.** Test out your principles with teams in different stages of the process from strategy to implementation. Insights can help you refine your principles and tools. Share their effectiveness more broadly to get others to begin using them.

Coda

- Experience principles help an organization produce mutually beneficial and differentiated customer experiences more predictably.

- Experience principles are not strict standards. They provide a common foundation for different teams to solve problems for customers while being true to their real needs and the connectivity and continuity you should create across all touchpoints.

- Your experience principles should emerge from the wisdom that you have compiled regarding your customers' needs. But don't create them in a silo. Engage your colleagues to craft principles that unite work across teams.

- Take great care in designing your principles for adoption. Treat them as a tool. Watch how they are used and keep trying new approaches to make them as viable and useful as possible.

A n "Experience Principles Refinement" workshop brings together stakeholders to pressure-test your draft principles. In this session, you will discover how your principles can be improved and address any misalignment among your key stakeholders. This workshop will inform additional actions that you need to take to get everyone on board. Remember: the value of experience principles increases exponentially when broadly used and followed.

Workshop Objectives

- Educate stakeholders on the value of experience principles.

- Review the process you followed to create your draft principles.

- Share progress to date.

- Work collaboratively to review, refine, and select experience principles.

Agenda

This workshop is designed to be completed in four hours, including a short break. Give yourself more time if you have a larger group of participants (more than 20). You will also need more time at the beginning of the workshop if you had little to no collaboration with your stakeholders in the research. In this scenario, you will need to go deeper into which research approaches and insights informed your principles.

TABLE 6.2   WORKSHOP AGENDA

Activity	Description	Duration
Introductions	Facilitate participants getting to know one another beyond just names and titles.	10 min
Review agenda and objectives	Share the activities for the day and what you want to accomplish by the end of the session.	10 min
Introduce candidate principles	Walk participants through your draft principles and the process that you followed to create them.	40 min
Refine principles	Capture participants' feedback and facilitate a discussion on how the principles may be refined.	60 min
Down-select	Have participants individually choose which principles should be taken forward in the process.	15 min
Break	Give people a rest while you get ready for the last activities.	15 min
Pressure test	Work with participants to review the voting and critique whether the highest voted principles work together as a system. Continue to refine.	75 min
Review and reflect	Review the workshop process and outcomes. Determine next steps.	15 min

Roles

- **Lead facilitator:** Workshop host and main facilitator for session activities

- **Co-facilitator(s):** Help(s) set up, break down, and assist in activities

- **Documentarian:** Takes photographs of the session to help nonparticipants understand the collaborative process

Participants

- Facilitators and experience mappers from research

- Owners of specific channels, products, or touchpoints

- Practitioners from relevant teams, such as branding, operations, design, and technology

Artifacts

- **Draft principles:** The output from your previous activities printed on large sheets so that you can write on and attach feedback and refinements during your session.

- **Process review presentation:** To provide context for your session, share a brief presentation on how experience principles will bring value and then explain the process you are following to create them. Including pictures from your earlier experience principle activities is an effective way to show the process and the rigor that has led to your session.

- **Brand principles:** If your organization has a set of brand principles, print them out and post them on the walls or distribute a copy to each participant. These will help you ensure that your experience principles align with your organizational persona.

- **Research artifacts:** Any artifacts that you have previously created—experience maps, ecosystem maps, and other models—can help ground discussion in what you know about your customers' experiences and how you envision them to be in the future.

- **Other principles:** When bringing together different teams, you will often discover they already follow a set of principles. Simplicity! Intuitive! Post them in the room to acknowledge their existence and to use them in alignment discussions.

Materials

- Self-stick easel pad (to create a wall canvas)

- Dots for down-selection

- Sharpies

- Sticky notes

- Camera

Preparing for the Workshop

As with the other workshops recommended in this book, how well you prepare and communicate will make or break the effectiveness of your session. Make sure that you have previously educated your collaborators and sold the value of experience principles (see the handy list earlier in the chapter). You want your workshop to be laser focused on getting feedback on your principles, not the process. You do not want the session to go off track by explaining in detail what experience principles are or defending their usefulness. People should be excited to collaborate on shaping a tool together, not being introduced to the concept for the first time.

Running the Workshop

It's important to manage consensus toward *what* your principles should be, not *how* each one will be worded. As you go through the workshop activities, encourage questions and make sure that everyone understands each principle's essence and what it would mean in practice. You will further refine them after the session, which will entail rewriting, further merging, or breaking apart your drafts. It's fine to get feedback on your detailed copywriting but caution the group that final editing will happen outside of the session.

Kick off your session by reviewing the value that experience principles will bring and what your process is to date. Then guide the group though the following activities:

1. Introduce candidate principles.

2. Refine principles.

3. Down-select.

4. Pressure test and iterate.

5. Review and reflect.

Introduce Candidate Principles

In a short presentation, share the process you followed to create the draft principles. Explain that the goal of this exercise is to familiarize everyone with each principle and then refine them as a team.

One-by-one, introduce each draft experience principle to the group. If you had a small team generating your drafts, assign a member of that team to present each principle, providing some of the insights that led to defining the principle. Also, briefly provide an example of what the application of this principle may mean in the future. This can be verbal or a simple sketch of a sample concept or photo from another experience that exhibits the qualities of the principle.

As you present, participants should capture their feedback and questions on sticky notes. You want everyone to understand and reflect upon all the principles before verbally critiquing. This will keep the session on track and reduce the "what about?" questions that the experience principles may address.

Refine Principles

After introducing the draft principles, open the discussion. You can have people attach their feedback sticky notes onto the printed versions of the principles as they discuss. As the discussion goes on, annotate your principles to reflect where refinements or key questions are arising. Circle words, underline phrases, and add to capture possible refinements.

Down-Select

Once you feel the essence of each principle is understood and refined as necessary, segue into narrowing down to a set of core principles via a simple dot-vote activity. As shown in Figure 6.6, give each participant four to six dots and ask them to place one dot per principle that should go forward in the process. After voting and a short break, review as a group and separate the top vote getters from the rest. Repeat the voting process as needed until you get within a range of 5–8 principles.

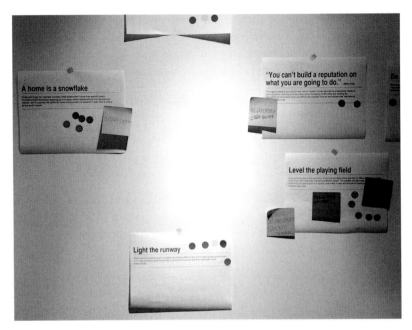

FIGURE 6.6
Using dot-voting to down-select to a set of 5–8 principles.

Pressure Test and Iterate

No experience principle is an island. Each should be understandable and useful on its own, but together your principles should form a system. Your principles should be complementary and reinforcing. They should be able to be applied across channels and throughout your product or service development process.

To ensure that each experience principle is solid and your system is strong, work with your participants to critique what made the cut in the dot-voting activity. This pressure test could mean further refining, removing, or even adding principles. Use the following questions as prompts to assess how well your principles work as a system.

- **Are any of the principles redundant?** If so, see if you missed a way to combine similar principles.

- **Do any of your principles contradict one another?** If so, you may need to return to your insights to clarify your priorities.

- **Do your principles align with your brand principles?** For example, if your brand aspires to be "authoritative," do any of your principles reflect how your future experiences reflect this attribute while connecting with the needs of customers?

- **Can all your principles be applied in any channel or medium?** If not, reword to ensure that they are not too narrow.

- **Do your principles speak to the breadth and depth of your product or service experience?** If not, go back to the principles that did not make the cut to address the gap.

- **Do you feel confident that you and others can use your principles at key decision points?** If not, simulate or pilot them to make sure that they are useful from definition through implementation.

- **Lastly, are all your principles clear and powerful as a decision-making tool?** If not, you may need to refine your articulation of what your principle is telling people to do.

Review and Reflect

Close the session with an open discussion of how everyone feels about your progress. Hopefully, you and your colleagues have narrowed down to a set that will work with some further refinements following the session. If you are not there yet, discuss how best to get there and if you need to bring the group back together again.

After the Workshop

Within a couple days of the session, play back to the participants where you ended up and what will happen next. Circle back with any stakeholders that you feel have yet to fully buy in to having common principles. You will need to keep splitting your efforts between making the principles and setting up your culture to embrace them.

CHAPTER 7

Identifying
Opportunities

W hen you look across the range of experiences that people have in their journeys, patterns will emerge. You will see commonalities in what people need and how they want to interact. You will also discover many gaps and inconsistencies in how your organization supports those needs, behaves in different channels, and provides clear pathways. In short, you will see missed opportunities to provide value and a lack of coherence in experience across time and space.

Understanding merely sets the stage for action. How do you and your colleagues determine where to focus and when? You begin with identifying opportunities rigorously and collaboratively.

Opportunities Are Not Solutions

Let's get this out of the way: opportunities are not solutions. Humans are natural problem solvers, and this instinct makes it easy in corporate environments to jump quickly to *how* to do something while skipping over *what* you are trying to solve. Stop us if you have heard this one before:

> You learn in your research that customers feel the onboarding experience takes too long. It's one of many insights, but it sticks out as a problem ripe for addressing. Immediately your colleagues start discussing how to reduce the number of screens. The logic: fewer screens equal less time; less time equals happy customers. Discussions turn into whiteboard sketches and requirements, and before you know it, a solution is on the fast track to execution.

This scenario plays out over and over in product and service teams: one business metric or a perceived customer pain point leading to hasty decisions while obfuscating better opportunities to improve or innovate an experience. In our example, the opportunity is defined cursorily as "How might we reduce the number of screens?" This narrow frame ignores other insights into customer needs and closes off the possibility of exploring other solutions.

It may seem obvious, but the road to bad product and service experiences is littered with solutions delivered without first asking: "What's the real opportunity here?"

What Is an Opportunity?

An opportunity is a set of circumstances ripe for creating positive change. Change can mean soothing customer pain points, extending your product or service to address unmet needs, or radically rethinking how those needs are met. Opportunities provide the fertile ground to create new value for an organization, its customers, and other stakeholders.

Identifying and prioritizing these opportunities should be done collaboratively and with rigor. The various sensemaking techniques from previous chapters can inform your understanding of organizational capabilities, customer needs, and the greater context that your product or service exists within. Based on these insights, opportunities can be framed properly to generate multiple ideas and potential solutions. This process ensures that you and your team frame the problem space accurately before imagining, much less making, possible solutions.

Orchestrating experiences means breaking away from business-as-usual, jump-to-a-solution approaches. It's about embracing collaboration and creating true alignment to focus on the needs of customers and the most important opportunities that will serve the entire organization.

Take Airbnb as an example. The genesis for the popular home-sharing service wasn't a reaction to business or technology trends but out of necessity. In 2007, founders Brian Chesky and Joe Gebbia found themselves short on money to pay for their rising San Francisco rent.[1] They knew hundreds of people were coming to the city for a conference in a city where hotel rooms were scarce and expensive. They recognized a real opportunity that they could potentially solve: supplementing their income by helping others stay for cheap. Chesky and Gebbia's initial solution was a marketing website, three airbeds, and a home-cooked breakfast. Since then, Airbnb has evolved from a small experiment to a sophisticated set of services around the travel journey, but the company's success initially occurred because it identified the opportunity of aligning host and guest needs.

Every context has its own unique forces that could influence what separates true opportunities from red herrings. In the case of Airbnb,

---

1 Morgan Brown, "Airbnb: The Growth Story You Didn't Know," growthhackers/growth-studies/Airbnb

geography, economics, and the founders' skills proved to be the right conditions to identify and solve for a real opportunity to create value. In general, there are three key requirements to check off when defining opportunities: value alignment, multiple possible futures, and the ability and resolve to change (see Figure 7.1).

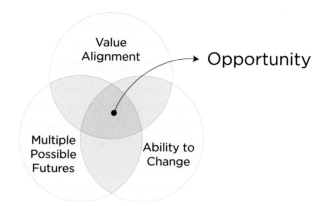

FIGURE 7.1
The three facets of opportunities.

Value Alignment

Value creation is a cornerstone of many ideologies making their way into large organizations. Value stream mapping, for example, is a lean approach for identifying and eliminating activities that result in operational waste in the delivery of products and services. In the context of orchestrating experiences, designers similarly put an emphasis on ensuring that activities—which are instantiated as touchpoints—provide a clear value.

In business-centric organizations, the answers to these types of questions can be shallow or one-dimensional. Customers will be happy because the application will take less time. Call center employees will be happy to deal with fewer unhappy customers. And, of course, the company will be happier if the Net Promoter Score increases. It's necessary to help your colleagues dig deeper.

It is important to clearly define and measure the business value of solutions, but a focus on experience means shifting the discussion from business value to *co-value*. Co-value means evaluating opportunities and solutions by how they will benefit all relevant stakeholders, not just the business. Overhauling an online application may increase conversions and decrease acquisition costs, but what value should be delivered to the applicant or to the employees who support acquiring and serving new customers? How would you define the opportunity differently from each stakeholder's perspective, not just the interests of "the business" (see Figure 7.2)?

BUSINESS VALUE • Increased revenue • Increased productivity	**CUSTOMER VALUE** • Decreased frustration • Increased happiness
EMPLOYEE VALUE • Increased skills • Increased job satisfaction	**SOCIAL VALUE** • Reduced carbon footprint • Improved health

FIGURE 7.2
Look beyond business value to evaluate potential opportunities.

Applying a co-value lens to the process of identifying and prioritizing opportunities is a critical practice to shift to a human-centered mindset in an organization. Also important is an iterative approach—from research to opportunities and from solution definition through execution. The concepts and methods outlined in previous chapters will help you and your team change the conversation about value. Here's a quick review:

- **Touchpoints and touchpoint inventories:** Evaluate current touchpoints or define new touchpoints by how they create value for the business, customers, and other stakeholders.

- **Ecosystems and ecosystem mapping:** Understand how different actors view, seek, and create value.

- **Journeys and experience mapping:** Identify gaps in the value that customers seek and what current solutions deliver at different stages and moments of the end-to-end experiences.

- **Experience principles:** Write guidelines for defining and making solutions attuned to customer needs and value while aligning with brand values.

Multiple Possible Futures

An opportunity should lend itself to many possible solutions. Let's return to our onboarding example, but this time with a better framing and outcome:

> *You learn in your research that customers feel the onboarding experience takes too long. This feeling applies to customers whose time to onboard varies from hours to days. Other insights from research reveal a lack of communication at key points that increase customer frustration, as well as a general confusion regarding the steps and information required to onboard. It's clear there is a more systemic problem at play. As a result, you and your team frame the opportunity as "How might we help get customers up and running easily and confidently?"*

As shown by this example, the framing of opportunities is critical to focus creativity and problem solving. The opportunity should be defined and worded to serve as a springboard to multiple possibilities, not an anchor to a specific solution (see Figure 7.3). Later sections of this chapter will walk you through how to frame opportunities properly with your colleagues.

HOW MIGHT WE...

FIGURE 7.3
Well-framed opportunities should inspire multiple possible solutions.

Ability and Resolve to Change

Even when there's an opportunity to create co-value in multiple ways, you must always do a gut check of whether your organization can affect change and has the resolve to do so. This can be tricky.

When orchestrating experiences, challenging business as usual is part of the game. You will identify potential opportunities that often require people to partner in new ways across organizational silos. You will need your colleagues to be open to reframing success from opportunities that they alone can own within their respective silos to ones that call for collaboration and shared ownership. Building rapport and partnerships with key stakeholders will help create the conditions to be able to affect change when you see an opportunity.

Breaking down silos helps open new possibilities, but you and your colleagues will need to be clear-eyed and recognize that conditions will never be ideal. Thus, you will need to identify any true constraints within your problem space. If you can take action, there's an *opportunity*. If you cannot take action—that is, if you cannot change something—it is a *constraint*. Seize your opportunities; embrace your constraints.[2]

In the context of orchestrating experiences, some examples of constraints might include:

- Your business strategy

- Regulatory rules that govern your activities and offerings

- Entities and events outside of your control, such as third-party services

- Risk tolerance

- Organizational structures, where stakeholders may be risk averse in co-owning outputs

You may have opportunities to work within or around constraints, but it helps to understand the difference when it comes time to create a plan of action for how to improve the end-to-end experience. For example, your insights may tell you that your customers don't like

---

2 Charles Eames said this better than we could ever dream to: "Here is one of the effective keys to the Design problem: the ability of the Designer to recognize as many of the constraints as possible...Each problem has its own particular list." As quoted in: "Qu'est ce que le design?" interview of Charles Eames by Mmn. L Aic. Answers at the Musee des Arts Decoratifs, Palais de Louvre.

giving their Social Security number during the application process because it makes them suspicious. However, for regulatory reasons, you cannot process the application without that information. You may then identify an opportunity to reframe or otherwise reposition the collection of this information. In this instance, you've done something important in identifying the constraint—and, instead of dismissing the insight as something you cannot change, you've created an opportunity.

Opportunities, Intent, and Timing

Value alignment, multiple possible futures, and the ability to change ultimately reflect the unique context of an organization and its ecosystem. When shifting an organization's mindset from individual touchpoints to customer journeys, it's critical to be clear on your overall intent and when you will take action.

There are three useful categories for defining and connecting opportunities to orchestrate end-to-end experiences better. They are the following:

- **Optimize the end-to-end experience:** Connect disparate moments into a connected system of channels and touchpoints.

- **Reimagine the end-to-end experience:** Extend the product or service experience to address unmet customer needs while emphasizing consistency and cohesion.

- **Innovate from the ground up:** Create new product and services designed as orchestrated end-to-end experiences.[3]

Optimize the End-to-End Experience

Any existing product or service experience typically has many opportunities for improvement. This should not be a surprise. Left to their own devices, different functional teams—marketing, product, design, technology, and operations—will have their own vision and priorities for optimizing within their area of responsibility. The

---

3 In defining these categories, we were inspired by the three horizons framework advocated for in *The Alchemy of Growth* and popularized by McKinsey & Company. See: "Enduring Ideas: The Three Horizons of Growth," www.mckinsey.com/business-functions/strategy-and-corporate-finance/ our-insights/enduring-ideas-the-three-horizons-of-growth

interdependency of these silos means well-intentioned point solutions likely will cause issues elsewhere in the customer's overall experience.

One common example: the lack of coordination between marketing and product or service teams. As a consumer, you have probably experienced a phenomenon that Brandon Schauer has labeled the *service anticipation gap*.[4] Marketing's traditional role is to create desire and anticipation for what a product or service will provide. Far too often, however, the delivered solution reflects a separation of vision, coordination, and execution among internal teams who support the same customer journey. For instance, imagine an airline that pours money into advertising a friendly flying experience but delivers poor experiences across checking in, boarding, and in-flight experience. How much revenue and customer happiness could be realized by connecting these dots, even incrementally?

Orchestrating experiences means changing this paradigm. It shines a light on numerous customer pain points hiding in plain sight once you frame customer engagement as an end-to-end experience to be designed collaboratively. The methods of this book—touchpoint inventories, experience mapping, and so on—support an important piece of work for modern organizations: optimizing the end-to-end experience.

Beyond Pain Points

Optimizing end-to-end experiences, whether coordinated or not, represents the bulk of work in most organizations. This is appropriate, because how customers engage with current offerings impacts an organization's near-term health and the ability to invest in future products and services. However, larger organizations should leverage design (or designers) beyond just alleviating pain points in the current experience. A sign of maturation is when designers partner to look beyond optimization and use the approaches like those outlined in this book to push into new areas that will create customer value through experience.

---

4 Brandon Schauer, "Serious Service Sag," adaptivepath.org/ideas/
   serious-service-sag/

Optimization in this context means systematically overhauling an existing product or service journey to be more consistent, cohesive, and complete. These changes often don't mean major new investments, but rather smarter use of existing or planned investments by orchestrating activities across teams. A few common examples:

- Removing customer touchpoints that add no value
- Changing existing touchpoints to work better as a system
- Creating new touchpoints that support core customer needs better
- Extending touchpoints into more appropriate channels
- Building better bridges between channels and contexts
- Applying common experience principles to all parts of the end-to-end experience
- Creating stronger starts and ends to a customer journey
- Attacking a low point and amplifying a high point
- Cooperating across silos to have different channels work together to serve a touchpoint
- Creating a smoother transition between journey stages

Many of these opportunities represent low-hanging fruit—many bumps in a customer's journey that can be corrected with small investments yet cumulatively produce a positive uplift in experience. Others may require more rigor to balance trade-offs across functional areas in support of the overall customer journey. And some opportunities may lead to new product or service touchpoints that meet existing customer needs more effectively.

For example, Rail Europe International found that customers greatly valued the current ability to build travel plans across different rail travel providers without having to go to multiple sites (see Figure 7.4). However, customers still found difficulty in creating itineraries because they could not visualize the physical locations of stations and other places they wanted to visit. Instead of jumping from booking site to booking site, they were juggling one booking site with maps, guidebooks, and other resources. This represented an immediate opportunity—they asked, "How might we help travelers visualize space and time more clearly when planning itineraries?" Overall, optimizing an end-to-end experience means shifting from improving touchpoints in isolation to designing the whole customer journey as a coordinated team.

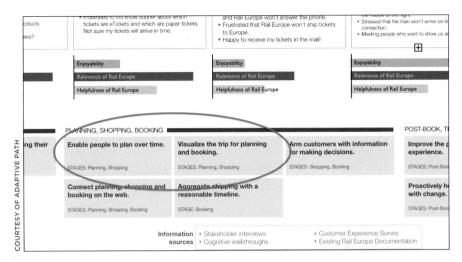

FIGURE 7.4

Optimization opportunities identified for Rail Europe.

Reimagine the Experience

Beyond optimization, there are opportunities for expanding or reimagining experiences to address a wider set of unmet customer needs. Here, the focus is not on which current customer touchpoints need to be improved or better connected, but on identifying opportunities to deliver new value. Opportunities that lead to reimagining parts or all of the end-to-end experience often result in new investments in people, processes, and technology. For this reason, an organization must do its homework to feel confident that acting upon these opportunities individually or in concert will likely create appropriate returns on investment for relevant stakeholders.

As noted in previous chapters, both ecosystem and experience mapping can reveal valuable insights into opportunities to solve for unmet needs. There are a few common patterns.

- **Ignored or underserved journey stages.** Many products and services are designed to support only use cases divorced from a greater context. For example, visiting a museum includes more than just experiencing the exhibits. The journey stages before and after offer great opportunities to provide new value and extend the museum experience.

- **Not serving the greater journey.** Instead of optimizing a current end-to-end experience, new opportunities may exist in a higher level of journey. Airbnb started with a focus on guests staying with hosts. Today, they focus on the overarching travel journey to provide more extensive value and differentiated experiences.

- **Unaddressed actors.** Ecosystem mapping often brings greater focus on other people that matter in a problem space. A common example is people—partners, family or friends, or third parties—who are part of the decision-making process. For example, in home buying, realtors may represent a new opportunity for engagement.

Reimagining goes well beyond the surface layer of an experience. The objective is to determine systematically how to redefine a portion or all of the *why*, *what*, and *how* of a product's service. This includes:

- The strategic rationale and intent (why)

- The value that will be created for stakeholders (why)

- A vision for the end-to-end customer experience (what)

- The role of different people, touchpoints, channels, processes, and technologies (what)

- A plan for how to evolve to the vision over time (how)

- The design and implementation of touchpoints and operations (how)

Innovate from the Ground Up

One of the tougher areas to identify involves opportunities to create innovative experiences while innovating with new business models. By default, this is where start-ups usually take advantage of an approach of orchestrating experiences. They don't have a mature offering to optimize or extend. Instead, they are hoping to innovate or disrupt an existing system.

A good example of new product and service innovation is UberEats (see Figure 7.5). Uber's core service—transporting people from A to B—was built upon a sophisticated infrastructure that orchestrated the just-in-time movement of vehicles across geographies. Much of Uber's value is this platform, and the company has been looking for new ways to leverage it. In 2015, Uber began experimenting with food delivery. While delivering food instead of people involves pick-up and arrival common in their core service, new challenges needed to be solved from orchestrating restaurant and food selection, to meal preparation, to partner management, and to drivers leaving their cars to complete the process.

FIGURE 7.5
The end-to-end UberEats experience was prototyped and piloted in three months.

To get a pilot in place quickly, an Uber team held a service design innovation workshop with colleagues to dig deeper into opportunities for providing a complete food delivery end-to-end experience.[5] These workshops then led to ethnographic research to understand the food delivery ecosystem: customers, restaurant employees, and drivers. With better insights in hand, the team was able to concept, design, and launch a service pilot (bootstrapped to the existing Uber ride app) in three months. Several iterations later, UberEats has evolved to a full service operating in dozens of cities with a stand-alone app.

Unlike startups, more established companies spend a great deal of time and energy on optimizing what currently exists. While these incremental improvements keep the train running, we have observed innovation teams center their efforts on new technologies or external competitive threats, not the needs of people and their experiences

5 Jessi Hempel, "The UberEats Standalone App Has Nothing to Do with Rides," www.wired.com/2015/12/ubereats-is-ubers-first-app-thats-not-about-rides

over time and space. Getting a cross-functional team aligned around a better understanding of both the ecosystem and journeys of customers primes the pump for *rethinking* how things are done.

The HomePlus case study from Chapter 3, "Exploring Ecosystems," is a good example of this. HomePlus did not simply try to improve the existing experience of going to the supermarket. They looked at their ecosystem with fresh eyes and found alignment with a common journey with which they could align—the daily commute. The resulting solution leveraged many of the operations needed for home grocery delivery wrapped in a unique shopping experience that required minimum behavioral change from customers.

In the end, organizations need to balance efforts and investments in experience across all three categories of opportunities. If you own or contribute to the end-to-end experience within a specific problem space, you should always ask these questions:

- What opportunities do we have to optimize the end-to-end experience to meet the needs of all stakeholders better?

- What opportunities are there to reimagine parts of the customer journey to create new value?

- What opportunities exist to disrupt how we and our customers could frame our relationships and the values we exchange?

AMAZON AND THE NEXT HORIZON

Amazon may be the paragon of identifying opportunities across all three categories. Amazon is known for optimizing every part of their experience. They also reimagine how their customers engage with that shopping experience, from introducing Amazon 1-Click, to extending the ecosystem beyond their digital channels, such as creating dash buttons for buying products as needed and in the context of when that need occurs (for example, buying detergent when your machine runs out). With AWS (Amazon Web Services), they identified the opportunity to take existing technical and data infrastructure investment and turn it into a whole new business—turning a cost center into a profit center. They rethought the actors in the journey, and they are constantly owning more parts of the shipping experience. Kindle, Prime, Echo, drone delivery, and so on—they are on a constant, obsessive mission to identify opportunities to optimize, reimagine, and reinvent.

Many approaches exist to identify and compare opportunities. The next section outlines a common design strategy approach for codifying opportunities as "How Might We?" questions. Techniques for prioritizing opportunities are also provided.

Identifying Opportunities

For identifying opportunities for end-to-end experiences, the overarching philosophies of the book apply to this step of the process:

- Look holistically across customer types, channels, touchpoints, and the context beyond your product or service.

- Perform qualitative research to make sense of your customers' needs, personal ecosystems, and experiences.

- Leverage touchpoint inventories, ecosystem maps, and experience maps to synthesize and communicate your growing understanding of your customers' broader journeys and discrete interactions with your product or service.

- Work collaboratively across functions throughout your sensemaking to create alignment and collective understanding.

Labeling Opportunities

Invitation stems—commonly called, "How Might We?" prompts—are an effective technique for framing opportunities. Pioneered in the 1960s by Dr. Sydney J. Parnes,[6] "How Might We?" prompts encourage lateral thinking and increase the quantity of possible ideas by posing questions. For example, if you have observed a pain point during customer onboarding, you could pose: "How might we make the onboarding process more efficient or steps clearer for customers?"

The key to crafting "How Might We?" prompts is to avoid going too broad or too narrow. Specifically, you should pull out any language that steers toward a narrower set of solutions. Table 7.1 shows some poor examples and how to reframe them.

As shown in these examples, you should avoid embedding solutions—such as specifying the channel, medium, touchpoint, or means (e.g., training)—in your prompts. They should inspire open brainstorming and idea generation well beyond the obvious.

---

6 GK VanPatter of Humantific documents the origins and open source status of this approach at **www.humantific.com/who-owns-how-might-we/**

TABLE 7.1 CREATING GOOD HOW MIGHT WE? STATEMENTS

Poor	Better
How might we create better aisle signage to help customers find products more easily?	How might we help customers find products more easily while in the aisles?
How might we use a mobile app to help customers keep doing product research when they leave the store?	How might we help customers continue their product research when they leave the store?
How might employees be trained to be more welcoming?	How might we provide a better sense of welcome when entering?
How might we educate customers in a graphical way on why it takes so long to do a return?	How might we set and manage customer expectations better when returning merchandise?

Prioritizing Opportunities

Numerous prioritization methods exist in design, business, product, and innovation literature. You can use simple methods—such as dot voting or the MoSCoW method[7]—to get a rough feel, but when possible, use an approach that uses at least two criteria to assess your opportunities. The criteria you use should be based on your strategic focus—optimization, reimagining, or innovation—and be clear to all participants. Here are two prioritization methods to consider for different contexts (optimization, imagination, or innovation). A third prioritization method—impact vs. complexity—that can also be used to prioritize opportunities is covered at the end of Chapter 8, "Generating and Evaluating Ideas."

Value vs. Urgency (Optimization or Reimagination)

Optimization efforts typically focus on immediate to near-term actions that you can take to address specific metrics related to your product's or service's end-to-end experience. Your objective in this exercise is to assess each opportunity against the co-value it could produce and how urgent it is to solve for sooner rather than later.

Optimization efforts typically focus on immediate to near-term actions that you can take to address specific metrics related to your

---

7 MoSCoW is a requirements prioritization method that can easily be extended to opportunities. For more, see en.wikipedia.org/wiki/MoSCoW_method

product's or service's end-to-end experience. This technique assesses each opportunity against the co-value it could produce and how urgent it is to solve for sooner rather than later. Figure 7.6 illustrates a simple model you can use to visualize and plot your analysis. The workshop following this chapter provides an example of how to use this method with your colleagues.

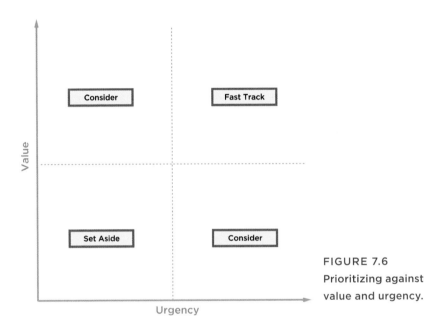

FIGURE 7.6
Prioritizing against value and urgency.

Satisfaction vs. Importance (Reimagining and Innovation)

This approach works best when part or all of your focus is smoothing out the rough edges of the end-to-end experience. In this case, timing or effort is less important than identifying opportunities to provide value outside of your current product or service paradigm. Uber's extension into food delivery and Airbnb's push into the broader travel experience are two good examples of this situation.

In this exercise, you will use a modified version of Opportunity Scoring from Anthony Ulwick's Outcome-Driven Innovation methodology.[8] Using a scale of 1 to 10 for both satisfaction and importance,

---

8 Ulwick's full approach is highly quantitative, but we're hacking it to create a collaborative workshop approach. See Chapter 3 in Anthony W. Ulwick, *What Customers Want: Using Outcome-Driven Innovation to Create Breakthrough Products and Services* (New York: McGraw-Hill, 2005).

discuss and rate each opportunity from the perspective of your customers. How ripe is the opportunity for a new solution? Did you learn in your research that other products and solutions already meet customers' needs? As you discuss, plot your items visually against the model illustrated in Figure 7.7.

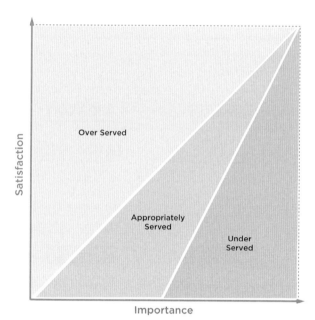

FIGURE 7.7
Opportunity scoring assesses opportunities against importance and satisfaction.[9]

For this method to work, you will need to have your insights from research handy to represent your customers' needs and perceptions of how well existing products and services meet those needs. This means it's critical to design your research to surface undermet and unmet needs within your customer base (or in new customer segments that you want to serve). Of the frameworks covered in Chapters 1–4, ecosystem maps are especially useful for this type of opportunity identification and prioritization. Ecosystem maps include products, services, and other people and things that customers may already turn to. For example, potential UberEats customers may already use food delivery services, so research into that space may reveal opportunities in portions of the journey that are more underserved than others.

---

9 Modified from Ulwick, *What Customers Want: Using Outcome-Driven Innovation to Create Breakthrough Products and Services.*

Communicating Opportunities

At some point, you and your colleagues will be ready to share more broadly the opportunities that you have discovered and prioritized. Here are a few approaches that you can use to get buy-in on priorities and to prepare your organization to jump smartly and confidently into solution mode.

- **Opportunity cards:** Making each opportunity, or recommendation, into discreet items helps break down some of the high-level critical details for the opportunity, such as channel or LOB ownership and key dependencies (see Figure 7.8). Just as important, it allows you to tie it specifically to the things that lead to the opportunity: the business value or customer need that was identified. This can provide traceability for people who become aware of the opportunity who weren't a part of the past work. Other stakeholders can see the justification for prioritizing this opportunity.

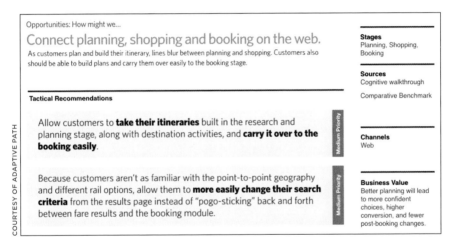

FIGURE 7.8

Opportunity cards are often half sheet (A5) or quarter sheet (A6) that provide some detail on dependencies or traceability for how you arrived at this opportunity.

- **Opportunities by stage:** Organize your opportunities by stage of customer journey or across two or more stages. (See Figure 7.12 in the workshop at the end of this chapter.)

- **Experience map annotation:** An alternate approach to show opportunities by stage involves taking your experience map and annotating it with your opportunities. You can call out the opportunities in a separate section of your map. Or you can create a version of your map fading back to the current state and overlaying your opportunities.

- **Opportunities by channel and stage:** You may have many opportunities that, regardless of how they are solved, apply to specific channels. In this situation, using a framework like a touchpoint inventory—channels as rows and journey stages as columns—will highlight the recommended focus in different channels across the end-to-end experience.

- **Opportunity map:** An opportunity map categorizes opportunities by theme and often includes other insights or information, such as experience principles (see Figure 7.9). This type of artifact provides stakeholders with an at-a-glance view of where design intervention can create better experiences and new value. The opportunity map can then support determining which opportunities to pursue, when to go after them, and which aspects of the customer journey would be impacted.

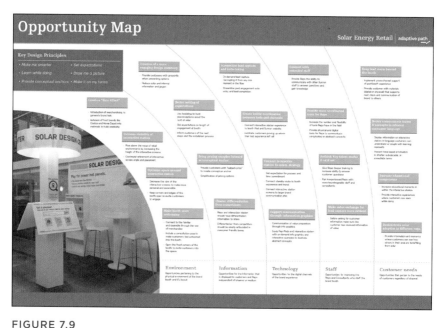

FIGURE 7.9

An opportunity map Chris and his team created at Adaptive Path for an energy sector client.

- **Ecosystem opportunities:** Similarly, an ecosystem map can be annotated with opportunities to show how new or reimagined products, services, other entities, or relationships can create new value.

One approach to visualizing your opportunities usually does not communicate the full story that you need to tell. Look to combine vantage points, such as by journey and by ecosystems, to help people see what you and your colleagues see—the best opportunities to create more value and better end-to-end customer experiences.

Coda

- An opportunity is not a solution. It is a set of circumstances ripe for creating positive change.

- Collaboratively identifying and prioritizing opportunities with rigor creates cross-functional buy-in and prevents fragmented efforts to jump quickly to solutions.

- There are three criteria to check off when separating real opportunities from red herrings: value alignment, multiple possible futures, and the ability to change.

- Opportunities fall broadly into three categories: optimize the end-to-end experience, reimagine the end-to-end experience, and innovate with new product and services.

- When identifying and prioritizing opportunities, use your experience maps and principles, and choose specific criteria (such as urgency, importance, complexity, or value) that support your opportunity category.

- Try different approaches to communicate your recommended opportunities visually and compellingly. Find a combination of approaches that tell the story you want people to buy into.

T his workshop leverages your experience maps, experience principles, and other sensemaking artifacts to identify and prioritize opportunities. Hopefully, you have involved a broad range of stakeholders in your discovery and research. Regardless, it is critical to have cross-functional representation in this workshop to ensure that you align around the most important opportunities and get broad commitment for action.

Workshop Objectives

- Identify opportunities based on customer needs across the end-to-end experience.

- Prepare your opportunities for ideation sessions.

- Prioritize your opportunities to determine what to act on now vs. later.

Example Pitch to Participants

This workshop provides an important bridge from research to ideation and action. Here's some language to encourage the right people to attend and play:

> While we're never done learning from our customers, it's time to use our new insights to determine opportunities for creating better experiences and value.

> In this workshop, we will use our experience map(s) as a tool to identify and codify opportunities for optimizing (in the near term) and reimagining (in the long term) our customers' end-to-end experiences. This process will include prioritizing opportunities based on their value and urgency. The output of this work will then be used in other sessions to generate ideas for seizing these opportunities together.

Agenda

This workshop typically takes a full day to complete, including breaks and lunch. In practice, you may want to schedule a second day (and possibly a third) to conduct some initial ideation immediately. See the workshop in Chapter 8, "Generating and Evaluating Ideas," for an approach that complements this workshop nicely.

TABLE 7.2 WORKSHOP AGENDA

Activity	Description	Duration
Introductions	Facilitate participants getting to know one another beyond just names and titles.	10 min
Review agenda and objectives	Review the activities for the day and what you want to accomplish by the end of the session.	10 min
Share key insights	Go back over the key insights from research and make sure that everyone is familiar with your experience map(s) and principles.	45 min
Break	Recharge!	15 min
Pull out the needs	Identify key customer needs by journey stage.	60 min
Identify opportunities	Identify and advocate for opportunities that should be addressed.	75 min
Lunch	Eat up!	45 min
Cluster opportunities and label categories	Find patterns in the opportunities and craft "How Might We?" prompts.	90 min
Document opportunities	Flesh out the opportunities and document them on opportunity cards.	60 min
Break	Rest up for the final push.	15 min
Prioritize opportunities	Rate and prioritize opportunities using a framework, such as value vs. urgency.	105 min
Reflect and determine next steps	Reflect upon the workshop process and outcomes. Determine the next steps.	10 min

Roles

- **Lead facilitator:** Workshop host and main facilitator for session activities

- **Co-facilitator(s):** Help(s) set up, break down, and assist in activities

- **Documentarian:** Takes photographs of the session to help nonparticipants understand the collaborative process

Participants

- Facilitators and experience mappers from research
- Owners of specific channels, products, or touchpoints
- Practitioners from relevant teams, such as branding, operations, design, and technology

Artifacts

- A large, poster-size printout of each experience map
- A tabloid-size version of your map for each participant
- Other relevant artifacts (ecosystem maps, personas, and touch-point inventories)
- Experience principles (posted by your map and handouts for each participant)
- Opportunity cards

Materials

- Small flag sticky notes
- Sharpies
- Square sticky notes
- Painter's tape (for the butcher paper or creating the journey framework)
- Self-stick easel pad or butcher paper (to create a wall canvas)

Preparing for the Workshop

Opportunities result from interpreting what you have learned and placing it within the context of your organizational goals and business strategy. When inviting colleagues to collaborate in identifying opportunities, you need to communicate this context explicitly. Be clear on whether you are focusing on optimization, reimagining, innovation, or some combination of the three.

Send out a summary of your key research insights and an overview of the workshop's agenda as a pre-read for your colleagues. This will help them hit the ground running in the workshop.

An important note about the experience map(s) that you use in the session: your map is a draft, not final. Test its usefulness and usability in the workshop. Once you understand its effectiveness, you should then update your map for future use.

Running the Workshop

During the workshop, you will guide participants from a high-level understanding of your key insights to an initial pass at prioritizing opportunities derived from those insights. We recommend breaking down this agenda into five distinct activities:

- Share key insights and strategic context

- Pull out customer needs

- Identify opportunities

- Cluster opportunities and label opportunities

- Document opportunities

- Prioritize opportunities

Share Key Insights and Strategic Context

If you have regularly engaged your colleagues in sensemaking and creating experience principles, this step can be a brief review. Go back over the key insights from research, walk through your latest version of your experience map, and make sure that everyone is familiar with your experience principles. Distribute duties for presenting these items to other attendees who participated in the research in order to get people engaged and collaborative.

In addition to reviewing your insights, remind everyone again of the context and any constraints that should be honored in the session. For example, you may have been asked to recommend improvements to an existing product or service to be implemented in the next six months. Or your goal might be to inform strategies and investments 12–18 months in the future. This context is critical because your collaborators might define an opportunity as something they could address the next spring, next quarter, or next year.

Pull Out Customer Needs

After you feel you have a good baseline understanding, break your participants into small teams. How you organize the teams depends upon a few factors. Some rules of thumb to keep in mind:

- If you have customer personas representing distinct behaviors and needs within your customer base, group participants by persona. Arm each group with specific maps that you have created to document these journeys.

- Each group should include someone who knows the research insights well. Your experience mappers will come in handy here.

- Create groups with a mix of roles, levels, and functions to stoke cross-functional collaboration.

Ask each team to review their experience map in detail and identify key customer needs by stage. Each need should be written on an individual sticky note. For example, a few needs that could emerge from an investing journey might be:

- A basic understanding of different investment products

- A clear explanation of how to open an account in laymen's terms

- A comparison of easy options

- The confidence to choose the best option for the customer's needs

- The access to account information 24/7

Then have the teams share out the needs that they have identified and place them below your poster-size map (see Figure 7.10). As the participants share out, cluster the needs that are alike. By the end of the activity, you should have a collection of needs that customers have within and across stages. Label your clusters and move on to identify your opportunities.

FIGURE 7.10
Identifying customer needs across the end-to-end experience.

Identify Opportunities

In this activity, each participant will identify and advocate for opportunities that should be addressed. Give each participant a tabloid-sized experience map and three-to-five sticky flags (see Figure 7.11). (You can buy these long, rectangular flaps or simply cut square sticky notes into several flags.) The number of flags depends on the complexity of your experience and the number of participants. The fewer the flags, the more important it is for participants to make a selective choice. This constraint helps the opportunities with the most potential to create value or take action to rise to the top.

Next, review the criteria for what makes an opportunity: value alignment, multiple possible futures, and ability to change. Reinforce the relevant customer and business needs, as well as the constraints that you reviewed earlier. However, don't worry about being too strict about constraints. You will resolve different perspectives on constraints when you prioritize later.

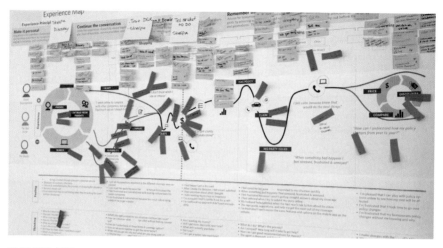

FIGURE 7.11

Pink flags identify opportunities. Blue flags indicate which experience principles might be applied to each journey stage.

Each person should review the map for 5–10 minutes, referencing additional insights, customer needs, and other information as needed. As participants identify opportunities, they should mark the opportunity area on their experience maps until they run out of flags.

What do opportunities look like? For this step in the exercise, they are simply anything related to the end-to-end experience that a participant believes should be addressed. Most participants' flags will end up on a particular moment or touchpoint. But encourage participants to put them anywhere on the map: on an empathy quote, on a piece of data, or anywhere they believe is critical to address. Doing this individually helps to ensure that each person isn't influenced by seeing what someone else (such as their boss) is doing.

Cluster Opportunities and Label Categories

As shown in Figure 7.11, next have each person share out their opportunities and place their flags on the larger experience map. Your role is to facilitate the discussion and help cluster similar opportunities on the map. Facilitate a dialogue on the patterns that emerged, making sure to review the outliers as well. Keep track of what emerges in the discussion in terms of the range of perspectives.

During this process, ask participants to discuss why that area of the journey should be addressed. Help the group articulate clearly what the opportunity is and why it matters. Referencing back to the needs discovered in your research and your experience principles will help ground the discussion in facts, not subjective preference. Also, steer them away from going into solution mode. For example, a travel experience team may have this type of interaction:

Facilitator: *We have a cluster around checking into the hotel. Why is this a thing?"*

Participant 1: *Our research showed us there's a high frustration level on checking in because it seems to take too long. Many people are so tired from their trip and just want to drop their bags in the room. And because they're tired, they forget to ask questions about getting on Wi-Fi or where the workout room is— which annoys them later.*

Facilitator: *OK, I think we can all imagine different ways to solve this individually, but for now let's identify or articulate what opportunities are here. It looks like there are more than one.*

Participant 2: *We need to make the checkout process faster for the guest.*

Participant 1: *At the very least, we should make checking in a more pleasant experience.*

Participant 3: *And how can we make sure they're loaded up with all the information they need to have a good experience without slowing them down?*

This isn't atypical of how a discussion will go. You will hear a lot of "we need," "we should," "how can we"—and that's good, because it means that people are thinking in terms of opportunities and not prescriptive solutions. Your job is to be alert and get these possible opportunities down and then make sure that you're identifying them.

After reviewing and clustering further the proposed opportunities, codify what the clusters mean and label them on larger sticky notes using the How Might We? method (see earlier in the chapter). For small sets of opportunities, you can facilitate a group discussion to write them. For larger sets, assign small groups to craft How Might We? prompts for a subset of the opportunities.

You now have a first pass at all the key opportunities that stakeholders collectively believe could be worth pursuing. You may have a handful, or literally dozens of opportunities. There should be no constraints, at this point, to the number of opportunities you identify.

Document Opportunities

Your final task for the workshop is to take a first pass at prioritizing the opportunities. Previous activities in the workshop likely caused a bit of a mess with sticky notes everywhere. A good way to transition to your prioritization step is to transfer your opportunities to something a little more formal than a sticky note. Figure 7.12 shows a useful approach in which you create a simple opportunity card that is then placed on a simple journey framework. Each card has a space for your How Might We? prompt, as well as space to articulate the potential value of the opportunity. More on value in a moment, but start with having your participants collaborate on creating a card for each opportunity.

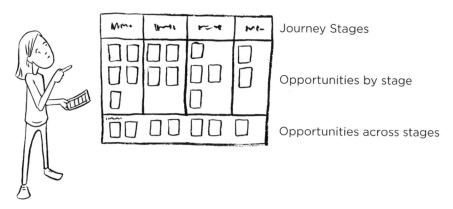

FIGURE 7.12
Preparing for prioritization.

Next, facilitate a discussion regarding the potential value that will be created going after each opportunity. If it is a small number of participants, you can work together on this. For larger groups, break into smaller teams to draft the value for each opportunity and then review and refine them together.

You should codify business value and customer value separately. You can also add spaces for employees or other stakeholders to analyze the value that they may receive. Table 7.3 gives an example of what these value statements might look like. At this stage, you do not need to be too precise in exact metrics or how much value would be returned quantitatively. When all the cards are filled in, place them back into your journey framework and get ready to prioritize.

TABLE 7.3 VALUE STATEMENTS

Stage	Research
How Might We…	Help customers continue their product research when they leave the store?
Business Value	Reduce risk of losing customer to a competitor
	Potentially add incremental downstream revenue (purchases following research) Improve Net Promoter Scores
	Insights into customer decision patterns
Customer Value	Convenience
	Reduction of effort (not repeating previous research steps)
Employee Value	Less pressure to answer all product questions and close the customer sale in store

Prioritize Opportunities

Finally, work as a team to prioritize the opportunities to get a feel for their relative value and your readiness to take action. Here's how to do so using the value-urgency framework introduced earlier this chapter:

After a few iterations to ensure that your points are distributed accurately, your items will fall visually into a few different categories. Fast-track items in the upper-right quadrant have the highest priority, while ones in the bottom-left can be set aside for now. The remaining opportunities will need more discussion to determine when and if to address them. Typically, these opportunities should be taken forward in the process (ideation).

- Count your opportunities and calculate a total number of available points using this formula: *Number of items x 3 (middle of a scale of 1 to 5) = total number of points.* For example, if you have 20 opportunities to rate, then you have 60 value points and 60 urgency points to distribute (20 x 3 = 60).

- Using large sheets or butcher paper, create the value-urgency matrix on a wall (see Figure 7.13).

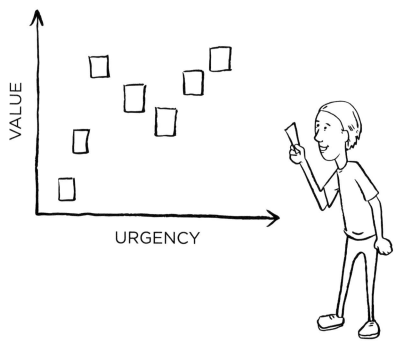

FIGURE 7.13

Collaborative mapping opportunities in a value-urgency matrix.

- Review each opportunity card, rating it on a scale of 1 to 5 for value. When discussing value, remember to assess each item on business, customer, and other relevant stakeholders.

- Next, plot each opportunity (again on a scale of 1 to 5) against how critical it is to go after it immediately or later in the future.

- Write the values on each opportunity card and keep track of your total points.

- Once everything is rated, see if you are over or under your target number. For example, you may have 60 points to distribute across 20 opportunities for value, but your total is 67. You would then go back through your opportunities and increase or decrease some of their values until they total 60.

This step can also be done in a separate session, especially if you want to expand the group to more colleagues who can help articulate and compare the value that each opportunity could bring to the organization, your customer, and other stakeholders. Keep in mind this is a first pass. You will likely need to have follow-up discussions with colleagues to finalize your prioritization.

After the Workshop

Following the workshop, iterate upon your opportunities and their relative priority. This could include additional discovery to further assess your criteria. For example, you may have some unresolved questions regarding the complexity of certain opportunities. Or you may decide to assess the importance and satisfaction of your opportunities from a qualitative standpoint. Make sure that you keep this process collaborative and get collective buy-in for your top priorities before moving on to explore potential solutions.

PART III

Vision and Action

Better understanding of your customers and aligning around the most promising opportunities should create confidence and excitement in your cross-functional team. It's critical to keep the momentum going. Many of your collaborators may start to drift toward defining solutions in silos—after all, that's business as usual. Don't let that happen! Your objective now is to orchestrate the process of turning opportunities into a compelling vision of the future that everyone wants to achieve.

This final part of this book will equip you to do just that. First, you will learn different methods for generating and evaluating ideas that work as a system, not disconnected solutions. Then you will learn techniques—visualizing future experiences, storytelling, and frameworks—for removing any ambiguity related to the outcomes that you want everyone to buy into. You will also get approaches for working with others to determine how to evolve to reach your ideal end state over time.

We will also look beyond strategy and share how to stay true to the intent of your vision and all of the insights behind it. You will learn how to make something in an orchestrated process to create touchpoints that do their job while connecting to a greater system. Because cross-functional teamwork is critical to orchestrating experiences, we'll close the book with advice on how to continue fostering collaboration and a shared, human-centered ethos in your organization.

CHAPTER 8

Generating and Evaluating Ideas

With your opportunities informed and framed as questions, you can now unleash your colleagues to address them with confidence. But how do you come up with promising ideas? And how do you wade through all those ideas to land upon viable solutions?

First, you must embrace the fact that people across your organization not only have a stake in future solutions, but they have ideas, too. Your colleagues have important viewpoints and knowledge, pre-existing solutions already in roadmaps, and the very human need to contribute to defining the future (not simply executing someone else's vision). Therefore, you need to build on the collaborative atmosphere that has been established while engaging others to generate and explore new ideas.

Generating ideas with many people of different skills, knowledge, and experience is critical at this stage, but it does come with some challenges. Many of your colleagues likely have lived through poorly facilitated brainstorming sessions that resulted in groupthink or dominant voices shouting out other perspectives. New collaborators may challenge prior research and the opportunities you have identified because they did not have a direct hand in it. And that's if you can get everyone to free up the time to participate. Your job, therefore, is to design working sessions and other activities that mitigate these challenges and produce quality ideas to further evaluate and choose. This chapter will equip you to do just that.

Leading the Hunt for Ideas

A plethora of books and resources exist on the topic of generating ideas. Advocates and detractors argue over the efficacy of brainstorming alone or in groups. Hundreds of proprietary approaches tout their methods as the most predictable ways to achieve innovative results. And then there's the old truism: "I get my best ideas in the shower."

Let's face it—ideas are mysterious. They can come at any moment during any phase of your initiative, project, or sprint. And most of these ideas—despite the refrain "there are no bad ideas"—end up being off topic, unviable, or simply never acted upon.

That said, you can successfully engage others in generating ideas and working toward agreed-upon solutions based on your identified opportunities. This process won't happen in a single workshop.

It requires careful planning, a variety of inputs and methods, and strong facilitation. It also takes a little creativity and a lot of flexibility. Let's look at four aspects of designing and managing collaborative sessions:

- Structure and focus
- Inputs and constraints
- Expression and form
- Evaluation and prioritization

Structure and Focus

As with any orchestration endeavor, structure and focus in your ideation activities are critical for a positive outcome. How you plan to engage your colleagues (and customers) depends in part on your context. If you have stakeholders across a broad geography, you may want to hold workshops in multiple locations or mix in remote sessions or individual ideation. A hierarchical culture may require you to increase the size of your sessions to include multiple layers of decision makers and influencers. A tight schedule could force you to hold open sessions based on availability instead of having ideal groups for specific sessions.

Regardless of your context, you should consider the following guidelines to set yourself up for success:

- **Communicate ahead.** As you engage a cross-functional team in discovery and research activities, you should communicate early and often how new ideas and solutions will be addressed later in the process. People are natural problem solvers, so this will help manage their expectations while nudging them not to jump to solutions too quickly.

- **Put emerging ideas in a parking lot.** When ideas inevitably bubble up, don't lose them! Gather emerging ideas in one place and save them until you are ready to move from sensemaking to solution definition. You can bring these into your workshops to be revisited, built upon, and evaluated along with new ideas that your sessions generate.

- **Hold multiple sessions.** End-to-end experiences have many moving parts and even more stakeholders. For both practical and quality reasons, don't attempt to tackle all your idea generation in one large (and very long) workshop. Instead, hold several sessions to explore different opportunities, engage specific stakeholders (who may be in different geographic locations), try different methods, or to simply marinate on the outputs of previous sessions as fodder for more ideation.[1]

- **Don't "blue sky" brainstorm—focus!** Collaborative ideation works far better with a clear focus, not through free-for-all spitballing. Leverage your opportunities to provide this focus. You might consider organizing sessions around specific opportunities by theme—such as by customer type, opportunity area, or journey stage—inviting participants with the most stake or subject-matter expertise (see Table 8.1).

TABLE 8.1 IDEATION BY TOPIC

Session	Opportunities	Participants
1—Product research and wayfinding	How might we help customers find products more easily while in the aisles? How might we help customers continue their product research when they leave the store?	Core team Store operations Floor associates Product Mobile Customer insights Enterprise information architecture Store environment team
2—Returning purchases	How might we make the returns waiting process less frustrating? How might we connect online and offline returns better?	Core team Store operations Returns associates Mobile Returns product manager Legal Process engineers
3—Entry experience	How might we provide a better sense of welcome when entering? How might we support customers on a time-sensitive mission in the entry experience?	Core team Marketing Target customers Store operations Floor associates Digital

---

1 See O. Goldenberg and J. Wiley, "Quality, Conformity, and Conflict: Questioning the Assumptions of Osborn's Brainstorming Technique," *Journal of Problem Solving*, 3, no. 2 (2011): 96–118.

- **Strategically engage your stakeholders.** Participants for each ideation workshop should be carefully selected to ensure that the proper functions are represented. People's time is valuable, and sessions need to be relevant to their responsibilities, expertise, or role. Make sure that no one leaves a session questioning whether to accept a future invitation.

- **Stay organized and keep everything.** Your sessions will generate hundreds of ideas. While most will end up on the scrap heap, don't abandon ideas that don't float to the top. Take pictures or scan all your outputs and keep them organized and accessible.

- **Have clear evaluation criteria.** Begin with the end in mind. Define how you will evaluate and prioritize at the beginning of your hunt for ideas. You should communicate this at any sessions as part of general context setting.

NO IDEAS LEFT BEHIND

In previous chapters, I shared my fondness for kicking off new initiatives with a workshop to capture stakeholders' current thinking on the problem space. These sessions are also a good time to gather many of the pre-existing ideas that people have for solutions. Often, I'm guiding people who have spent months or years saving ideas and waiting for the time or money to do them justice. Gathering these early on helps bring these ideas out of the shadows. Most of them do not make it through the process (once the problem space is properly reframed), but it's good to know if any stakeholders (or myself!) are anchored to pet ideas. It's even better when a pre-existing idea gets honored once its appropriateness becomes clearer.

Inputs and Constraints

Opportunities give a specific focus for ideation in and across sessions, but they aren't your only inputs. The many insights and frameworks that emerged during sensemaking now become tools to help your colleagues explore solutions creatively. Touchpoint inventories, experience maps, and ecosystem maps provide proper context to optimize or reimagine the end-to-end experience. Personas and other models ensure that the needs of people remain top of mind and inspire better ways to serve various stakeholders.

Most critically, experience principles should be used throughout the ideation process. They can be combined with other inputs—opportunities, journey stages, unmet needs, channels, or technologies—to prompt a range of creative solutions. Throughout this chapter, several examples of using principles to generate and evaluate ideas are provided.

In addition to sparking new ideas, these inputs serve as important constraints to keep ideation focused and productive. This is a delicate balance. Well-framed opportunities—"How might we…"—provide a springboard to go beyond overly constrained problem statements, and human-centered frameworks encourage you and your colleagues to set aside personal viewpoints and biases. However, all these inputs and variables can be overwhelming. Table 8.2 shows examples of combining different inputs to constrain and focus idea generation. For any opportunity, however, you should mix your inputs in different ways to see what leads to the best results.

TABLE 8.2 FOCUSING IDEA GENERATION

Prompt	Input/Constraints
How might we help customers find products more easily while in the aisles?	Customer journey type (mission or research) + experience principles
How might we help customers continue their product research when they leave the store?	Journey stages (before, during, after) + experience principles
How might we make the returns waiting process less frustrating?	Journey stages + analogous inspiration
How might we provide a better sense of welcome when entering?	Personas + channel
How might we support customers on a time-sensitive mission in the entry experience?	Journey stages + technology

One question that always comes up that you'll want to plan for: "What about feasibility?" Your objective at this stage is to produce a large quantity of possible new solutions, so you should not constrain yourself to what your organization can or probably does now. However, you do want to stay within some boundaries, if only to honor the laws of physics or the natural abilities of people! Here are some tips on managing the question of feasibility:

- **Be clear on your timeline and intent.** Are you looking to optimize a set of touchpoints in the next three months or instead look years into the future to reimagine the end-to-end experience? This context will help people feel out their boundaries, but encourage them not to let perceived feasibility overly constrain their ideas.

- **Focus on experience.** Prompt colleagues to come up with ideas for the best possible experience, not the most likely experience (given how they interpret feasibility).

- **Work backward from ideal.** Once you have ideas to work with, you can begin to evaluate them iteratively against feasibility (and other criteria). Your eventual solutions may not be the ideal represented in the original ideas, but they can retain the original kernel that addressed the opportunity. Your solution may also have its own evolution plan to become closer to the ideal over time (see Chapter 9, "Crafting a Tangible Vision").

- **Build new prompts.** Ideas that push beyond perceived feasibility boundaries can be turned into new prompts or challenges. For example, an idea to provide product research recommendations using a mobile app could be explored using the prompt: "How might we provide personal product recommendations without the use of new technology?"

Expression and Form

In addition to playing with different inputs, you can employ a variety of methods to generate ideas. The following three methods (see Figure 8.1) are highly effective in the context of collaborative sessions for idea generation for end-to-end experiences: visual brainstorming, crafting stories, and bodystorming.

  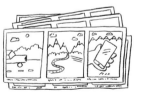

Visual Brainstorming   Bodystorming   Crafting Stories

FIGURE 8.1
Three effective ways to generate and explore ideas for your opportunities.

NOTE COMBINING METHODS

Following this chapter, an example workshop is provided showing one way to combine these methods to generate and evaluate ideas.

Visual Brainstorming

You have likely participated in brainstorming sessions in which participants write down ideas on sticky notes that are then organized by affinity and labeled. As noted earlier, this kind of ideation has as many detractors as advocates, with research to back up both perspectives. That said, brainstorming, when done correctly, is a good method to generate the seeds for some real solutions, as well as a constructive way to engage various stakeholders with different skills and viewpoints.

Consider the following when using brainstorming for end-to-end experiences:

- **Play with different inputs in timeboxed rounds.** As noted earlier, structure and focus are critical to any idea generation sessions. Brainstorming works best in short, intense bursts of activity followed by time to evaluate and reflect. A good approach is to divide your session into rounds, each with a different opportunity or combination of variables. Rounds could focus on each stage of the journey, a different persona, or a subset of experience principles. Each round should have a set time limit (typically, 4–6 minutes). For example, "How might we help customers continue their product research when they leave the store?" could be approached in a couple of different ways to prompt new ideas (see Figure 8.2).

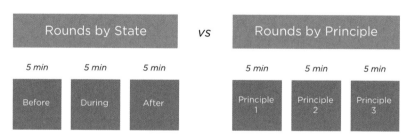

FIGURE 8.2
Two different approaches to designing rounds in a visual ideation session.

- **Go for quantity.** Each round of ideation should result in multiple ideas per participant. As in other brainstorming approaches, go for quantity over quality and feasibility. Encourage participants to spend less time adding details to ideas and more time getting the next one out of their heads.

- **Show the experience.** While brainstorming often involves writing ideas down on sticky notes, words can be ambiguous. Expressing ideas visually communicates the nuances of an idea more clearly. Have participants name, describe, and draw each idea to make sure that the full concept is captured. As shown in Figure 8.3, a quarter sheet (of A4 or 8.5" x 11" letter) provides enough space to express ideas visually while not encouraging unnecessary details.

FIGURE 8.3
Show, don't tell.

- **Start individually and then share.** Avoid "popcorn" style brainstorming in which participants throw in ideas at the same time. This approach leads to dominant voices taking over the session or groupthink. Instead, let each person generate ideas alone each round, and then have participants take turns sharing their ideas.

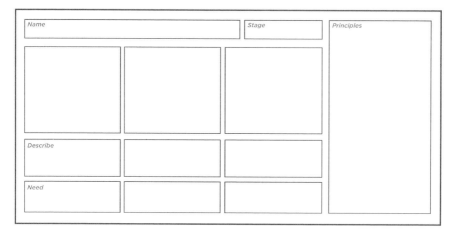

FIGURE 8.5

An example of a storyboard template for idea generation.

- **Pull out the ideas.** Once you have a bunch of stories generated, you can mine them for individual ideas within them. You will typically see some of the same ideas of *what* to do with different ways of *how* to do it, ideas in one channel or medium that could be moved or extended to other channels, or ideas in different stories that can be combined and built upon.

- **Pair with visual brainstorming.** Another way to use stories: pair them with visual brainstorming to connect and help ideas evolve. The workshop following this chapter illustrates one way to combine these methods.

USING TEMPLATES

When using stories to connect individual ideas, I recommend creating templated concept cards in quarter sheets or half sheets of A4 or letter. Each card should have room to identify the stage of the journey that the idea addresses, the specific opportunity (or "how might we") being addressed, and other details, such as what channel, media, or other resources (such as staff) are involved. This isn't so important when doing the visual brainstorming, but when the ideation activity can produce dozens of ideas, having your cards coded like this makes a huge difference when sorting through them later. For example, you can easily cluster ideas by stage or opportunity, or have discussions about the channels or media involved.

Bodystorming

A third effective approach is to put aside paper and pen and use your voice and body. Sometimes called *bodystorming* or *service storming*, this approach involves acting and improvisation in small teams to generate, connect, and build upon ideas (see Figure 8.6). The point-of-view shifts from third-person omniscient to first person, as participants experience directly what various customer touchpoints may be like to interact with, the flow through different moments, and the emotions interactions invoke.

COURTESY OF RICHLAND LIBRARY

FIGURE 8.6
Generating new ideas through acting.

While some participants may be resistant at first to bodystorming, the benefits are numerous. In addition to simulating what a customer may experience, acting and improvisation engage different parts of the brain than other idea-generation methods, boosting creativity.[2] Getting up and playing creates a different energy, helping you and colleagues to break out of typical modes of work interaction.

---

2 C. J. Limb and A. R. Braun, "Neural Substrates of Spontaneous Musical Performance: An fMRI Study of Jazz Improvisation," *PLoS ONE* 3, no. 2 (2008): e1679. doi:10.1371/journal.pone.0001679

Improvisation also has a unique form in which one simultaneously presents a problem, generates ideas, and tests the efficacy of those ideas.[3] Without any tools but your bodies, this approach is also flexible and fast, supporting multiple iterations of generating and evolving ideas in a short amount of time.

Consider the following when bringing improvisation and acting into your idea-generation sessions:[4]

- **Warm up.** Get your participants warmed up using a series of improvisational exercises. (Good ones are easily found online.) In addition to loosening people up and checking for participants' comfort levels, these exercises will reinforce the core improvisational concepts of not overthinking what to do (Just do it!) and building on ideas (Yes, and!).

- **Work in small teams.** Using your opportunities and other inputs to organize around, divide into small teams to generate ideas together. Participants should build upon each other's ideas, simulating an experience by embodying different actors and touchpoints.

- **Play with ideas before building a narrative.** Give teams time to play around with different ideas before moving too quickly to a cohesive story. Encourage them to keep looking at the opportunity using different variables (principles, channels, personas, and so on) before locking onto a specific experience to evolve.

- **Adapt to a narrative structure.** After exploring ideas, help teams shift into constructing narratives by giving them a simple structure. This could be three chronological scenes (as with the storyboarding technique), a problem-resolution story, or contrasting current-state and alternate future solutions.

- **Capture what happens.** The ephemerality of acting out experiences means that you have to capture the outputs in another medium. Common approaches are to video the session, take pictures and later build into an annotated storyboard, or have other participants write down what ideas stand out to them.

---

3 Colin M. Fisher and Teresa M. Amabile, "Creativity, Improvisation, and Organizations," in *The Routledge Companion to Creativity*, ed. Tudor Rickards, Mark A. Runco, and Susan Moger (Oxford, U.K.: Routledge, 2009).

4 Tip of the hat to Jamin Hegeman who many of these tips originated with during our work together at Adaptive Path.

- **Combine with other methods.** Improvisation and acting can also help connect and evolve ideas generated by other methods. You can take individual ideas from visual brainstorming into improvisation, create storyboards based on your improved ideas, or act out your storyboards and then watch them evolve.

Evaluation and Prioritization

At some point, you will need to rein in your ideation process and start selecting the most promising concepts with which to move forward. You may have a sense for some of the best ideas already. Perhaps they bubbled to the top in individual sessions. Or you may have seen common themes emerge across sessions that indicate where to focus.

Transitioning from what you *might* do to what you *should* do can be tricky. For end-to-end experiences, your proposed solutions will impact many parts of the organization. For example, going forward with an idea requiring marketing, product, technology, and operations to coordinate their activities will generate many questions about feasibility and trade-offs in each function. This is why cross-functional collaboration is so critical before, during, and after generating new ideas. The more that key stakeholders understand and buy into where you are collectively heading, the easier it will be to get down to brass tacks.

Making sense of the many proposed ideas and concepts, therefore, follows the patterns recommended throughout this book. These include:

- Involve a broad range of colleagues.
- Leverage simple frameworks and principles to aid decision-making.
- Be clear on your focus, whether it be optimization, reimagining, innovation, or some combination of the three.
- Keep everyone centered upon ideas that deliver value to people, not just the business.
- Look for connections that bridge moments, touchpoints, and channels.

While structured sessions can produce great results, they have limitations and challenges. Getting the right people, in the same place (physically or virtually), and with the proper context and energy requires careful planning and coordination. Additionally, ideas for an active product or service can come at any time. Capturing and evaluating these ideas is an ongoing process rather than a planned stage in a project plan.

Fortunately, you have other options to inspire, find, and connect ideas from across your stakeholder ecosystem. Using experience principles, journey models, ecosystem maps, "how might we's," and other tools, you can equip disparate stakeholders to generate ideas for making better end-to-end experiences. Here are some gathering approaches to consider:

- **Collect existing ideas.** Whether in the context of a new project or adopting new ways of working, ideas for how to make a product or service better will exist already. These could be documented or simply tacit knowledge. Invite your colleagues to send you any pre-existing ideas and then map them to your new frameworks, such as experience principles, opportunity maps, or journey models.

- **Share experience principles.** Socializing experience principles and offering them as tools for others to use can help an entire organization produce ideas asynchronously that share a common DNA. You can then gather them and find potential solutions to evaluate, connect, or prioritize.

- **Socialize "How might we?" opportunities.** The structure of "How might we?" prompts— questions to answer—make them great tools for unguided ideation. Paired with experience principles, these opportunities can be shared broadly to nudge teams toward the high-value focus areas.

- **Adopt frameworks.** The frameworks covered in earlier chapters should provide a common foundation for generating ideas. Journey models and ecosystem maps provide context for how changes in one part of the problem space could affect others. They also provide simple, common structures—stages, moments, relationships—that disparate teams can leverage in their area of responsibility while connecting to the greater whole.

- **Design ideation kits.** Collaborative workshops have the advantage of providing a facilitated structure in which people of different backgrounds and skills can contribute. To increase the odds that colleagues will use appropriate methods and frameworks, consider designing ideation kits. These kits should include clear instructions and well-crafted tools. You can also design them as a game to be played by one or more players. Figure 8.7 shows an example of a kit in action.

- **Be ready to collect.** Before you introduce new prompts and tools into your culture, have a plan for how to access emerging ideas. This could be as simple as a shared folder or as elaborate as an idea management solution. Regardless of your approach, build in easy ways for people to share their ideas, as well as stories of how they have used your tools.

- **Close the loop.** Lastly, it's important to communicate back to people who offer their ideas. Let them know what you are doing with them and what's next. Also, get feedback on your process and tools to improve your approaches over time.

FIGURE 8.7
A design kit in which principles, strategic goals, and other inputs can be used to spark new ideas and capture them on small cards.

In addition, it is important to be rigorous in your evaluation and selection of ideas. This ensures that others can trace back your eventual solutions to the concepts, opportunities, and insights that gave birth to them. Here are a few tips for keeping organized and working with others to land upon the best ideas to act upon.

Play, Prototype, and Connect

While each idea should be evaluated on its own, it's important not to lose sight of how they may connect in various ways to create greater value. You should iterate looking at the parts (ideas) and the whole (multiple ideas that collectively create better end-to-end experiences). These iterations begin in your workshop sessions and should continue as you circle around the most promising ideas. See the workshop following this chapter for an example of this approach.

You should also build in iterations with your customers and employees to validate that your concepts are on the right track. This could be as simple as creating storyboards of key scenarios and paper prototypes of key features and touchpoints. Or you could hold codesign sessions with customers, front-line employees, and other stakeholders to role-play or construct new concepts to meet their needs.

Service blueprinting is also a good tool to use at this stage of the process. You can use blueprints to work with others to explore the feasibility of concepts you have documented in storyboards or through acting. See the next chapter for an overview of this approach.

Codify Your Ideas

To make it easier to compare and connect ideas, you should design a classification approach. You should put this in place as early as possible, because it may impact how you design your templates or store the outputs from your workshops and other approaches. For example, you might add a space for "stage" on your visual brainstorming templates to be able to see or document all the concepts by stage more efficiently.

You likely will have a slightly different list of things you want to track or describe. That said, Table 8.3 lists common facets that should be helpful in being able to evaluate ideas from multiple useful angles. An example for each facet is also provided.

TABLE 8.3 EXAMPLE IDEA SCHEMA

Facet	Description	Example
ID	Unique identifier	001
Name	Unique name	Augmented Reality aisle wayfinding
What	Textual and visual details for what the idea is and how it is experienced	An augmented reality mobile camera data overlay that a customer can use to locate shopping list items by aisle
Who	Persona, customer role, or other stakeholders	Authenticated customers with mobile account
When	Stage or moment	Shopping the store
Where	Channel and/or physical location	Aisles and departments in retail channel, mobile app, web
How	Operations, partnerships, key technologies	Store operations, mobile app dev, digital team, merchandising, marketing
Why	Value to business, customers, employees, and other stakeholders	Business: more items move from shopping list to purchase; Net Promoter Score (NPS) Customer: time saved finding items Employees (store): help with wayfinding requests
Connects To	ID numbers for what other ideas this is similar to or could be combined with	007, 103, 105
Opportunity	Opportunity or "How might we?"	How might we help customers more easily locate the items that initiated their shopping trip?

Depending on your context, the robustness of your organizational approach will vary. A smaller project or end-to-end experience may only require some detailed lists or large sticky notes on the wall. If you are dealing with dozens of ideas or a more complex product or service, spreadsheets are great for itemizing and describing all your ideas. They are especially useful for sorting and filtering ideas by facet. Figure 8.8 shows one example of this approach.

	Journey	Peril to Precarious Stage 1	Precarious to Choice stage 2	Choice t... Stage 3
Ideas	**barrier type**		Journey stages affected	
Build a Budget	Situational	Overspending		
	Emotional	Stress leading to avoidance		
	Experiential	Negative past experiences with other tools		
	Psychological	Not knowing where/how to start		
	Psychological	Belief that I can't budget		
	Psychological	Perception of budgeting as too restrictive - seeing it as limitation not tool		
Reduce discretionary spend	Behavioral	Overspending on self		
	Social	Desire for a certain status or lifestyle		
	Psychological	Not foregrounded / not top of mind		
	Financial	Comfort with a small amount of savings		
	Situational	Overspending on luxury items for dependents		
	Financial	Having no goals or plans		
	Financial			Having vag...
Automate savings	Psychological/ Emotional	Fear and lack of control over money		
	Situational	Variable income		
	Psychological/ Emotional	Belief one can't save even $1		
	Situational	Credit debt is so high that they are budgeted to the penny		
	Psychological	Belief that I can't make it to the end of the month		

FIGURE 8.8
Idea spreadsheet.

USING SPREADSHEETS

I tend to go the spreadsheet route, even for smallish projects, because it allows me to evaluate ideas from different angles very quickly. Spreadsheets can also be used in combination with InDesign's data merge feature to automate making tools and visualizations. For example, it's helpful for making cards with each idea on them to use in a prioritization exercise.

Rate for Value and Feasibility

After you have identified the most promising ideas, your next task is to rate each one based on its value and feasibility. This part can be tricky, because most organizations have multiple ways of measuring value and impact. Lean on your cross-functional team again to find a rating system that will work for your needs. Before rating or prioritizing any ideas, you must find how you will collectively define criteria for what makes something relatively valuable or feasible.

Here are a few steps to consider that will help you do this effectively.

- **Get the lay of the land.** Bring stakeholders from relevant areas together to compare how they each measure value and determine the feasibility of different solutions. See if you can find key commonalities and contradictions.

- **Define common value and feasibility scales.** Work with your team to explore a common set of criteria for value and feasibility. For example, you may identify separate metrics for business value (improved NPS, creating efficiency, generating revenue, and reducing call center volume) and customer value (feels more confident, reduces effort, and increases enjoyment).

- **Get the right stakeholders to rate each item.** Once you have common scales, you will need to engage stakeholders who have the knowledge to compare the value and feasibility of your ideas. You may do this through a series of workshops or conversations. If you use the spreadsheet approach recommended previously, you can use it to document the evaluation.

Prioritize

At some point, you will need to end your process of evaluating ideas and make some decisions. Work with your colleagues to finalize your analysis of which ideas and future experiences will make the cut. The prioritization approaches covered in the previous chapter can be repurposed here, as well as the "Value vs. Complexity" approach in the sidebar that follows. Then it's time to pull all your threads together, craft your vision, and present your plan to the organization (see Chapter 9).

More often than not, the business will want to know the level of complexity of each idea so that investment and effort can be weighed against the potential value. In these cases, you will want to prioritize against relative value and complexity. This method uses many of the same scarcity distribution and facilitation approaches as the value-urgency method (see the "Opportunity Identification and Prioritization" workshop preceding this chapter), but with a couple of tweaks. Here are the steps:

1. **Define your value scale.** As covered in the "Opportunity Identification and Prioritization" workshop, value should be rated on a scale of 1 (low) to high (5). Value should be calculated weighing outcomes for the business, customers, and (when applicable) employees.

2. **Define your complexity scale from 1 (low) to 5 (high).** Complexity should consider your efforts to define, design, and implement a solution based on the idea. It should also reflect how much the organization would need to contribute to a potential solution.

3. **Draw your scale on large sheets of paper (or using tape to create your axes).** Number your Y-axis from 1 to 5 going bottom to top. For complexity, invert the numbers so that 5 (high) is to the left and 1 (low) is to the right. Figure 8.9 shows the beauty of inverting the X-axis. High-value, low-complexity ideas will go to the upper-right; low-value, high-complexity to the bottom-left.[5]

4. **As with the value-urgency method, use the scarcity formula** (*Number of items x middle of your scale = total number of points*) to assign a point limit and then rate each item individually. Refine your scoring until your value and complexity for all items equals your target number of points.

---

5 This method was a favorite at Adaptive Path and taught as part of our design strategy course. David Gray has a great walkthrough of a similar approach—the Impact Effort Matrix—in this video: www.youtube.com/watch?v=_grj-UKUAVM

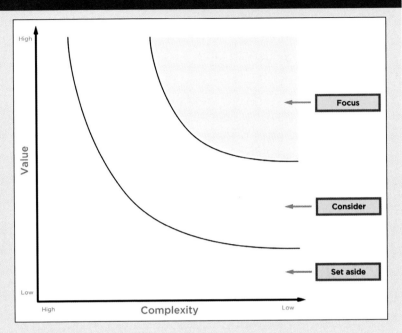

FIGURE 8.9
Prioritizing against value and complexity. Note that the complexity high-low scale is inverted.

This visualization approach will force items into three categories. In the upper-right model are ideas to focus on to get the biggest bang for the buck. The middle category will contain ideas to further consider as higher value items will likely require more sophisticated or costly solutions. The rest of the items should be set aside as you pursue the other opportunities.

Coda

- Cast a wide net for ideas, engaging stakeholders across your organization. This can be done through workshops or through independent activities.

- Be rigorous. Stay focused on your high-priority opportunities, provide structure through frameworks and toolkits, and don't lose sight of your customers' needs and experience principles.

- Mix methods. Visual brainstorming, improvisation, and crafting stories each tap into creativity in different ways and can be used in different combinations.

- Stay organized. Define a common way to catalog and describe ideas so that you can evaluate them individually or in combinations.

- Evaluate the parts and the whole. Define common criteria for rating individual ideas, but continue to evaluate them as a system that produces great end-to-end experiences.

REMOTE WORKSHOPS

Before moving on to the last workshop of the book, I'd like to put in a good word for remote workshops. While it's more effective to get people in a room together to collaborate, your timeline or budget may not accommodate this idea. Here are a few tips when you need to go remote:

- **Keep it hands on.** While remote collaboration tools (in which you type and move objects around digitally) have some benefits, they lack the tactile interactions that come with analog tools. A better approach is to use video to see one another and show your work, while still having people work through exercises with paper tools.

- **Give yourself more time for activities.** Everything takes longer to do in remote sessions due to lagged communications and synthesis steps that require more time in this format. You may have to split what would be one in-person workshop into a couple of shorter sessions to keep peak focus, energy, and attention.

- **Design templates.** Without you in the room, people need more instruction and structure to work effectively. For this reason, avoid blank sticky notes as much as possible. Design simple templates with instructions that help people understand the form their ideas should be documented in.

- **Leverage mobile phones or scanners.** Many ideation methods follow a generation and then evaluation cadence. In remote sessions, have participants work individually and then send in photos or scanned documents of their work. Give them a break, and then magically print and cut their work and place it on a large board. You can then walk through the items on camera, moving and organizing them as people give input and see the results.

- **Train cofacilitators.** If possible, assign and prep cofacilitators at each stakeholder location.

The following workshop illustrates how multiple methods, each covered in depth in Chapter 8, can be combined to collaboratively generate and evaluate ideas. You should experiment with how you sequence these (or other methods) to find the right approach for the project at hand. You also could hold multiple shorter sessions employing one method per session. That said, combining methods allows you to attack your opportunities from multiple angles and build upon your ideas in each iteration.

Workshop Objectives

- Generate a large quantity of ideas inspired by your opportunities.

- Evolve and connect ideas to produce concepts for meeting the needs of customers better across an end-to-end experience.

- Refine your end-to-end experience concepts and document them to share with other stakeholders and customers.

Agenda

This workshop typically takes six to eight hours, depending on the number of opportunities you want to explore and how many participants you include. It can be broken into multiple smaller sessions if needed. This example agenda is for an eight-hour session.

TABLE 8.4 WORKSHOP AGENDA

Activity	Description	Duration
Introductions	Facilitate participants getting to know one another beyond just names and titles.	15 min
Review Agenda and Intended Outcomes	Share the activities for the day and what you want to accomplish by the end of the session.	15 min
Introduce Opportunities	Share the opportunities that you will focus on in the session.	30 min
Visual Brainstorming (1)	Individually generate ideas inspired by your opportunities.	60 min
Break	Give people a rest while you get ready for the last activities.	15 min
Visual Brainstorming (2)	Choose a subset of your ideas to take forward in the workshop.	30 min
Improvisation	Use acting to connect, evolve, or generate new ideas within the framework of an end-to-end experience.	90 min
Lunch	Eat!	60 min
Craft Stories (1)	Create storyboards to document one or more future end-to-end experiences.	75 min
Break	Recharge!	15 min
Craft Stories (2)	Share storyboards and capture feedback.	60 min
Review, Reflect, and Next Steps	Review the workshop process and outcomes. Determine the next steps.	15 min

Roles

- **Lead facilitator:** Workshop host and main facilitator for session activities
- **Co-facilitator(s):** Help(s) set up, break down, and assist in activities
- **Documentarian:** Takes photographs of the session to help nonparticipants understand the collaborative process

Participants

- Core team

- Owners of specific channels, products, or touchpoints

- Practitioners from relevant teams, such as branding, operations, design, and technology

- Front-line employees (if applicable)

Artifacts

- Printouts of relevant frameworks and models, such as your experience map, current-state blueprint, touchpoint inventory, and personas

- Opportunities printed or displayed on-screen individually

- Experience principles (handouts for each participants)

Materials

- Stickers for dot voting

- Quarter sheets (A6 or cut from 8.5" x 11" paper) for visual ideation

- Storyboard templates

- Sharpies

- Sticky notes

- Self-stick easel pad (to create a wall canvas)

- A camera (still and video)

Preparing for the Workshop

To have a good session, communicate your focus, objectives, agenda, and supporting documentation to participants at least one week beforehand. This is especially important for colleagues who were less involved in your opportunity identification activities. Communicating the purpose and outcomes helps more introverted personalities feel less put on the spot during your session. Since you may be using some new methods, also consider including pictures and example outputs of what you will be asking people to take part in. Demystify the process as much as possible.

Running the Workshop

In this workshop, you will divide your group into smaller teams of four to five people. Make sure that each team is cross-functional and multilevel. First, review the agenda and the opportunities that you will focus on. Then guide each team to generate and explore ideas in three iterations: visual brainstorming, bodystorming, and crafting stories (see Figure 8.10). A subset of the ideas produced is then taken forward into the workshop process.

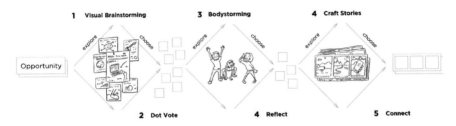

FIGURE 8.10
From opportunities to connected moments over time.

Visual Brainstorming

In this first activity, each participant will generate ideas individually in several rounds. Give each person a stack of quarter sheets (A6) and Sharpies. Remember to encourage everyone to visualize their ideas, as well as name and describe them. Consider making a template for your quarter sheets (see materials list above) to reinforce this approach.

DO A WARM-UP

It's always good to get people comfortable with visualizing their ideas before brainstorming. Take a few minutes to have people warm-up by sketching simple shapes and objects. You can also give them an opportunity to practice, such as "How might we make our break room a better employee experience?" or "How might we celebrate the end of this project?" Have fun with it!

Typically, 30 minutes is enough time to generate a large quantity of ideas while not overtaxing your participants. Each round should be

233

four to six minutes, so you should have time for five to seven rounds before moving on to the next step. The structure for each round should be as follows:

- **Introduce the focus.** You can design each round in many ways. For example, each round can focus on a different opportunity. Or you can take one opportunity and spend rounds exploring it using different lenses, such as journey stages, experience principles, or personas. Read your focus aloud and provide additional context to make sure that everyone understands its intent.

- **Play music.** Get the energy level up by playing some upbeat music (but not too loudly to be distracting).

- **Start ideation.** Each participant will begin capturing their ideas on quarter sheets (A6). Keep an eye out for anyone who is stuck putting pen to paper. Encourage them to write down a first idea quickly to get into a flow. More and better ideas will follow.

- **Give signposts.** Provide participants with a heads-up when you reach the middle part of the round and again with one minute left.

- **Discourage oversharing and talking.** This brainstorming approach allows people to generate ideas individually before critiquing everyone's ideas as a group. It is fine for participants to introduce their concepts briefly—"a wayfinding robot"—but make sure they don't have extended conversations. After all, they only have five minutes or so per round, and you are going for quantity.

- **Call time and immediately jump into the next opportunity.** Keep the energy up by moving quickly to the next round.

After completing all the rounds, ask participants to share their ideas within their small teams and then select ones to take forward into the next activity. Here's a simple approach to do this:

- **Get people up.** It's good at this point to have people on their feet. Post some large sheets of paper on the walls (or cover tables) to create a workspace.

- **Pick five.** Each participant will have many ideas to share, but ask them to select five to share with the team. This is in part to avoid people waiting for one person to share dozens of ideas. If there is time, they can share additional ones after everyone has presented their top five.

- **Share and organize.** Have each participant share their top ideas. If teammates have a similar concept, they should jump in and add to it. As sharing continues, participants should cluster similar ideas and organize them by opportunity, journey stage, or other relevant categories.

- **Dot vote.** When all the ideas are shared, each team should do a quick dot vote to identify the most promising ideas. Remind everyone to use your experience principles as part of their evaluation criteria.

Improvisation

Once you have some good ideas to work with, it's time to do some acting. The objective of this activity is to explore how to connect, evolve, or generate new ideas within the framework of an end-to-end experience. You should break this activity up into the following steps:

1. **Give a structure.** Ask teams to create an end-to-end experience. Give them a specific amount of time (no more than five minutes). Refer to earlier in the chapter for tips on additional ways to structure the improvisation.

2. **Get organized.** Have each team take their top ideas from the first activity and briefly discuss how they may relate to one another. If they haven't done so already, organizing their concepts by journey stage will help show options to sequence them.

3. **Start playing.** It's important to get participants playing with their ideas rather than talking about them. Encourage participants to just start improvising and see where it leads.

4. **Connect, evolve, and add.** As each team improvises, they should naturally connect and evolve different concepts. They should also generate new ideas as they feel their way through what would make a good experience.

5. **Direct and prompt.** Facilitators should engage with each team, giving them feedback and recommended adjustments.

6. **Share, rewind, and capture.** After shaping their end-to-end experience concepts, have each team perform while other teams take notes on what they are seeing. Critique each concept before moving on to the next one. Facilitators can also work with each team to

rewind their concepts to iterate on specific moments. For example, moving a touchpoint to a different channel ("What if they called a customer service agent?") or reworking specific interactions ("Try making a recommendation sooner in the flow").

Craft Stories

In this last iteration, have each team return to their tables and reflect on what they learned through improvisation and the feedback they received. Their next objective is to create storyboards to document one or more future end-to-end experiences that trace back to your original opportunities. This activity works like this:

- **Make decisions.** Based on earlier iterations, each team determines its final concepts and how to express them using one or more storyboards. For example, a team may want to produce two storyboards, each showing the experience of a different persona. Or they may produce one storyboard showing many moments across a journey.

- **Create storyboards.** With each team, participants should create storyboards detailing an end-to-experience that contains their recommended concepts. See earlier in the chapter for storyboarding tips.

- **Review, refine, and reflect.** Finally, have teams share their storyboards with one another. As they do, discuss similarities and differences—such as touchpoints, features, interactions, and moments—across the stories. Use sticky notes to capture feedback and questions.

After the Workshop

When the dust settles, you will have a set of end-to-end experience concepts that contain many ideas within them. You will collect additional stories and ideas as you continue ideation in other sessions or by using distributive methods (see Chapter 8, "Going Beyond Workshops"). Keep everything organized while beginning to identify common themes, ideas, and questions. This will come in handy when it's time to further evaluate all your options to determine the best strategy to use to move forward.

CHAPTER 9

Crafting a
Tangible Vision

W hen you work in a small business, such as a start-up, you can get everyone to play off the same sheet of music more easily. The larger your organization, however, the greater the challenge of understanding the end-to-end experiences you want to enable and why. Hierarchy, functional silos, and distributed teams create communication and collaboration barriers. Strategy is distributed in slides with terse bullet points that get interpreted in multiple ways. The vision for the end-to-end experience is lost in a sea of business objectives, channel priorities, and operational requirements. The result: painful dissonance when the dream was a beautifully orchestrated experience.

This chapter is about working with others to craft a tangible vision for your product or service–a *North Star*. These approaches will help your organization embrace a shared destiny and collaboratively create the conditions for better end-to-end experiences.

The Importance of Intent

The use of the word *intent* has increased dramatically in the halls of most large corporations. You may have intent owners or leaders in your organization, or intent statements as part of your strategy and execution process. Intent is an important concept to understand and align with to get things done, especially with the complexity inherent to orchestrating end-to-end experiences.

Strategic Intent and Lean Management

In the late 1980s, management consultants Gary Hamel and C. K. Prahalad studied the reasons Japanese companies were eclipsing their Western competitors in innovation and business outcomes. They coined the term "strategic intent" to codify how these organizations focused their employees on the same target. Instead of a generic mission statement, there was a simple, inspiring rallying cry. Yearly strategic planning was replaced with pairing near-term goals with the freedom for employees to determine the steps to achieve them.[1] Hamel and Prahalad argued that these practices motivated employees to find inventive ways of creating great outcomes despite relatively scarce resources.

---

1 G. Hamel and C. K. Prahalad, *Competing for the Future* (Boston: Harvard Business School Press, 1996).

In the decades since, many corporations have begun to embrace the concepts of strategic intent, as well as its close sibling, lean management. If you work in a medium- to large-sized organization, you likely see the tentacles of lean making their way into every nook and cranny—small, cross-functional teams, kanban boards, value stream mapping, SMART goals, and so on. The uniting philosophy behind these tactics is to empower small teams to deliver upon strategic intent through extreme focus and collaboration, as well as to streamline or remove processes that don't directly result in customer value. In this way, lean management is one of the primary means to drive to the destination evoked in the strategic intent.

Commander's Intent and Agile

Another strain of intent common in organizations derives from the military: commander's intent. In this context, intent is a commander's concise statement for the purpose and desired end state of a military operation. Well-crafted intent "must be understood two echelons below the issuing commander" and "focus subordinates on what has to be accomplished in order to achieve success."[2] While this sounds top down, commander's intent sets the context for a dialogue between those responsible for conceptual approaches and those crafting detailed execution plans (see Figure 9.1).

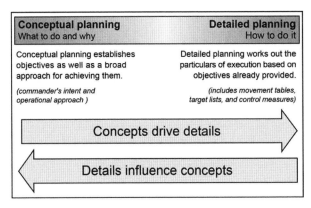

FIGURE 9.1

The relationship between intent and execution from the U.S. Army's *The Operations Process* (ADRP 5-0) field guide.[3]

---

2 U.S. Army, *The Operations Process*, (ADRP 5-0. Washington DC, Army Publishing Directorate, 2012). https://fas.org/irp/doddir/army/adrp5_0.pdf

3 Ibid.

As a philosophy, commander's intent reflects a move away from command and control toward crafting a clear vision and empowering semi-autonomous action. It's no surprise that this type of intent would inspire other organizations grappling with increased complexities and rapid change. You see these dynamics in the adoption of agile approaches in more established organizations. In agile development, for example, a product owner provides the commander's intent to support agile teams, who then have the latitude to determine how best to define and sequence tasks to reach the objective.

Ambiguous Intent and Experience Design

Organizations should strive to inspire employees to stretch while providing them with more agency to achieve important strategic objectives. Teams should look for ways to work smartly and flexibly, not follow rigid, unchangeable operating procedures. These approaches, on paper, embrace human ingenuity and the complexity of the problems that they are trying to solve.

In practice, however, intent applied within the context of product and service definition runs into many issues if your objective is to have effective end-to-end experiences. These include the following:

- **Words are ambiguous:** Intent is communicated through words, often in just a few concise points. People across the organization may read or hear the same thing, but each may envision a slightly or dramatically different solution or experience to each the business objectives.

- **Just the facts:** Success is defined as business results (more customers, greater profits, or increased NPS) and a list of features (mobile check-in, personalized recommendations, or self-service help) without a vision for the customer experience and the role of different channels and touchpoints.

- **Incomplete value:** The benefits to the business are clear, but the value to customers and other stakeholders is absent or uninformed.

- **Cascading communication:** Even in relatively flat organizations, communication from leadership to employees or from strategy to execution loses important nuances as the vision is filtered through the lens of functional leaders and managers operating in organizational silos.

- **Domains of control:** In most organizations, no one owns the end-to-end experience; they own the brand, channels, touchpoints, processes, and technologies. These leaders are measured on the performance of their piece puzzle, not higher-order metrics for the quality of customer journeys. In this context, ambiguous visions are easy to ignore, pay lip service to, or de-prioritize.

- **Fire and forget:** Drafting an intent statement or a strategy document, no matter how well communicated, is just the beginning of steering an organization toward better end-to-end experiences. Increasing your chance for success requires ongoing communication and collaboration, as well as adaptability, because execution reveals deficiencies in even the best of strategies.

Overcoming these deficiencies requires augmenting intent with a clear articulation of future customer experiences. In other words, intent needs a tangible vision.

Defining Your Vision

A tangible vision communicates examples of desired product or service experiences, as well as how the organization might achieve this end state over time. Unlike intent statements and requirements, it shows—largely from the customer's perspective—how a well-designed and orchestrated system of touchpoints can create better outcomes. As a process and a set of artifacts, it helps you and colleagues do the following:

- Clearly frame what value will be created for customers, your business, and other stakeholders through better orchestrating of end-to-end experiences.

- Help each functional group look outside of their functional sphere and see how they fit in the greater whole.

- Show where channels, features, touchpoints, capabilities, and moments must integrate to result in holistic experiences.

- Maintain empathy for customers as teams across the organization make critical decisions in designing the channels and touchpoints for which they are directly responsible.

- Act as a reference point for future action, guiding decisions that should align with intended experiential outcomes for customers.

- In keeping with the spirit of intent, help unite and empower internal stakeholders to play their role in making the future a reality.

A handy analogy for a tangible vision is the North Star, Polaris. Also known as the lodestar ("guiding star" in Old English), the North Star is used in celestial navigation because it lies nearly in a direct line with the North Pole, and thus, being at the top of the Earth's rotation, appears fixed as other stars appear to rotate around it. It's important to note that the North Star is not a destination; it's used as a constant against which to navigate toward a destination.

As with intent, defining a North Star for product and service experiences doesn't mean figuring out every detail. Your North Star should guide—not prescribe—methods of execution. It must frame for the organization qualitatively the types of experiences that will meet customer needs moment by moment, channel by channel, and journey by journey. A North Star provides enough detail to inform and align downstream channel and touchpoint design, but not so much detail that others feel they are simply painting within predefined lines.

It is important to continue to collaborate with others across the organization as you formalize your strategy and hang your North Star in the sky for others to follow. Hopefully, you have been working with and communicating to a diverse, cross-disciplinary team all along. Why? You are instigating a paradigm change that many organizations desire but struggle to make happen.

Previously, a call center worried just about the experience that customers had when calling. It was relatively easy with that function to rally around an operating model based on customer service principles. Similarly, the web team focused on the website experience, the mobile group on mobile, and on and on. Since it is unlikely one person owns an entire journey or end-to-end experience, buy-in from leaders and their teams across the organization is critical for your North Star to cut through the corporate din of competing visions and objectives.

Your tangible vision is an important bridge, from what *is* to what *could be*. It sets the table for intentional orchestration of the customer experience and invites the organization to take their seat. The planks of this bridge are:

- **Stories from the future:** Future-state customer narratives communicated with enough clarity to socialize and be understood across an organization.

- **Service blueprints:** A prototype of how key customer pathways could be delivered operationally in alignment with your experience principles.

- **Capability descriptions and future-state touchpoint inventory:** Details of discrete capabilities (aka features) that are critical for delivering upon the value proposition in and across key customer moments, as well as a framework defining touchpoints in all channels envisioned to support the customer experience.

Your experience principles, opportunity maps, and other outputs from your strategy work will also help people understand and buy into your vision. As you will see, they and the overall value proposition should be woven into your vision. Let's now look at these three planks in detail.

Stories from the Future

You have probably noticed that narrative plays an important role in orchestrating experiences Finding patterns in the stories you collected from customers uncovers the gap between your current product or service experience and what your customers need. Repeating and sharing those stories builds empathy in cross-functional teams. Storytelling and improvisation provide a customer-centered form to generate and create new ideas.

Therefore, it should be no surprise that stories are an effective vehicle for recommending what customers should experience in the future. First-person narratives, told from the perspective of your customers, show the interactions and outcomes that your organization should rally behind. These stories illustrate the specific roles channels and touchpoints should play moment by moment. They also provide a tangible example of how your product or service will fit in your customer's context. This holistic storytelling is critical to ensure that colleagues understand your vision and its efficacy. As executive coach Harrison Monarth put best, "A story can go where quantitative analysis cannot: our hearts."[4]

How does one create and communicate these narratives—these stories from the future? The approaches described in Chapter 8, "Generating and Evaluating Ideas," apply here: show the experience from the customer's perspective; visualize, don't describe; explore the experience from different vantage points; and reinforce context.

---

4 H. Monarth, "The Irresistible Power of Storytelling as a Strategic Business Tool," **hbr.org** digital article, March 11, 2014. Accessed 25 September 2014, from: https://hbr.org/2014/03/the-irresistible-power-of-storytelling-as-a-strategic-business-tool

In terms of form, storyboards work well to communicate your stories from the future (and are relatively low effort to produce). Other formats—such as videos, posters, and narrated storyboards—are also very effective. Often, combinations of these forms work well for communicating to various audiences and in different contexts. Regardless, what you decide to place into your stories should be traceable back to the insights and experience principles.

BUILDING ALIGNMENT THROUGH STORYTELLING

Stories are an important tool to build alignment and focus. I've often seen how even low-fidelity sketches of customer narratives get across important points of functional coordination that requirements or program plans never do. Stories are also easily repeated and socialized, which helps spread and maintain customer empathy.

Consider the following guidelines in order to create compelling and effectives stories from the future.

- **Cocreate your stories.** As mentioned earlier, define your stories as a cross-functional team. (This should flow out of your idea prioritization.) Your goal is to show how an experience harmonizes across channels and touchpoints, so it's critical to keep collaboration strong and get the buy-in of their relative functions (see Figure 9.2). You should also put these stories in front of your customers to get feedback and improve your conceptual stories.

FIGURE 9.2
Creating stories from the future collaboratively builds organizational trust and buy-in for your intent.

- **Provide a range of stories.** In addition to showing future experiences from a customer's perspective, make sure that you share stories of different kinds of people in different situations. However, your goal is not to create dozens of potential scenarios. Instead, include a set of stories that establishes a good understanding of the range of key experiences, as well as the flexibility that will be necessary to be built into channels and touchpoints to accommodate the varying needs and contexts of your customers.

- **Emphasize emotion.** Your stories should not merely focus on future actions and interactions, but also the emotional context. They must communicate the human dimension of your vision and reflect how future experiences will foster customer emotions. Your stories must also depict the critical moments and interactions in which your product or service will have a positive emotional impact.

- **Be specific, but focus detail where it matters most.** You want others to believe your stories from the future. Use the stories and insights from your design research to bring richness and realism to them. However, avoid granular details that paint too fine of a picture of features and touchpoints. Remember, you want to leave plenty of room for others to design these details while adhering to the greater system conveyed in your tangible vision.

- **Show different solutions working in tandem.** Focus your storytelling on showing how a system of touchpoints can create the pathways that customers will follow in the future. Communicate how consistent, continuous experiences will result in greater value to both customers and the business. In this sense, you are like an astronomer unveiling the connections that will transform individual stars into a more powerful constellation (see Figure 9.3).

- **Mind your time horizon.** Each story should paint a picture of how intent manifests as valuable experiences in the future. How far into the future? It depends upon your context. You may be helping others understand experiences that will result from optimization work over the next six months, or your stories may put a stake in the ground for customer stories that may play two to three years into the future. In the latter case, you can create stories that show the evolution of the experience at different points to inform near-term to mid-term work (see, "Determining Your Evolutionary Path" later in this chapter).

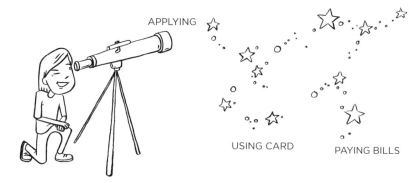

APPLYING

USING CARD   PAYING BILLS

FIGURE 9.3
Rather than a North Star for each major channel or touchpoint, your objective is to show the constellations that unite them in service to the journeys of customers.

- **Show clear connections to what and why.** Include additional details and annotations to help others understand why these stories are important and what it will take to bring them to life. Effective approaches include noting your experience principles, showing which opportunities are being addressed by moment, and listing the capabilities required to enable each moment to happen (see Figure 9.4). Also, consider explicitly calling out the value created for different stakeholders by story or by moment.

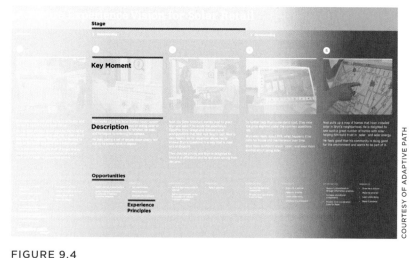

FIGURE 9.4
In this example, opportunities and experience principles are correlated with each key moment of a retail journey.

Airbnb is one of the most public examples of a business using stories to focus its strategic intent and execution. Inspired by Walt Disney, Brian Chesky, a cofounder and formally-educated designer, hired illustrator Nick Sung to produce storyboards depicting the key moments of three Airbnb journeys: the guest, the host, and new employees. Each panel is about the context and human emotions in which Airbnb can play a role now or in the future. They aren't just pretty, inspirational art; they are tools.

Why make storyboards? Chesky wanted his quickly growing company to understand the organization's intent—create great end-to-end travel experiences for both hosts and guests.[5] This decision, it appears, was an important one for the young start-up. CTO Nate Blecharczyk, put it this way:

"The storyboard was a galvanizing event in the company. We all now know what frames' of the customer experience we are working to better serve. Everyone from customer service to our executive team gets shown the storyboard when they first join, and it's integral to how we make product and organizational decisions. Whenever there's a question about what should be a priority, we ask ourselves which frame will this product or idea serve. It's a litmus test for all the possible opportunities and a focusing mechanism for the company."[6]

---

5 Anthony Ha, "Brian Chesky Explains How Snow White Pointed the Way to Airbnb's Future," TechCrunch. Accessed December 16, 2016. https://techcrunch.com/2012/07/18/airbnb-brian-chesky-snow-white/

6 Nathan Blecharczyk, "Visualizing the Customer Experience," Sequoia (website), https://www.sequoiacap.com/article/visualizing-customer-experience/

Service Blueprints

Stories from the future depict key examples of holistic customer experiences, but they do not tell the whole story of your vision. To make your intent clear and actionable, you need to articulate how new or improved operational components—people, processes, and technologies—can form an effective end-to-end experience architecture. In other words, your vision for *how* to increase orchestration backstage to deliver the front stage experiences more predictably, which is communicated in your stories.

As discussed in Chapter 3, "Exploring Ecosystems," the method of service blueprinting can help you at this stage. If you created blueprints in your discovery, then you have familiarized yourself with issues and opportunities related to your current operations. You and your colleagues can now use future-state service blueprints to prototype more granular details of your envisioned customer pathways and what operations will need to do to support them (see Figure 9.5).

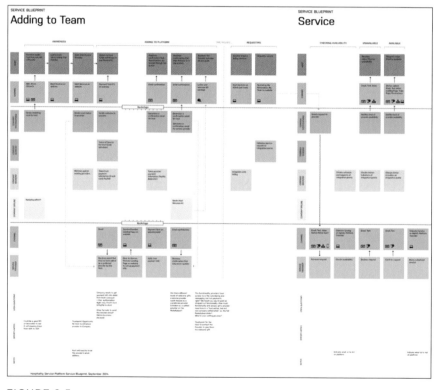

FIGURE 9.5
A future-state service blueprint.

EXPERIENCE BLUEPRINTING FOR PRODUCTS

We have referred often to "product or service or experiences" to signal the broad application of the book's
concepts and tools, regardless of label. This holds true
for service blueprints. In some organizations in which
I have consulted, I referred to this method as "experience blueprinting" when the term *service* proved to be
a distraction to some stakeholders. In the end, it's more important that you prototype how multiple touchpoints, channels, and
other operational capabilities are orchestrated to deliver end-to-
end experiences. What you call it (and how you connect it with
other frameworks) is up to you.

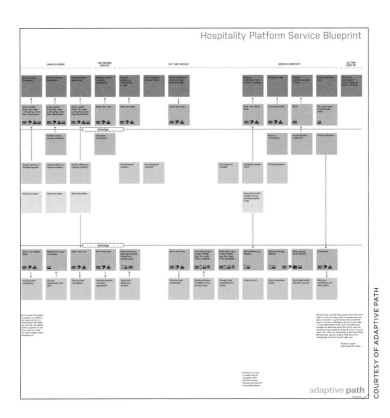

As there is a growing body of literature around the practice of service blueprinting, what follows is not an exhaustive how-to process. If you have never done a service blueprint, we recommend you dig deeper into the method.[7] Once you have the basics down, consider the following guidelines to design your blueprints in coordination with the rest of your tangible vision.

- **Get the right people in the room.** A blueprint gives a bird's-eye view of how different functions—technology, process design, training, product, marketing, and so on—may be called upon to contribute their expertise, time, and energy. Get these stakeholders in a room with some sticky notes and get to work. You can add things, remove things, or move things around as you explore how to deliver the intended experience. Together, you will see the chain reaction of different operational choices, allowing you to have focused conversations on what will work best.

- **Work outside-in.** Solution development often begins with what is operationally efficient or technologically supportable. Blueprinting flips this approach on its head. Your blueprints should derive from working through how a customer would successfully navigate an end-to-end experience, detailing the touchpoints and channels that they interact with along the way. Your individual ideas and storyboards should inform the scenarios and potential experiences that you blueprint (see Figure 9.6).

  Once you have the front-stage details drafted, challenge your colleagues to find operational solutions to enable that experience. Frame this activity as its own "How might we?" For example, "How might we define operations to deliver the intended customer experience?" This is similar to the concept of challenges in strategic intent. In this case, the desired customer actions and outcomes set the intent, while employees are asked to use their ingenuity to find operational solutions to deliver upon it.

---

7 One good resource: *Guide to Service Blueprinting* by Nick Remis and the Adaptive Path Team at Capital One. You can download it for free here: https://medium.com/capitalonedesign/download-our-guide-to-service -blueprinting-d70bb2717ddf

FIGURE 9.6

Beginning the service blueprinting process on a whiteboard with sticky notes.

- **Focus on key customer pathways.** Choose scenarios to blueprint that reinforce key recommendations in your strategy and help tell the overarching story of what the future will be like for your customers and organization. Typically, so-called "happy paths" will appropriately flesh out your vision, but use your judgment. If you're currently having issues with service recovery, then your blueprint may show how some customer journeys may get off track and also detail how your customers will get back on track in the future.

- **Reinforce your journey framework.** Your tangible vision needs to establish a common framework for designing and evolving your end-to-end experiences. Make sure that your blueprints call out the stages and moments that you identified in your research and are refined in your ideation. Refer to Figure 9.5 for an example of this approach.

- **Don't feel tied to the basic blueprint framework.** If you do some research, you will find multiple service blueprint frameworks. Sometimes service evidence is the top row, each channel has a row, or touchpoints are placed between the customer actions and front-stage staff (our preferred standard approach). You should experiment with what works best in your organization.

- **Highlight the big rocks.** Any vision will have recommendations that are more critical or more challenging to execute. Consider highlighting these big rocks in your blueprint. For example, place a star icon on key touchpoints or put thick outlines on high effort process changes. Keep it simple, and these details can help others read and understand your blueprint better.

- **Tie to operational roadmaps.** As you prototype different operational solutions, you likely will explore leveraging existing, in-progress, or completely new processes, roles, and technologies. Perhaps there is a new customer relationship management (CRM) solution being planned for 18 months out, or store ops is splitting a general retail role into two new roles. It may be useful to call out these planned but moving targets to indicate that you have connected those dots or to reinforce the criticality of these planned changes to your vision.

- **Show multichannel options.** Your blueprint may include touchpoints that customers can experience in their channel of choice, such as receiving a confirmation by text, push notification, or a phone call. Make sure that you indicate this option on relevant touchpoints, as well as define what technologies and processes make this choice possible.

- **Call out key metrics.** As part of your vision work, you will need to indicate how value is created and where you can insert indicators to measure performance. Consider including key metrics in your blueprint to show important places to measure the impact of experience and operations.

- **Combine with or connect to other artifacts.** Finally, the classic boxes and arrows blueprint does not have to stand on its own. Simply combining your stories and blueprints creates a powerful combination of showing experience and supporting operations. Also, consider cross-referencing your blueprints with other artifacts, such as a future-state touchpoint inventory or evolution map.

Capability Descriptions

In Chapter 2, "Pinning Down Touchpoints," we defined features as a subset of touchpoints that deliver a unique value or experience. This is closer to the marketing use of the term (although we recommend using human-centered approaches to identify and design features). However, end-to-end experiences contain many more moving parts than features. We call this super set of solution parts *capabilities*.

A capability is the thing that *your organization must be capable of doing* in order to enable a particular moment within a given stage of your journey. You can reframe most things you consider features as capabilities—such as thinking of the ability for customers to upload a profile photo. The reason for doing this is to keep those "features" on the same playing field as things that aren't typically thought of as features. For example, "What are the most important capabilities for our call center during pre-onboarding?" In this case, the ability to create a seamless transfer from one representative to another might not be thought of as a feature, but could be considered a capability. Also, among the moments you support, uploading a profile photo and supporting seamless call transfers could be thought about in the same way. If you work in a purely digital environment, you may not need to reframe features as capabilities, but in a cross-channel, cross-functional environment, capabilities unify the different things you need to do. A capability encapsulates an operational component that supports the experience, such as the touchpoints, channels, processes, or roles.

Many of these capabilities will have come up in different activities and discussions that have led to your vision. You now need to define them more formally. Documenting your capabilities should be a collaborative effort. When defining each capability, consider the following:

- Describe the capability in enough detail that it can be understood by anyone across the organization.

- Identify the channels needed to support that capability.

- Map the capability back to a specific stage of the experience.

- Surface any major dependencies to enable the capability.

- Identify accountability for that capability.

When you bring people together to do this, the core team likely will take a stab at drafting the capabilities. The group can work together to ensure that each capability is articulated clearly, with little abstraction, and can prioritize the set of capabilities, typically along the lines of business benefits, customer benefits, and feasibility. Figure 9.7 illustrates how to use small cards to facilitate the definition and prioritization process. In prioritization, you may not get to every capability. Focus on the ones that are most important, documenting more details for capabilities that may be needed in the near-term. Further prioritization and sequencing of capabilities will then occur in evolution mapping (see "Determining Your Evolutionary Path").

FIGURE 9.7
Capability cards.

As you identify and prioritize capabilities, you should map them to your Stories for the Future and blueprints to indicate the moments to which they align. This enables you to identify and discuss dependencies better. This is where having the cross-functional group together will be key. Lastly, with everyone in the room, you can determine who is accountable for each capability.

Future-State Touchpoint Inventory

It is also helpful to explicitly define the collection of touchpoints that must be created to support or trigger customer actions. Some of these touchpoints will appear in your stories and blueprints, while others from your ideation and prioritization may not. Don't lose this good thinking!

Chapter 2 introduced the touchpoint inventory framework and the discovery approach of itemizing and organizing key touchpoints by channel and journey stage. This same framework can be used to document your future-state touchpoints. When crafting your vision, you probably have not identified all the touchpoints that customers will need. However, create an initial inventory with your known touchpoints. This will help colleagues begin to take responsibility for defining, designing, and maintaining the touchpoints for which they are responsible. Here are a couple of approaches to document an initial future-state touchpoint inventory based on your ideation and vision work.

- **Simple:** This approach leverages the framework used in your current-state touchpoint inventory, but is updated with your latest definition of journey stages. Your channel rows should also reflect what channels you will leverage in the future. In this approach, it is also useful to distinguish new touchpoints from existing touchpoints.

- **Detailed:** You can get much more detailed in your future-state inventory. You can break out your stages into discrete moments to document when touchpoints play a role in more granularity. Your detailed inventory can also highlight the expected impact to existing touchpoints, such as reimagined, modified, or as is. Figure 9.8 shows one approach to this type of documentation. In even more detailed inventories, connections between touchpoints and design direction are included. Your simple stage-channel framework (at a glance) should refer to these detailed spreadsheets (specifications and intent).

	A	B	C	D	E	F	G	H	I	J
1										
2			Channels			Journey Stages and Moments				
3	ID	Touchpoint	Digital channels		Phone channels	Exploring my options			Making my decision	
4			Acme.com	Acme mobile	Acme sales	Looking casually	Making a list	Researching more closely	Narrowing down	Getting a second opinion
5	T1	Weekly specials	Existing	New	Sunset	YES		YES		
6	T2	Product stories	Reimagined	New				YES		
7	T3	Product FAQs	Existing	New				YES	YES	
8	T4	Ask an expert	New	New	New			YES	YES	
9	T5	Compare to competition	New	New	New		YES	YES	YES	
10	T6	Share list	Reimagined	Reimagined	New		YES			YES
11										

FIGURE 9.8

Part of an example-detailed touchpoint inventory. It maps each touchpoint (same intent, different design per channel) to channels and moments within journey stages.

Charting Your Course

In larger organizations, optimizing an end-to-end experience involves working with multiple groups, dealing with legacy systems, and navigating a complex political landscape of competing priorities. You should recommend a strategy of starting small, learning, and adapting, but also provide guidance for how work across multiple fronts will eventually coalesce into a holistic experience.

This is a balancing act. For example, say that you have crafted a vision for a better end-to-end experience for ordering online and picking up in store. This new customer journey will require changing or creating touchpoints in multiple channels. Operations will need to design processes, marketing will create new collateral, and the learning department will develop employee training. Your stories, blueprints, and other artifacts will give these efforts a tangible vision of what to aim for in execution. Yet, you must enable flexibility to address yet unknown constraints, implement and refine iteratively, and inform other work efforts.

Given these dynamics, you must define how to take intentional steps toward your vision while leaving room to learn and adapt along the way. This guidance is delivered in the form of an *evolution map*. As you will see below, an evolution map shares many best practices with a good product roadmap but takes a broader view than a product and its features. It informs disparate products, technology, and operational roadmaps to align them in support of the North Star (Figure 9.9). Most importantly, an evolution map has an experiential bias to ensure that customer needs stay front and center over time.

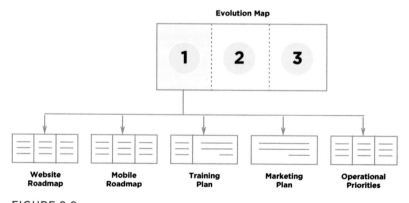

FIGURE 9.9

An evolution map provides context for other roadmaps and plans.

Determining Your Evolutionary Path

While creating your vision, you and your collaborators will swim in ideas, potential solutions, opposing priorities, possible stories, and feasibility questions for some time (see Figure 9.10). At some point, your strategy will become clear. A pathway will present itself that embraces known constraints, delivers value to stakeholders, and feels achievable by your organization. Your evolution map documents this recommended course of action.

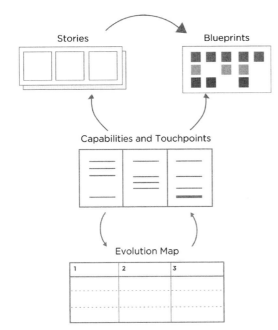

FIGURE 9.10
Through multiple iterations, you can settle upon your vision and the pathway to improve the end-to-end experience over time.

If you have experience with developing roadmaps, then you know there is a natural tension between acting now and building support for larger investments of time and money. Defining near-term action (in part driven by quarterly and annual cycles in corporations) often displaces architecting and committing to solutions that require more time to bear fruit. Orchestrating experiences, however, requires breaking down this organizational muscle memory. Your vision orients others to the horizon; your evolution map frames actionable steps to move together in the desired direction (see Figure 9.11).

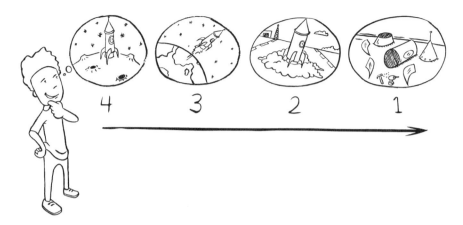

FIGURE 9.11

Through multiple iterations, you can settle upon your vision and the pathway to improve the end-to-end experience over time.

Your mantra must be "work backward from our vision." In practice, this means taking your envisioned end state—as communicated in your stories and blueprints—and determining how to move in that direction over time. This mindset derives from the work of the University of Waterloo's John B. Robinson. In his research at the intersection of environmental change and public policy, Robinson outlined an approach—called *backcasting*—for defining a desired future and then determining the most viable actions to take to attain it. His method moved the emphasis from predicting possible futures to analyzing the effort and investment required to live into a future that you would like to see.[8] Matthew Milan, CEO of software innovation firm Normative, helped to widen its application to information architecture and user experience.[9]

In the context of product and service experiences, your nascent vision provides examples of end-state outcomes from which to backcast. Backcasting for orchestrating experiences has one differentiation: where traditional backcasting often identifies multiple future state hypotheses, here you typically have a singular vision of the future toward which you want your capabilities to evolve.

---

8 John B. Robinson, "Futures Under Glass: A Recipe for People Who Hate to Predict Futures," Futures 22, no. 8 (1990): 820–842.

9 Matthew Milan has been inspired by the "big backcasting" of Robinson and simplified it as a facilitated workshop session for information architecture. https://www.slideshare.net/mmilan/backcasting-101-final-public

BACKCASTING FOR ORCHESTRATING EXPERIENCES

Backcasting often involves identifying multiple possible futures and then mapping the opportunities and barriers that exist on the path to those futures. When you're orchestrating experiences, you typically have a singular vision (or set of vision stories) that define the future experience you want to support and the capabilities needed to support them. Backcasting used here is specifically designed to orchestrate the evolution from the baseline current state to a more singularly desired future state.

You could also use backcasting earlier in the process when you're defining that future state and look to see which path is better—more achievable, more competitive, etc.—among multiple future state possibilities.

It's important to reinforce here that this is an iterative process. As you define your stories of the future, your blueprints, and your capabilities, you are still circling around a vision that your organization will commit to. As you begin to map a potential evolutionary path, you will naturally sharpen your vision as the feasibility and impact of different options become clearer. In each iteration, however, the key is to let the desired future drive your analysis so that your intent isn't lost along the way.

Evolution planning can easily wrap you and others around its axle with so many variables at play—competitive pressures, feasibility, effort, timing, dependencies, and so on. To avoid this, lean heavily on the journey framework that has emerged through your sensemaking and vision activities. While your stories from the future will take several iterations to achieve, journey stages and moments (and customer needs within them) provide a consistent structure to plan and coordinate improvements to the end-to-end experience over time.

Take air travel as a case. As a service experience, technology advancements and increased security requirements have transformed how passengers plan a trip and get to their destination. These changes, however, sit upon a more consistent architecture of moments—choosing a destination, booking your flight, going to the airport, checking in, and so on. If you were tasked with an air travel initiative today, you would look to transform these moments to improve them, rethink their sequence, or replace them.

Your journey framework can serve as a table of contents for your product or service experience evolution. Working backward from your stories of the future, you should weigh different options for when and how to address each journey stage and moment. This means asking questions such as:

- Which journey stage(s) and moment(s) will you address first? Next?

- For each moment, will it remain the same over time, change once, or evolve in a series of steps?

- When will you introduce new moments, or remove an existing one?

- When will your key features be introduced? Will they be executed in phases?

- How will your channel strategy evolve? Can you leverage some channels for interim solutions?

- What big rocks—new platforms, channels, roles, and so on—must be tackled (and when) to enable moments and touchpoints?

- How will you work with major dependencies? Do you need interim solutions to deliver value while waiting for your capabilities to line up?

As you explore how your stages and moments will evolve, you will naturally begin analyzing how the roles of various channels, key touchpoints, and capabilities will also change independently or in concert. Some of your decisions may be driven by implementation constraints, while others may fall later in your plan due to dependencies, urgency, or value.

For example, your long-term vision may be to partner with Lyft to schedule a pick-up service to the airport when booking a flight. The optimal solution would involve changes to several channels, backend integration, training, and other efforts. While this is not feasible to tackle fully in the near-term, your challenge is to identify manageable steps that you can take to move toward your vision for this "schedule a ride to the airport" moment (see Figure 9.12). The plan for this moment, of course, impacts the evolution of later moments, such as "leaving for the airport" and "arriving at the airport."

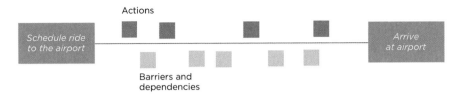

FIGURE 9.12
Backcasting booking a ride to the airport.

Throughout your evolution mapping activities, use your experience principles to pressure-test your options for initial or interim solutions. For example, your vision for a hotel service experience may include personalizing room amenities based on a guest's profile. This solution is not achievable now due to technical reasons. Yet, one of your experience principles is "to fit like a glove." Reviewing your near-term evolutionary stage against this principle helps to reveal this gap. You and colleagues can then challenge yourselves: "How might we make the guest's room fit like a glove within our near-term technical constraints?"

Mapping out how to evolve moments, as well as the entire journey, is hard work, but keep focused on your intent and framework to navigate the unavoidable ambiguity. Eventually, a sequence of actions will emerge, as well as how to organize them into phases. You are then ready to document your evolution map.

Communicating Your Evolutionary Pathway

You have many options for designing your evolution map. As with other artifacts, you should choose an approach appropriate for your culture while crafting it to stand out from the pack. Common forms include a large canvas, a series of slides, a book, or a combination of all three. Get creative!

Regardless, make sure that your evolution map works in concert with your stories from the future, blueprints, capabilities, and other documentation. Cross-reference as much as you can so that people can easily dig into the details without getting confused on the big picture. Your vision and evolution map package should tell a story that inspires others to follow your recommended course of action and stay in alignment with your tangible vision.

While the form of your map is up to you, consider the following guidelines to ensure that you communicate the important details of each phase on the pathway ahead of you clearly.

- **Organize by phases with themes.** As in a roadmap, you should organize your evolution map into distinct phases with clear entrance and exit criteria. Each phase should have a theme that communicates its intent. For example, you may come to the realization that your first evolution will focus on updating your content strategy because it will not require new investments in operational infrastructure. The theme of this first stage, therefore, might be defined as "improving customer communication." You may also determine that you can do better data collection to enable new interactions and value. So, your second stage might be called "getting smarter."

- **Don't align to dates.** Avoid giving each phase a specific time frame, such as first quarter. An evolution map should show a sequence of phases and the relative length of phases. You should not tie your phases to dates. Leave that to more detailed program planning to nail down details of timing and funding.

- **Communicate value and measurement.** Within each phase, break down how your efforts will result in better experiences that deliver measurable value to various stakeholders. This is especially critical in the early phases in which business and technical outcomes often push out to later (or never) the value that is to be created through customer experience. By being explicit about value in each stage, you will reinforce that customer (and other stakeholder) value is a key part of your success criteria.

- **Align to stages and moments.** As covered previously, your evolution map should call out when you will address each journey stage and moment. Communicate clearly the focus of each phase, as well the individual evolutionary path of specific moments (see Figure 9.13).

- **Call out features, channels, touchpoints, and operations.** You should show how the role of channels will change in each phase, as well as what the plan is for key features and touchpoints. Each phase should also note operational changes—technologies, processes, and people—required to support the intended experience. Refer people to your capability descriptions and future-state touchpoint inventory for the nitty-gritty details.

FIGURE 9.13
Example of an evolution map.

- **Define ownership, accountability, and dependencies.** Many functions and groups will be needed to put your plan into action. Make sure that you annotate your map with who will be involved in each step, what you will ask of them, and what any major dependencies will be.

- **Know what you want to learn.** Finally, the spirit of a tangible vision and evolution plan is to adapt to changing circumstances while not losing sight of your original intent. Be explicit as to what you want to learn in each phase to validate your original course of action. This will help ensure that your evolution map evolves with new evidence.

Coda

- Many organizations have adopted practices built on defining strategic intent and unleashing employees to achieve it. In end-to-end experience design, this intent is delivered through creating a compelling, tangible vision.

- Stories from the future depict intended customer experiences, highlighting how different moments, channels, and touchpoints deliver value across time and space.

- Service blueprints, touchpoint inventories, and capability descriptions document the architectural components (and connections among them) to deliver the intended end-to-end experience.

- Backcasting can help you define an evolution map that delivers value at each phase while staying aligned with your North Star.

- Stay collaborative throughout the process to ensure that cross-functional buy-in occurs for the vision and commitment that follows your evolution map.

Designing the Moment

A vision and plans are critical to aligning stakeholders to work toward the same end-to-end experiences. Your frameworks will provide each execution team with good context for their work. These artifacts define and communicate the moments that you want to bring to life, as well as the role of different touchpoints and channels. Your experience principles provide a common set of criteria to inspire and critique your work.

However, these orchestration efforts will be for naught without action. It's now time to make the future. But what does it mean to *make* something in an orchestrated process? Does each functional group follow its business-as-usual approach to create requirements, define features, and make content, user interfaces, printed materials, and so on based on the relevant medium? No! It's now everyone's responsibility to design and execute toward the same *customer moments*.

MACROINTERACTIONS AND MICROINTERACTIONS

In this sense, a moment is a *macrointeraction*—a collection of interactions that collectively shape a key part of an experience. For example, going through the checkout line to make a purchase at a store is a macrointeraction, while using the POS payment device for your credit card is an interaction. The beep that tells you to pull your chip-enabled card out of the slot is an even more granular level of interaction (a *microinteraction*, as coined by Dan Saffer).[1] This hierarchy of interactions is good to keep in mind when defining how each touchpoint and associated interactions support the larger moment.

Designing moments well requires multiple iterations. Through trial and error, each touchpoint, should be refined to work well on its own and in concert with other touchpoints that make the moment possible. This chapter provides guidance on how to use different forms of prototyping to explore different design approaches for moments that make up an orchestrated experience. Chapter 11, "Taking Up the Baton," shares techniques for orchestrating the people that design and develop these moments.

---

1 We highly recommend Dan Saffer's book, *Microinteractions: Full Color Edition: Designing with Details* (Sebastapol, CA: O'Reilly, 2014).

Prototyping Options

Due to the breadth of end-to-end experiences, it's rare that one prototype will do the job of exploring and validating design solutions.
Some prototypes will help you design how multiple touchpoints connect to create a customer pathway, while others will go more deeply
into the interactions within one moment. Prototypes can focus exclusively on the customer's experience, or on how people, processes, and
technology behind the scenes make those experiences possible. What
follows are the various options that you can pull from to test various
dimensions of your product or service iteratively. These dimensions
are not mutually exclusive. Use them to inform the direction that you
take your prototyping.

Horizontal vs. Vertical

Horizontal prototypes broadly reflect the narrative flow of a product or
service experience, while not going deeply into any one moment or
interaction (see Figure 10.1). Horizontal prototypes help you assess
how well different moments (touchpoints) and features meet the
customer needs and deliver your overall value proposition. Validating these prototypes with stakeholders, customers, and front-line
employees then informs individual concepts as well as how they
work together as a system.

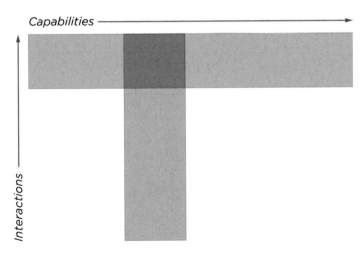

FIGURE 10.1

Horizontal prototypes will test a broad collection of capabilities while
vertical prototypes go deeper in a narrow scenario, but are detailed in
testing interactions and functionality.

Horizontal prototypes can take on many forms based on your needs and context. Paper mock-ups, interactive digital artifacts, storyboards, and other approaches can be used to express features and touchpoints that make moments possible. For example, prototyping new experiences for checking into a hotel may involve making a storyboard of key moments across multiple journey stages and contexts, or perhaps paper mock-ups and digital simulations of specific touchpoints in the order they would be experienced. For more complex experiences, your prototype may need to zoom out to show a bird's-eye view of the entire service (or product). This is called *service modeling*, with business origami (see Chapter 3, "Exploring Ecosystems") being one distinct form. As Figure 10.2 shows, service modeling helps you lay out the broader experience landscape and constantly reference, explore, and incorporate new ideas as stakeholders and customers provide feedback.

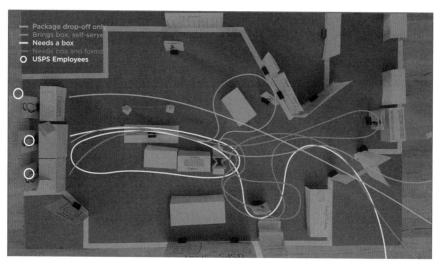

FIGURE 10.2
Service modeling used for design and connecting moments.

SERVICE MODELING

Service modeling may seem best suited for experiences for prototyping physical environments, but it's also great for prototyping use cases of digital services in context. Digital channels—such as kiosks or dedicated software terminals—that live exclusively in retail stores, warehouses, bank branches, medical facilities, car dealerships, and so on can benefit from having a physical model to identify opportunities to inform the digital touchpoint.

Regardless of the form you choose, remember to focus your horizontal prototyping on the flow of the end-to-end experience. This form of prototyping aids cross-functional teams in designing together. At this stage of experience design, the details of interactions and content are less important than how various channels and touchpoints may work in coordination to support customers over time. Horizontal prototypes help you express to customers how they may experience these future journeys.

When you want to go deeper into a specific moment, channel, or touchpoint, *vertical prototypes* provide the right lens to make, test, and refine important details. As with horizontal prototypes but even more so, their form depends upon the channels and context of interaction. For example, mobile touchpoints that help customers find and book rooms from anywhere would likely be simulated in an interactive prototype. A series of conversations at the front desk, on the other hand, may be validated using role-playing with customers and employees. In either case, the goal is to bring to life specific interactions with high levels of fidelity and interactivity.

Vertical prototypes are also useful for exploring how different touchpoints come together to create moments in a specific context. In a health clinic, for example, you may envision a new flow of moments that connect your arrival to meeting with your doctors. To iron out the details of interactions, language, and hand-offs, you might build a physical prototype of the environment (kiosks, check-in areas, seating, and so on) along with a digital simulation of the kiosk touchpoints and role-playing of person-to-person interactions. These types of prototypes trade depth for breadth, enabling you to refine more granular details within and across touchpoints (see Figure 10.3).

FIGURE 10.3

Concept evolution for an immersive physical experience for a store-within-a-store concept.

In Context (or Not)

Many people think of prototypes as things—products or communications in various media—to be tested in a controlled environment, such as a lab. Based on this conventional wisdom, organizations tend to gravitate toward usability studies and focus. However, lab studies may be convenient for researchers, but customers don't live in rooms with people watching them through a two-way glass. Our advice: test each prototype within the context for which it is designed.

You can make a prototype to test in any environment, but *contextual prototyping* intentionally focuses on validating designs in the context in which they will be experienced. For instance, a team may be responsible for designing the digital aspects of an in-store kiosk, but testing in the hectic environment of the store (rather than the lab) pressure-tests the validity of the design better. A good example of this approach was Nordstrom Innovation Lab's sunglass iPad prototype. In their study, captured in a compelling process video, a prototype was conceived, created, and iterated in the eyewear department in collaboration with customers and employees.[2] This approach not only benefited from designing in context, but also led to strong results in only one week.

A contextual prototype can be of any fidelity, as long as it helps you understand and incorporate how you can tune your design better to fit a specific context. And, of course, you can combine multiple contextual prototypes of different touchpoints to validate how these new design interventions serve customers individually and collectively.

Technical vs. Experiential

Technical prototypes provide the means to ensure that a product or service can do what it promises. Traditionally, a technical prototype might be about whether the technology worked. At Fitbit, this could mean testing whether the sensors needed to track data fit on a wrist. For Google, a technical prototype may validate that predicative search is indeed predicative. Technical prototypes take critical jobs that the product or service needs to do—track or predict—and prove it's possible before going too far with other aspects of the design. This makes sense because you don't want to center your value proposition on something that can't be done!

In product design, technologists typically own these types of prototypes. But increasingly, as experience design points to connected devices, embedded technologies, and new ways of interacting (such as voice interfaces), designers must concern themselves with what's possible. This is one reason why cross-functional collaboration is critical to both designing well and efficiently. But this isn't limited to technology. Designing to support experiences across digital and physical touchpoints is more broadly about feasibility, of which technology is one facet.

In experiences that are based on personal information or data from consumers—such as healthcare or financial services—testing an experience through a prototype where the information isn't the consumer's data presents a challenge. People have a hard time responding to an experience where the information isn't their actual

---

2 As of this date, you can view this video on YouTube at **www.youtube.com/ watch?v=szrOezLyQHY**

information. In this context, a technical prototype might mean hacking together an Excel sheet to test an experience of a financial application or in an estimating flow. The experience is limited, but a person can use his or her real data—showing the feasibility of having that data be relevant to the consumer.

In a service experience, a technical prototype might be about operational testing. You may create an immersive physical experience (vertical prototype), where you want to test out not only the front stage experience, but also work out how backstage elements could support that experience. You are testing if the backstage operations feasibly work to support the frontstage experience.

An *experiential prototype* (also, experience prototype) lets you test how a product or service is experienced, in which case that prototype may not work from a technical perspective. In product design, this is often called a *Wizard of Oz* prototype. To the user, it should feel like a high-fidelity experience, while the behind-the-scenes system is simulated. In other words, your prototype does not technically work, but your test participants can respond to an experience as it would work. This approach can be used to simulate a single technology (e.g., a database or integration point) to what will eventually be a coordinated system of people, processes, and technologies.

PALM PILOT AND THE EXPERIENTIAL PROTOTYPE

The founder of Palm Pilot famously walked around with a block of wood covered with printouts that represented screens, along with a wood "stylus."[3] He would go so far as to pull this block of wood with static printed screens out in meetings and mimic writing on the "device" to capture a meeting in his calendar or adding a contact. This is an experiential prototype. Separately, Palm Pilot made many technical prototypes to test if they could easily (enough) sync data between the device and a PC, or if the resistive screen and stylus could support accurate data entry (see Figure 10.4).

---

3 More on the early Palm Pilot experience prototype: www.wired.com/1999/10/the-philosophy-of-the-handheld/

FIGURE 10.4
Examples of Palm's technical and experiential prototypes.

Interactive vs. Narrative

Perhaps when you hear the word *prototype*, you think of things that can be put in front of people to test interactions—interfaces with features and functions. For example, it might be a physical object with buttons, levers, and other controls. But remember all those stories, blueprints, and models that you created during ideation and North Star visioning? Those are also prototypes. They're something you've made to answer a question—"How might we...?"—that can be validated to inform even better solutions. Framed as a prototype, these mostly serve for internal use, getting buy-in across stakeholders. But you can also walk customers or users through storyboards and other static artifacts to prompt a dialogue around what will best meet their needs.

The Prototype Value Proposition

How will you know that what you design connects to what you realize you *need* to design? Through your orchestration, you've created *traceability* that links your design decisions to your original insights. Your vision work framed each moment and the value it should create for customers, employees, and your organization. Your vision was informed by principles, which were applied to characterize opportunities, which were based on insights from journey-based research.

As you make and test your prototypes, don't lose sight of this critical *throughline*. Each touchpoint should have a raison dêtre—a clear why, what, and how that supports the value proposition of one or more moments. As you share and validate your prototypes, anyone, particularly stakeholders who aren't always involved in the process, should be able to easily see why this solution is appropriate. Figure 10.5 shows one approach—a prototype value proposition worksheet—for making this throughline more tangible and measurable.

Keep these earlier concepts in mind:

- **Touchpoint type:** Working with your touchpoints, you'll start to see that you can categorize them into common types based on the role they play. When you are making something that tests one or multiple touchpoints, make sure that you define that role these touchpoints play. If your prototype is required for the user or customer to interact with, then usability is paramount since people will see it as something they have to do. For example, entering billing and shipping information at checkout is a necessity. If the touchpoint is about enhancing the experience, then you know that it may be about delighting or overdelivering value (a cherry on top).

- **Experience principles:** Experience principles, at this stage, will help teams judge or measure their designs. Unlike heuristics (which can help guide design decisions), these principles are contextually specific to the opportunity that your prototype is addressing. As you identify what to make and how to craft your prototype, you should know specifically what subset of your experience principles (usually one to three) are most relevant to that moment and its supporting touchpoints.

- **Touchpoint heuristics:** As covered in Chapter 2, there are some intrinsic characteristics that can define any given touchpoint. When you identify your *touchpoint type*, you can identify what heuristics are most important for that touchpoint. For example, in an enhancing touchpoint, being delightful may be the overarching heuristic. If the touchpoint is identified as critical, then being valuable and relevant may be the sentiment you want to engender.

TOUCHPOINT:

Stage: **Channel(s):**

Describe Touchpoint

Present State

Customer Doing	Customer Thinking	Customer Feeling

Rail Europe Doing	Rail Europe Thinking	Rail Europe Feeling

Context

Information & Insights	Challenges

Innovation / Opportunities

Success Criteria and Capabilities

Success Criteria for Rail Europe's Business	Key Capabilities to Support This Touchpoint

Key Experience Attributes

Disposition #1	Disposition #2
1.	1.
2.	2.
3.	3.
4.	4.
5.	5.

FIGURE 10.5

Prototype Value Proposition worksheet (stage, opportunity, type, experience principles—throughline).

Putting It Together

Chapter 2 used the analogy of touchpoints as a coordinated system of featured and supporting players on the stage of experience. That chapter highlighted some examples from the travel experience through an airport. Let's unpack another airport moment to explore how prototyping can help answer the overarching question: "Is everyone playing their part, and well?"

Increasingly, Automated Passport Control (APC) kiosks are replacing human agents and the tasks they perform when international travelers pass through customs (see Figure 10.6). These tasks include scanning your passport, asking questions, entering data, checking a database, and stamping you through (or, if you're unlucky, being held for more questioning). Most of what these agents do is data entry, so a kiosk may make the process seem more efficient and convenient. However, there are things that only an agent could do, up to this point, such as match the face of the person with the face on the passport.

Passport control is one moment in a journey that may have started many miles and days earlier, and won't end after this moment passes. The identified opportunities for this moment include: make passport

FIGURE 10.6
A bank of APC kiosks.

control *easier* for select travelers; *faster*, which benefits travelers and the airport; and *cheaper* for the border protection agency through staff reduction.

Imagine that your team is designing the interface for this new kiosk, and there are various touchpoints you would like to test. Even though you are testing digital flows, accounting for the physical environment is critical. There is the arrangement and location of the kiosks in contrast to the traditional agent-supported passport lines; information that helps people know what to do; as well as the physical kiosk, which has a camera, a sensor to read passports and documents, a sensor for fingerprints, and a receipt printer. Given the rich environment, you don't want to limit yourself to a controlled lab environment testing your screens.

What prototyping approach should you take?

- Access to the security environment is limited, so you might first refine your narrative storyboards and build smaller-than-scale models to create a horizontal prototype. This approach allows you to explore how your new touchpoints may fit within the larger journey and the environmental context of border control. Where are the kiosks located? How many are there? How are they arranged? How would people know to queue up to use them?

- Your team would then want to work more vertically to see how all the touchpoints work together with the onscreen flow. Here, an immersive experience prototype at scale would help test how the screens complement the scanners and vice versa.

- Technical prototypes could be used to validate that the facial recognition software works.

- You may create a contextual prototype that's placed at the border control area to ensure that you get real feedback about how the kiosk is used in context. When distracted by signage, agents, and roped lines, do people still know what to do? You may see travelers doing a lot of looking at travelers at other kiosks to try to reassure themselves that they are doing things correctly. At what points do they do that?

These different prototypes collectively help test both the flow among touchpoints and interactions with discrete touchpoints. Answering questions, scanning fingerprints and documents, taking a picture, and retrieving a receipt must all work individually and as a system to ensure the best experience. Taking your picture using a camera and the screen is a required touchpoint, and it is also a sequential touchpoint, where there are multiple actions that need to take place (see Figure 10.7). Can this required activity be designed to minimize any sense of burden? Can the sequence of actions feel seamless and intuitive? How do you minimize a sense of intrusion or "big brother" suspicion?

FIGURE 10.7
Having your photo taken through Automated Passport Control.

You also have experience principles, such as "treat people humanely" and "familiar as shopping online," to guide and test your design decisions. A kiosk may feel like a great alternative to being in front of a person looking at you suspiciously. But you're also asking people to do more on their own. When testing, there will be some finer usability issues you may identify, but as a new moment, it's important to judge your prototypes based on how well they meet your principles and deliver on the intended value proposition. If you introduce this new moment, in what way does your testing help you validate its value? Quicker process or less uncomfortable human interactions? Thinking in these terms helps to ensure that what you make has a strong focus on what's important for the customer and business.

Coda

- Think both horizontally and vertically. What do you need to prototype in order to test broader sequences in a journey and fine-tune key moments?

- Stay collaborative. Prototyping experiences is still a cross-functional endeavor that should involve key stakeholders.

- Know your audience. Consider if you're making something to explore and validate with end-users, or if you need to demonstrate how something works to get internal buy-in.

- Connect to a value proposition. Be aware of the throughline from original customer need to your testable prototype.

Taking Up
the Baton

Increasingly, business leaders understand the critical nature of customer experience to their bottom line. Walk the hallways of your organization, and you will likely hear phrases such as customer-centric, Voice of the Customer, and Net Promoter Score. You will see proclamations that all experiences should be simple and seamless while wowing your customers. You may also notice increased investment in human-centered approaches, such as design thinking, as well as skill sets needed to plan, design, and implement customer touchpoints.

These developments indicate good intent (and great demand for designers!), but most organizations still struggle to understand customer needs effectively or translate that understanding into well-designed end-to-end experiences. Why? In our work, we have seen many barriers, including:

- Talented people of all disciplines still work in silos, unable to see or contribute to a compelling experience vision.

- Customer research is insourced and outsourced, keeping decision makers and practitioners at arm's length from people's real needs.

- Strategy and planning remain largely tied to specific channels, products, and functions, not customer outcomes.

- Execution has become more iterative, yet agile is largely driven by business and technical considerations, not the needs of people.

- Organizations are trying to become more collaborative, but employees lack a shared language and philosophy for the role of customer needs, experience, and design in achieving business objectives.

Our objective for this book was to share a mindset and methods for taking on these challenges. There is no silver bullet. It takes hard work, inspired leadership, grit, and a little luck to orchestrate experiences. Yet, we have seen individual teams and entire organizations make great progress through employing the approaches outlined in previous chapters. We hope you and your colleagues will be able to do the same. To that end, here is some final advice for gaining traction in your organization.

Embrace Your Context

There are many paths that you can follow to influence how your team or organization orchestrates experiences. These paths each begin at the same point—your unique context. You may work in a relatively small company with touchpoints that you can count on a few hands, or you might have thousands of fellow employees with multiple business units, products, and services. Your organization may be hierarchical or flat, collocated or spread across a large geography, and have a mature or nascent design group.

Regardless of your situation, you need to take stock of the current state of your product or service experiences, your would-be collaborators, pre-existing plans for the future, and how work gets done in different organizational pockets. Here are a few ways that you can get started.

Document Your "As-Is"

For reasons stated earlier, you and your colleagues probably lack an understanding of all the moving parts of the current end-to-end experience. This makes everyone's work more difficult and less effective. For example, product and marketing teams may have the same goal of increasing customer knowledge, yet not realize that they have duplicated efforts due to a lack of visibility into each other's work. Customers eventually feel this pain through too many options, conflicting information, or touchpoints that simply don't connect.

This is where you can make an impact immediately. Part I, "A Common Foundation," introduced approaches that help people see the big picture. Here's a quick summary of where you might begin. Each approach will deliver immediate value with relatively low effort and expense. They will also help establish language, concepts, and frameworks to build upon later.

- **Create a touchpoint inventory.** Get a cross-functional team together and map your touchpoints by channel and journey stage (see Chapter 2, "Pinning Down Touchpoints"). Align around the purpose and efficacy of each touchpoint. Try to identify ways to collaborate more effectively across journey stages and channels.

- **Gather existing principles.** Track down principles (or guidelines) that different groups use to guide work. Partner with colleagues to establish a common set of principles, either by synthesizing existing ones or doing new research with customers (see Chapter 6, "Defining Experience Principles").

- **Catalog current personas and journeys.** Locate all relevant personas and experience maps floating around. (You will likely be surprised at how many you find.) Work with others to rationalize these into a foundational set of customer archetypes and journeys to support cross-functional strategies and planning. At the same time, you will uncover gaps in knowledge that may lead to new customer journey research (see Chapter 5, "Mapping Experiences").

- **Make a current-state blueprint.** Select a critical customer pathway (such as onboarding) and create a current-state blueprint. Make sure that you invite a cross-functional team. You might also consider annotating your blueprint with upcoming operational changes that may impact the experience in the future (see Chapter 3, "Exploring Ecosystems").

- **Look at the numbers.** Get your hands on any scorecards, reports, or other data that can help you understand the range and quality of your touchpoints. Then you can augment your touchpoint inventory, experience map, and service blueprint.

TAKE A SERVICE SAFARI

Service safaris are a common method in service design, and they involve experiencing a service firsthand. Invite colleagues to explore several end-to-end experiences (both your own and competitors) to record how well they can navigate across channels and touchpoints, what moments work and do not, and how the experience makes them feel. You can then look for patterns across safaris, as well as identify some potential opportunities for improvement.

Identify (and Get Close to) Your Internal Stakeholders

Better end-to-end experiences depend upon the right people in your organization aligning behind a common cause. But who are these people? Do they see the value in end-to-end experience and design? How open are they to collaboration? To make progress, you need to find out the answer to these questions while building rapport and trust. Here are a few tips:

- **Create a stakeholder map.** As detailed in Chapter 3, a stake-holder map visualizes the people, roles, and relationships of an ecosystem. You can use this method to visualize your internal stakeholders. These likely include channel owners, product managers, operational leaders, marketing managers, and many others. Leverage your company's organizational chart and directory to start your discovery.

- **Be a roadmap detective.** Program roadmaps often list the own-ers of an initiative's various projects and tasks. Many of these people may be relevant to your work. You may discover, for example, a marketing manager is involved in several onboarding projects that can help you understand marketing's strategy for that journey stage better. In this way, roadmaps (and quarterly plans) can help you build out your stakeholder map and refine your plan for creating critical relationships.

- **Meet and greet.** Using your map, meet as many of your stake-holders as possible. You can use short 15-minute meetings (over coffee, for example) to put a face to a name. Share your intent of helping others work more effectively to help customers have bet-ter end-to-end experiences. Invest in maintaining and expanding this network.

- **Ask about their goals and success criteria.** When meeting stake-holders, ask directly what their current goals are and how their success is measured. For example, a mobile app product owner may be tasked with doubling the number of user accounts. The operations team, meanwhile, is expected to decrease call center handling time. Understanding these underlying drivers can help you identify common goals and conflicting priorities.

- **Take a pulse check.** Let's face it, not everyone sees the value in designing for experience or collaborating in the manner outlined in this book. You should gauge your stakeholders' openness to what you're selling. A good tactic: as you learn their goals, give examples of how the specific orchestration methods can help achieve their goals.

Learn How Stuff Is Made

We all start somewhere. Maybe you are trained in interaction design but trying to get into strategy, or you have worked in digital your whole career but want to have a greater impact in other channels.

Regardless of where you began or what you know today, you will need to get smarter on how different functions think and go about their work.

What does this mean in practice? You need to understand how stuff—products, services, processes, touchpoints, technological solutions, and so on—get designed and made in your organization. This involves learning both craft and process. For example, consider the CVS Target example back in Chapter 2. Here are a few examples of what you could learn:

- **People:** Are there a common set of principles behind how they interact with customers?

- **Tools:** How are work tools created to support employee tasks and the overall customer experience?

- **Marketing:** What is the process for defining marketing strategies? Who is responsible for making touchpoints in each channel?

- **Software and technology:** How do point solutions (such as adding register prompts or new applications) get made? How often are releases done? How long does it take to get modifications to software or technology platforms to get approved and executed?

- **Physical environment:** Who owns how a department is laid out and designed? What is their process for making changes?

- **Processes and policies:** How are different processes defined, documented, and implemented? Who defines policies and what are the processes for changing them?

Designing for end-to-end experiences becomes easier the more you know the answers to questions like these. It arms you with the knowledge to talk shop with collaborators, earning their trust and proving that you can understand and empathize with how they get their work done. You also become more effective in analyzing the value and feasibility of solutions outside of your core discipline. For example, you may know the ins and outs of digital product design and implementation, but now you understand the process that operations follow to implement changes to a physical environment or employee roles. Most importantly, this knowledge increases your ability to facilitate the design process within cross-functional teams.

Building your knowledge of how stuff gets made will happen through both experience and study. Our best advice is to ask lots of questions. Be curious about your colleagues and seek out ones who will share how they think about their work. The more you learn, the more dangerous (in a good way!) you will become.

Orchestrate Change

Throughout this book, we've intentionally used "orchestration" as a double entendre. In one sense, orchestration means holistically designing a system of moments, touchpoints, channels, and more. Orchestration, however, also applies to the process of collaborating with your colleagues. Instead of playing independently, you harmonize for the benefit of your customers' experiences and your organization's objectives.

Earlier chapters provided guidance on orchestrating the process to create your North Star. This section lays out four approaches for keeping the momentum as you scale that orchestration mindset into implementation and beyond. In concert, these activities—which we call *experience orchestration*—help increase visibility and encourage collaboration across multiple execution teams tasked with creating different touchpoints, processes, and other solutions. Experience orchestration can be a role, but works best when leaders and managers commit to working collectively to create more coherence and continuity within the customer experience.

Start Small

Once you have a vision, the more difficult work of orchestrating experiences begins— executing across multiple fronts with competing priorities while not losing sight of your vision. Don't underestimate this challenge. It will take time to communicate the vision, build trust, align in-flight work, and try new ways of working across channels. You also will need to build confidence in management that this new paradigm will lead to better results.

For these reasons and more, start small. Below are a few options to consider. The common thread among them is changing small portions of the customer experience to be in alignment with your vision. These efforts can be accomplished in prototypes, pilots, or small experiments. In addition to helping you learn what solutions will work best, you will also forge new ways of working across teams that will pay off when you attempt a larger program of work.

For these examples, a fictitious installation service will be used to make these approaches more tangible.

Build a Bridge

End-to-end experiences are supported through many individual connections—touchpoint to touchpoint, moment to moment, back-stage to front stage. Your North Star vision shows examples of critical connections, but these will take time to create. To start small, identify one or two new bridges that you can build. Figure 11.1 provides some common approaches to consider.

For example, a cross-functional team redesigning an in-home installation service might have a vision for personalizing call center, online, and in-home interactions. To start moving toward their North Star, this team focused on the bridge between capturing installation preferences and reviewing the personalized plan before installation began. The team also limited its scope to building only the connection between the call center and in-home channels (leaving other channels where preferences could be set for later phases).

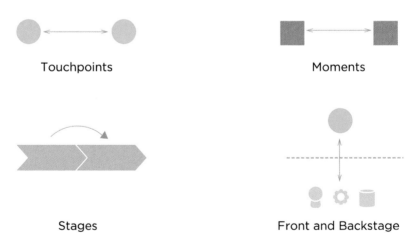

Touchpoints   Moments

Stages   Front and Backstage

FIGURE 11.1
Making one or two connections helps you test new approaches and build confidence.

Make a Touchpoint Consistent Across Channels

In some cases, you may want to begin by improving consistency of a key customer touchpoint that is delivered via multiple channels. Try to choose a touchpoint that, once changed, will have a clear measurable customer and business value. These types of efforts also help show the benefit of creating a common touchpoint architecture across channels.

In our installation example, design research revealed that customers were receiving conflicting and difficult-to-understand status messages in multiple channels. The team decided to tackle this touchpoint—*learn my status*—by defining common messaging standards, including language, timing, and frequency. They then partnered with channel owners to implement these changes for text messages, push notifications, emails, and automated calls.

Attack a Leverage Point

When you map end-to-end experiences, you often find a severe emotional low point that screams to be addressed. Fortunately, you now have the context of the full journey and your vision for improving it over time. In these cases, a good strategy is to address that low point first (see Figure 11.2), as this will improve the customer's lasting impression of their entire end-to-end experience.[1] The key is to do so in alignment with your experience principles and long-term vision.

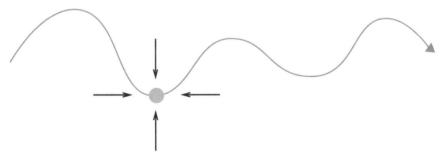

FIGURE 11.2
Starting with the low point of an experience can alleviate customer frustration and improve their overall lasting impression.

---

1 See the work Dan Kahneman and his peak-end rule.
   http://www.vwl.tuwien.ac.at/hanappi/TEI/momentsfull.pdf

Back to our installation service team. Call center complaints backed by experience mapping research had revealed that the moment of choosing what services and equipment to be installed was frustrating and confusing. These emotions carried into the rest of the experience, as well as cases of buyer's remorse following the installation. The team chose to attack this moment. They created and tested concepts both online and in the call center, using their experience principles and vision for guidance.

Add or Resequence Moments

Because process design often dictates customer flow, you may find instances in which the sequence of moments does not optimally support customer needs. Similarly, your customers may have needs not addressed by any of your existing moments and touchpoints. A good place to start could be to experiment with rearranging the moments in a customer pathway or introducing a new stone in that moment altogether (see Figure 11.3).

FIGURE 11.3
Re-architecting with the sequence of moments.

For example, the installation service team prototyped in a service blueprint a concept for reimagining all the moments of the installation experience. This was a large endeavor, requiring new technologies, touchpoints, roles, and processes. To start small, the team focused on re-architecting the moments from just before the installer's arrival through the service follow-up. Using a pilot in one market, they resequenced the moments following the installation, as well as added a new moment (with supporting touchpoints) prior to the appointment. The team worked within the constraints of what could be implemented and tested in two months.

Fake the Backend

Operational investments often dictate when (or if) significant improvements to end-to-end experiences can be made. New platforms, retraining employees, and redesigning business processes cost time and money. It also requires making trade-offs, such as deprioritizing other changes. To make a stronger business case, as well as learn to fine-tune your vision, consider starting with a pilot that fakes the backend. In this approach, you will test the key features and value proposition of your product or service, while working around current operational limitations.

In the case of our installation service, the team had envisioned a sophisticated customer relationship platform to collect data for use in tailoring interactions across channels. There were questions about this investment, and it certainly wasn't going to be developed in the near term. The team decided to run a limited pilot partnering with the digital, call center, and installation teams (see Figure 11.4). The

FIGURE 11.4
Faking the backend helps you test new experiences without waiting or building the case for significant changes to your operations.

digital team would build a web form that some customers would interact with earlier in their journey. Instead of storing the data in a new system, an email would be sent to a call service agent. The call center agent referred to this information when following up with the customer, and then appended notes to the job record. The installer followed the current process of referring to the job record to prep for future appointments. Finally, the installer personalized the in-home installation based on this new information.

Make a Rough Cut

Let's return to the installation service example cited earlier. After making some progress with their pilots, the initiative team received funding to redesign the end-to-end experience. This would involve teams from digital product, technology, operations, customer service, field service, legal, marketing, and many others. Each function had its own way of defining solutions and implementing them. The digital product and technology teams ran Agile, but other functions still used waterfall. The marketing team outsourced production work to agencies. Program management tracked and reported the status of each project, but no one directed or reviewed whether all this effort would result in a great end-to-end experience.

This is a common scenario. In this environment, producing quality end-to-end experiences requires smart and effective collaboration. You (personally or with other team members) must continually provide execution teams with context and feedback, as well as listen to them and adapt your design as their work reveals new challenges. A tangible vision will remind everyone where you are headed. Your experience principles will provide a common language to inspire solutions and evaluate work. However, distributing these tools will only go so far in nudging all the work in the same direction. There are simply too many details and considerations to anticipate.

Filmmaking provides inspiration for how to engage and collaborate in a distributed execution team environment. While film is a linear art form, most productions do not shoot scenes in the sequence in which they will be viewed. This creates an economy of budget and time, but also creates challenges in keeping consistency in art direction and performance, as well as continuity across shots and scenes. After shooting early in the editing process, a rough cut is assembled to get a feel for the overall film, the sequence of shots, and the best takes to use. In animation, rough cuts are constructed regularly to see the status of each scene and the flow of the narrative. Some scenes are complete; others have temporary animation or sound. Regardless of how complete each part of the film is, seeing the pieces strung together as a story helps identify issues with consistency, continuity, and flow.

FILM AND EXPERIENCE

In helping organizations orchestrate experiences, I've taken a lot of inspiration from the art and craft of film-making. Filmmaking, like designing complex experi-ences, is a team sport. While producers and the director oversee the vision, budgets, and resources required to make a film, many specialized roles contribute to the final product. From scriptwriting, to costume and set design, to lighting and sound, and even the craft table that keeps the troops fed, hundreds of people can be involved. A film production is not unlike an army that decamps on location in a state of organized chaos. Along the way, thousands of decisions are made that contribute to a creative triumph or a forgettable failure, a block-buster or a bomb.

Designing experiences that span channels and touchpoints shares many of the same challenges, and film production approaches can help immensely. Storyboards can be used to create concepts or to previsualize experiences. Rough cutting can help everyone see the work in progress and adjust accordingly. Continuity tracking will aid the identification of inconsistencies across moments. In concert, these methods help everyone understand the intended holistic experience that their individual efforts will manifest.

Creating rough cuts (or rough cutting) for end-to-end experiences is a great vehicle for gathering your collaborators and taking stock of what the result will be for customers. Like the filmmaking technique, a rough cut arranges an in-progress or completed work in a sequence that customers will experience. This should be done at regular inter-vals throughout execution, as well as after release to review metrics and plan future iterations.

The following is one approach for rough cutting with your col-leagues. It assumes that you have created storyboards visualizing the moments that you want to create for customers. In the absence of storyboards, you can use simple scenario steps (on sticky notes), service blueprints, or other artifacts that provide an outline of the customer's pathway. (Note: This is an in-person approach, but virtual sessions can also work if you can't get people in the same room).

- Post your storyboard panels on the wall.

- Ask teams to bring their latest work. These could be mock-ups, requirements, sketches, screen shots, process designs, and so on—anything showing where they are in their process. It's also helpful to have your touchpoint inventory handy to make sure that you cover all the parts of each moment.

- As a group, walk through the end-to-end experience. For each moment, remind everyone of the intent for the moment, as well as how it fits with the moments before and after.

- Review and discuss the different posted artifacts moment by moment. In our installation example, perhaps the mobile product team shares their latest sketches for requesting service, while the business architect shares the data model for a claim. Remember to refer to your experience principles to help guide and spark feedback.

- In some cases, the posted artifact may be a jumping-off point to review a working prototype or detailed designs in a document.

- During the review, participants should write down feedback and questions on sticky notes (see Figure 11.5). This keeps things moving, as you can save longer discussions for after the walkthrough.

FIGURE 11.5
A rough-cut walkthrough.

- All participants should be looking for opportunities to create better consistency and continuity in the customer's journey. This could be language, interaction approaches, tension between process and experience, and so on.

- Finally, end the session with a review of decisions and action items. Commit to coming back together again. (Scheduling a meeting every two to three weeks is a good cadence for most projects.)

The dialogue during your rough cutting will reinforce teamwork, surface issues, make trade-offs clearer, and ultimately lead to better designed end-to-end experiences.

Lean into Your Journey Framework

When you observe how work gets defined, organized, and assigned in most companies, you see some interesting patterns. Three common ones that make orchestrating experiences particularly challenging include the following:

- **Chopping up the funnel:** Functions are organized around awareness, acquisition, onboarding, and servicing. Work happens independently, but each silo tries to influence the others to prioritize their dependencies.

- **Product quarterbacks:** Product management works as a federation of owners (or quarterbacks), often with divergent visions of the customer experience. In multiple instances, we have seen seven to eight product managers, with little to no coordination, who own different portions of the product experience.

- **Operations-centric:** Business process design—through value-stream mapping and various Six Sigma approaches—drives decisions on how customers (and employees) interact with the organization. As a result, product and service design are heavily constrained by these operation-centric architectures.

In each of these cases, ownership for what will become different stages, moments, or pathways of the customer experience is distributed. Each function creates plans to reach its objectives—create more awareness, reduce call center complaints, increase usage—but a holistic customer journey is typically not a shared objective. The resulting experiences reflect this fragmentation. Thus, an end-to-end experience has many masters, but no single owner.

This is beginning to change in some organizations. Jobs titled "journey manager" and "product journey manager" are cropping up in the U.S. and Europe. While their responsibilities are far from standard, these roles share a common intent of defining strategy and organizing work around the customer journey, not channels, technologies, or funnel stages.[2] As the role spreads and teams are formed around them, our hope is that human-centered design will influence how customer journey management is practiced.

In the absence of this role, you and your colleagues will need to work together to increase focus and collaboration on the end-to-end experience. Your journey stages can be used as an organizing framework for spurring cross-functional communication, coordination, prioritization, and (eventually) strategy. Consider the following steps:

- **Map projects to journey framework.** A great starting point is to create visibility into all the in-flight or planned projects that will impact the end-to-end experience. Stakeholder conversations, roadmap reviews, and workshops are good ways to track down relevant projects. To communicate what you've found, use your journey framework to show which projects align with one or more of your stages and moments. Figure 11.6 shows this approach using storyboards.[3]

- **Seize opportunities for collaboration.** By showing the relationship of work to the customer journey, you can see opportunities for connecting efforts that impact the same stage or moment. For example, you may find several unconnected projects all working on improving onboarding, each with a different intent. This could result in a workshop to share insights, an experiment based on a common journey framework, or a formal project.

- **Prioritize and plan together.** Strategy is all about making smart trade-offs, given limited resources. To develop better end-to-end experience strategies, your journey framework can be used to facilitate cross-functional priorities. Using a similar matrix as a touchpoint inventory, Figure 11.7 shows one approach to visualizing these trade-offs.

---

2 For a good analysis of the value behind this trend, see David C. Edelman and Marc Singer, "Competing on Customer Journeys," *Harvard Business Review*, November 2015, https://hbr.org/2015/11/competing-on-customer-journeys

3 This example is inspired by the work of Maria Cordell, Bryn Bowman, and their project team at Adaptive Path.

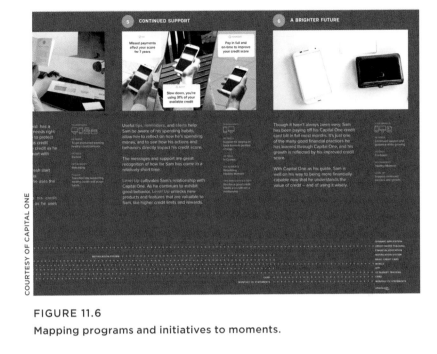

FIGURE 11.6

Mapping programs and initiatives to moments.

Cross-Channel Blueprint

A tool for planning user tasks across multiple channels.

	Lookup	Explore	Compare	Organize	Purchase
Print Catalog	Low priority Table of contents Index	High priority Immersive photography	Low priority Flip pages back/forth	N/A Flip pages back/forth	High priority Order by phone Order by mail Order online
Website	High priority Search box	High priority Browse by category	High priority Table view of selected items	High priority Favorites Wish list / gift registry	High priority Standard checkout Expedited checkout Order by phone
Tablet App	High priority Search box Voice input	High priority Catalog-like browsing experience	Medium priority Table view of selected items	Medium priority Favorites Wish lists	High priority Expedited checkout Standard checkout
Mobile App	High priority Search box Voice input Barcode scanner	Medium priority Browse by category	N/A Impractical due to screen size	Low priority Add items to favorites and wish list, but limited ability to edit	High priority Expedited checkout
Physical Store	High priority Clear signage Store map Helpful staff	High priority Wander the aisles	Medium priority Compare side by side Ask staff	Low priority Gift registry / wish list	High priority Attendant-assisted Self-checkout Scan-as-you-go
Shared Assets	Product taxonomy All channels powered by a single set of categories		Compare engine Web & tablet powered by one component	Universal Favs Favorites list shared by web, tablet, mobile	Checkout workflow Universal checkout process for web, tablet, and mobile

FIGURE 11.7

An example of communicating priorities across channels and journey stages.

Spark Change

Organizations are creatures of habit. You and like-minded colleagues must work to help others break the muscle memory of how problems are framed and work gets done. This change occurs interaction by interaction, project by project. Through hard work, infectious passion, and results, you can show others that there is better way.

Once you start making an impact, amplify your work as widely as possible. Tell stories. Invite others to play. Mentor or encourage others to take up the baton. As key leaders and other influencers join the cause, the change you want to see will gain momentum.

As your journey begins, consider these three approaches:

- **Share stories.** New approaches often get criticized by others as being too academic, too costly, or simply redundant. This resistance is partly fear of the unknown. As you create examples of orchestrating experiences, share them with others to demystify the process. This may be through case studies, presentations, or events. For example, at the close of a project, have your cross-functional team members invite peers to share how you approached the work and its outcomes.

- **Train others.** To create change at scale, you will need to equip others to work differently. This can start with informal or formal training sessions to introduce key concepts and methods. It's important to be strategic when you determine whom to invite to training to spread experience orchestration more widely. Get people onboard excited to change the culture, not simply further their own agenda or personal brand.

- **Make tools.** Another effective practice is to make and distribute toolkits that guide others through using new methods. Adaptive Path took this approach to spread service design throughout Capital One. Through publishing a guide to service blueprinting and a set of supporting tools, they were able to touch hundreds of employees and equip them to try service blueprinting on their projects.[4]

- **Build a community of practice.** As more people get first-hand experience, these converts will help spread these new ways of

---

4 Adaptive Path's *Guide to Service Blueprinting* is available to download online at https://medium.com/capitalonedesign/download-our-guide-to-service-blueprinting-d70bb2717ddf

working into their teams and future projects. It's important to keep this excitement and interest building. Consider creating a community of practice to support one another and share progress. Simple tactics such as creating a Slack channel or regular lunch-and-learns can go a long way toward building momentum for more wide-spread adoption.

Start with You

In the beginning, you and others may have to stretch beyond your current responsibilities to influence your organization to adopt new ways of working. New roles, however, will eventually need to emerge to facilitate design orchestration. We have seen (and helped define) some of these roles for the organizations that we have worked with. Titles such as journey experience designer, cross-channel architect, end-to-end experience designer, service designer, and many others are becoming a bit more common. Increasingly, organizations will need these roles to step into the ambiguity of how to orchestrate experiences. Our advice: as you push into uncharted territory, don't be afraid to label the new roles you play as their value is understood.

Positioning yourself to play a greater role in orchestrating experiences requires more than technical knowledge of concepts and tools. As you have probably noticed, a lot of this work involves guiding and collaborating with people from all walks of life, both inside and outside of your organization. These soft skills often separate good practitioners and leaders from great ones; they will be even more critical as organizations become more flat, matrixed, and (by necessity) collaborative.

Here is a brief overview of five key skills that you should work to build over time.

- **Empathy:** Empathy is more than a fashionable trend; it's a critical 21st-century skill. Indi Young, in her excellent book on empathy, wisely notes that greater empathy can transform organizations, but this change occurs through people building their own abilities to listen and empathize with one another.[5] Your ability to practice the methods of this book will be greatly improved as you sharpen your own empathy.

---

5 We highly recommend Indi Young's *Practical Empathy* (New York: Rosenfeld Media, 2015).

- **Facilitation:** Facilitating others through the design process requires confidence and skill. Seek out books, classes, and mentors to reflect upon and evolve your facilitation skills. Steal from the best, while developing your own style. You should approach this role as a service.

- **Improvisation:** You will run into many unforeseen challenges as you attempt to orchestrate experiences. A basic framework may not quite fit the context. A carefully planned workshop may end up being the wrong approach to get the job done. Approach these moments as a hurdle, not a wall. To get more comfortable thinking on your feet and embracing current conditions, consider taking improvisational theater. A good improv class will teach you to be more present, improve your listening and empathy skills, and tackle obstacles creatively as they arise.

- **Storytelling:** Earlier chapters reinforced the power of story in informing and inspiring others, as well as understanding and improving people's experiences. Storytelling is an invaluable skill in today's organizations, providing a critical counterbalance to big data and other approaches that can remove human context from strategic insights. Make it a habit to reflect on your storytelling approaches and look for new ways to expand your palette. Read books on the storytelling craft. Take classes. Most importantly: experience stories in all media and reflect on the techniques that make them work.

- **Visual communication:** It's trite, but true: show, don't tell. This includes sketching concepts, cocreating models with research participants, as well as visually communicating concepts in various artifacts. Whether you cannot draw a straight line or are a master illustrator, hone your visual communication skills. Take in-person or online sketching classes. Find a style that works for you to express concepts quickly. Push through the fear of drawing in front of other people. Be an advocate for visual communication and get people with great skills (who are often left out of strategic design work) deeply embedded into your project.

BUILDING EMPATHY FOR STRANGERS

I constantly get inspiration from all forms of storytelling to bring into my personal practice. Brandon Doman's *Strangers Project* (see Figure 11.8), for example, invites people to share their personal stories as part of a curated experience toward creating greater understanding and empathy. I now use similar curated environments to make the stories of customers—and how to collect them through qualitative research—more accessible and impactful.

FIGURE 11.8
Curating and sharing stories.

Take It from Here

Thirty years ago my older brother, who was ten years old at the time, was trying to get a report on birds written that he'd had three months to write, which was due the next day. We were out at our family cabin in Bolinas, and he was at the kitchen table close to tears, surrounded by binder paper and pencils and un-opened books on birds, immobilized by the hugeness of the task ahead. Then my father sat down beside him, put his arm around my brother's shoulder, and said, "Bird by bird, buddy. Just take it bird by bird.

—Anne Lamott,
Bird by Bird: Some Instructions on Writing and Life[6]

We believe the mindset of orchestration—of experiences, of touch-points, of people—will create better outcomes for organizations and those they serve. It may seem like an enormous task to shift pro-cesses, habits, and cultures. We certainly see this as a long game. Yet, moment by moment, journey by journey, and initiative by initiative, you and others can create the change that you want to see.

Take up the baton. Play well with others. Make beautiful music together.

---

6 Anne Lamott, *Bird by Bird: Some Instructions on Writing and Life* (New York: Anchor Books, 1995), 18–19.

INDEX

bridge, building, 288

bridge touchpoints, 28–29, 35

business ecosystems, 57–59

business metrics, for research, 128

business origami, 77–78, 268

C

call center, channel data for
research, 128

call center touchpoint, 39–40

capabilities, 253–254, 267

channel data, for research, 128

channels, 3–20

building an orchestra, 18–19

changing channel-centric
mindset, 15–19

customers moving across, 9–12

defined, 4

defined as destinations, 13, 15, 18

defined by interactions, information,
and context, 12–13

as ecosystem entity in customer
journey, 101

intent of touchpoints, 25

as moment enablers, 13–15

in opportunity identification, 188

organizations structured by, 5–9

touchpoint consistency across, 289

in touchpoint workshop, 51

touchpoints by channel, 32–33

types of, 4–5, 7

Chesky, Brian, 171, 247

co-value, 172–173

commander's intent, in crafting
tangible vision, 239–240

communication, visual, as skill to
build, 300

competitive relationships, as type of
experience ecosystem, 67

complementary relationships, as type
of experience ecosystem, 67

concept cards, templated, 216

constraints

compared to opportunities,
175–176

in idea generation, 209–211

context

as building block of end-to-end
experiences, 97, 102

channels defined by, 12–13

research for experience map,
125–127

contextual prototyping,
270–271, 277

conversations as touchpoints, 39

cooperative relationships, as type of
experience ecosystem, 67

creativity inspiration, with experience
principles, 154

current-state service blueprints,
40, 76, 284

customer building blocks of end-to-end
experiences, 97

doing (behaviors), 100

feeling (emotions), 98–99

thinking (perceptions), 100

customer-centered approach,
in ecosystem model, 71

customer journeys. *See* journeys,
customer

customer relationship management
(CRM), 22, 93

customers
as actors in experience
ecosystems, 60
learning their stories through
research, 118–130, 142–143
moving across channels, 9–12

CVS, 35–36, 286

D

data, using in customer
relationships, 93

decision-making, with experience
principles, 154

design principles, compared to
experience principles, 150, 151

designing the moment, 265–279
air travel experience
example, 276–278
contextual prototyping, 270–271
horizontal *vs.* vertical
prototypes, 267–269
interactive *vs.* narrative
prototypes, 273
macrointeractions and
microinteractions, 266
prototype value
proposition, 273–275
prototyping options, 267–273
technical *vs.* experiential
prototypes, 271–272

detailed touchpoint inventory, 42–44

directed storytelling, in experience
map, 124, 136–137

DNA of the journey, 96

doing (behaviors), as customer
building block of end-to-end
experiences, 100

Doman, Brandon, 301

dot-voting, 166–167, 235

E

Eames, Charles, 175

ecosystem maps
for idea generation, 220
modeling an ecosystem, 70–73
in opportunity identification, 173,
180, 186, 189
other approaches, 74–78
as tool for strategy and design,
73–74
uncovering the components, 69

ecosystems, 55–86
as building block of end-to-end
experiences, 97, 101–102
business ecosystems, 57–59
experience ecosystems, 59–68.
See also experience ecosystems
mapping, 69–73
modeling, 70–73
workshop on landscape
alignment, 80–86

efficiency, with experience
principles, 154

emotional relationships, as type of
experience ecosystem, 67

for prototype value proposition,
274, 278

workshop, 162–168

experiential prototypes, 272

F

face-to-face customer research,
122–125

facilitation, as skill to build, 300

factors, of experience ecosystems, 62

faking the backend, 291–292

feasibility

  in idea generation, 210–211, 225

  of technical prototypes, 271–272

featured touchpoints, 28, 253

feeling (emotions), as customer
building block of end-to-end
experiences, 98–99

filmmaking, 292–293

first-person documentation, 127

Fitbit, 271

forced provocation, 74

future-state service blueprints, 248

future-state touchpoint
inventory, 254–255

G

gallery tour, 130, 148

Gebbia, Joe, 171

good, defined, 150, 153

Google, technical prototyping, 271

government agencies, as actors in
experience ecosystems, 61

granularity of channels, 17

H

Hamel, Gary, 238

handoffs, 28–29

happy paths, 251

Home Depot, 65

HomePlus, 64, 74, 182

horizontal prototypes, 267–269

horizontal servitude, 5

"How Might We?" prompts,
183–184, 196–198, 220, 250

hub of empathy and understanding,
journeys as, 94–97

hypothesis workshop for experience
map, 116–117

hypothesizing an ecosystem, 70

I

idea generation, 205–236

  bodystorming, 211, 217–219

  crafting stories, 211, 214–216, 236

  evaluation and prioritization,
219, 222–227

  expression and form, 211–219

  forced provocation, 74

  improvisation, 217–219, 235–236

  inputs and constraints, 209–211

  leading the hunt for ideas, 206–207

  prioritizing, 225, 226–227

  structure and focus, 207–209

  value and feasibility ratings,
225, 226–227

  visual brainstorming, 211, 212–213,
216, 233–235

idea generation (*continued*)

workshop, from ideas to narratives, 230–236

workshops, going beyond, 220–221

workshops, remote, 229

ideation kits, 220–221

impact *vs.* complexity prioritization method, 184

importance *vs.* satisfaction prioritization method, 185–186

improvisation

for idea generation, 217–219, 235–236

as skill to build, 300

influencer relationships, as type of experience ecosystem, 67

information, channels defined by, 12–13

innovation, in opportunity identification, 180–183, 186

intent

ambiguous intent and experience design, 240–241

commander's intent and agile, 239–240

in experience map, 110–111

importance in vision, 238–241

strategic intent and lean management, 238–239

of touchpoints, 25–26

interactions

channels defined by, 12–13

in experience ecosystems, 65

macrointeractions and microinteractions, 266

in moments made of journeys, 89–90

interactive prototypes, 273

interactive voice response (IVR) system, 39

intercepts, as research method, 126–127

interviews, in call centers, 40

invitation stems, 183–184

J

jazz, compared to experience principles, 152–153

job titles, 296, 299

journey framework, mapping projects to, 296

journey map, 109

journeys, customer, 87–103

as building block of end-to-end experiences, 97, 98

defined, 23, 30, 88–89

end-to-end experiences, 97–102

getting started, 102

as hub of empathy and understanding, 94–97

made of moments, 89–90

in opportunity identification, 173, 179–180, 187–188

stage definition in touchpoint workshop, 51–52

stages of, 30–31, 33

types of, 90–92

value of, 92–94

products

  as actors in experience
    ecosystems, 61

  as ecosystem entity in customer
    journey, 101

  vs. services, 8

prototype value proposition,
  273–275

prototyping options, in designing
  the moment, 267–273

  contextual prototyping, 270–271

  horizontal *vs.* vertical
    prototypes, 267–269

  interactive *vs.* narrative
    prototypes, 273

  technical *vs.* experiential
    prototypes, 271–272

Q

qualitative research

  on customer emotions, 99

  for experience maps,
    69, 118–127, 135

  synthesizing data, 127

quality control, with experience
  principles, 154

quantitative research, for experience
  maps, 128–129

question map, 130

R

Rail Europe, 34, 41, 129, 178–179

regulations, as factor of experience
  ecosystems, 62

regulatory relationships, as type of
  experience ecosystem, 67

relationships

  as ecosystem entity in customer
    journey, 102

  in experience ecosystems, 66–67

repair/recovery touchpoints, 28–29

research

  beginning, 18

  crafting experience principles in
    place of, 154–155

  learning customer stories for
    experience map, 118–130

  origami in, 78

  using existing knowledge, 115

retail industry, virtual shopping in
  South Korea, 64

ride-a-longs, as research
  method, 126–127

roadmaps, 285

Robinson, John B., 258

roles, in experience ecosystems, 61

rough cutting, 292–295

S

Saffer, Dan, 266

Samsung, 58

satisfaction *vs.* importance prioritization method, 185–186

scarcity formula, 226

Schauer, Brandon, 177

secure authentication example,
  11–12

T

tangible vision. *See* vision, crafting a tangible

Target, 35–37, 286

technical prototypes, 271–272, 277

technology trends, as factor of experience ecosystems, 62

thinking (perceptions), as customer building block of end-to-end experiences, 100

throughline, 274

time, as context in customer journey, 102

timeboxed rounds, 212

toolkits for teaching, 298

touch, 22

touchpoint heuristics, for prototype value proposition, 274

touchpoint inventory

of customer experience, 32, 34

documenting current state, 283

future-state, 254–255

lean *vs.* detailed, 41–44

in opportunity identification, 173, 188

workshop, 46–54

touchpoint name, 43

touchpoint type, for prototype value proposition, 274

touchpoints, 21–54

cataloging and communicating, 41–44

consistency across channels, 289

customer journeys, 23, 30–31

customer moments, 26–28

defined, 7, 22–23, 25

as ecosystem entity in customer journey, 101

framework, by channel, 32–33

framework, by moment, 30–32

identifying, 33–41

intent, 25–26

measuring value in journeys, 93

reporting and evaluating, 29–30

roles of, 28–29

workshop, 46–54

traceability, 273

training others, 298

transactional relationships, as type of experience ecosystem, 67

transcripts of calls, 40

travel experience, 91–92, 96

Twain, Mark, 106

U

Uber/UberEats, 180–181, 185, 186

Ulwick, Anthony, 185

urgency *vs.* value prioritization method, 184–185, 199–201, 226

V

value alignment, in defining opportunity, 172–173, 199

value rating, in idea generation, 225, 226–227

value stream mapping, 172

ACKNOWLEDGMENTS

Both Authors Would Like to Thank

For their patience and guidance: Lou Rosenfeld and Marta Justak

For their knowledge, friendship, generosity, and inspiring work (much of it featured in the book): Jamin Hegeman, Brandon Schauer, Maria Cordell, Amber Reed, Iran Narges, Todd Wilkens, Paula Wellings, Tracey Varnell, Julia Moisand Egéa, Henning Fischer, Nick Remis, Ayla Newhouse, Jessica Striebich, Chris Wronski, Evi K. Hui, Toi Valentine, Nick Crampton, Katie Walker Wilson, and Bryn Bowman

For helping us share examples of work: Brandon Schauer, Lucy-Marie Hagues, and Melanie Huggins

For his inspiring body of work and thought-provoking foreword: Marc Rettig.

For his amazing illustrations: Nick Madden

For their invaluable reviews, critiques, and support: Samantha Starmer, Jess McMullin, and Andy Polaine.

Chris Would Also Like to Personally Thank

I want to thank Todd Wilkens, Brandon Schauer, Alex Berg, and Patrick Quattlebaum for their mentorship, partnership, and making me a better designer.

And Patrick Warmly Thanks

I would like to thank Jamin Hegeman, Brandon Schauer, Stephen Taylor, Andrew Hinton, Maria Cordell, and (of course) Chris Risdon for their inspiration and thought partnership. My growth as a designer is attributed greatly to collaborating with all of you.

I would also like to thank the many clients, designers, and others whom I have worked with throughout my career. Thanks for your trust and willingness to play.

Finally, thanks to my wife, my mother and father, the Quattlebaum family, the Hankins family, and the Dunaway family. Your love and support made it possible for me to spend many a night, weekend, and holiday writing this book.

ABOUT THE AUTHORS

Chris Risdon is director of design for peer-to-peer carsharing service Getaround. Previously, Chris was head of design for Capital One Labs and a design director for Adaptive Path, the pioneering experience design consultancy. Chris has introduced and advanced new methods in design, teaching thousands of design professionals and students. He holds an MFA in design from the Savannah College of Art and Design and is an adjunct professor at the California College of the Arts, teaching interaction design and service design to the next generation of designers. Follow him on Twitter @chrisrisdon.

Patrick Quattlebaum, is a designer, management consultant, and founder at studioPQ. He helps organizations experiment with and adopt collaborative approaches to designing service experiences and the operations that support them. He has held multiple design leadership positions, including managing director at Adaptive Path and head of service design at Capital One. He is also a passionate design instructor, having taught thousands of practitioners in North America and Europe. He holds an MS in Information Design and Technology from the Georgia Institute of Technology. You can follow him on Twitter @ptquattlebaum and @studiopq.